*Presented to*

_____

*From*

_____

*Date*

_____

# WHEN THE DAY BREAKS

CHRISTIAN ART
PUBLISHERS

Published by Christian Art Publishers
PO Box 1599, Vereeniging, 1930, RSA

© 2000
First edition 2017

Cover designed by Christian Art Publishers

Images used under license from Shutterstock.com

Devotions written by Nina Smit

Unless otherwise indicated, Scripture quotations are taken
from the *Holy Bible*, New International Version® NIV®.
Copyright © 1973, 1978, 1984 by International Bible Society.
Used by permission of Zondervan Publishing House.
All rights reserved.

Scripture quotations marked *The Message* are taken from
*The Message*. Copyright © by Eugene H. Peterson 1993, 1994, 1995.
Used by permission of NavPress Publishing Group.

Set in 11 on 13 pt WeidemannBook
by Christian Art Publishers

Printed in China

ISBN 978-1-64272-091-4

20  21  22  23  24  25  26  27  28  29  –  11  10  9  8  7  6  5  4  3  2

*And we have the word of the prophets made more certain, and you will do well to pay attention to it, as to a light shining in a dark place, until the day dawns and the morning star rises in your hearts.*

2 PETER 1:19

# Together with Jesus

Lord Jesus,
In this year, teach me to walk with You day by day
with my hand in Yours.
Thank You for the assurance that if I do this,
I will find no challenge too great
and no obstacle insurmountable.
I want to leave my entire life in Your hands
and trust You completely.
Show me the right way
and take care of me in the year ahead.
Please provide for each of my needs
and when I am occasionally doubtful,
send the light of Your Word as a lamp to light my way.
Thank You for the promise that You will be with me,
that You will help me up when I fall,
that You will lead me like a shepherd.
Teach me to wait for You,
to cling to the hope that I profess,
because I know for certain that You will do
what You have promised.
I pray that in this year You will,
through Your Holy Spirit who lives in me,
enable me to live according to Your instructions
and to comply with Your commandments.

*Amen.*

# Commit your life to the Lord

> Delight yourself in the LORD and he will give you the desires of your heart. Commit your way to the LORD; trust in him.
>
> PSALM 37:4-5

Psalm 37 is a song of the future, a song about God's promises to His children who find themselves in the midst of difficult circumstances. Even though we may face crisis situations, we know that we can continue to live and work peacefully in the year ahead, because the God in whom we trust will always care for us.

On the threshold of a brand-new year why not try to do a few of the things that the psalmist suggests:

- ☀ Trust in God for the year ahead, do what is good and continue to live and work in peace (see v. 3).
- ☙ Delight yourself in the Lord, and He will provide the things that you desire (see v. 4).
- ◈ Entrust the management of your life to God, and He will take care of you every day (see v. 5).

We are often upset by the fact that things go so much better for unbelievers than for us. But the psalmist knows full well that suffering often draws us closer to God.

There is no guarantee that you will skip through the year ahead without problems. But your circumstances do not determine your happiness. Happiness resides in the hearts of people who are in step with God. If you undertake to follow God's commandments, God Himself will give you His joy and peace in your life.

*Heavenly Father, this year I want to commit my life to You and trust only in You. Grant me Your joy, and care for me daily. Amen.*

# The right path for the New Year

> The mouth of the righteous man utters wisdom, and his tongue speaks what is just. The law of his God is in his heart; his feet do not slip.
>
> PSALM 37:30-31

If you want to be truly happy in the year ahead, you need to be willing to comply with God's conditions for your life. You must do what God tells you to do in His Word and walk the path through the new year together with Him, with your hand in His.

In Psalm 37:30-37 we find a profile of what God's children should be like. Test yourself against these requirements:

※ God's children should be people who trust in the Lord and who speak wisely. After all, God's children are often known by what they say and, of course, by what they do *not* say!

❦ God's children are people who not only speak justly, but who also act justly. They are people who carry the law of God in their hearts. This implies that you know God's will for your life, and that you will be willing to submit your own mind and will to God's will.

Can you say in all honesty that God's will determines your entire life?

If so, He promises that your direction on the path of the new year will be certain. You will know where your journey will lead you in the new year. And God's promises not only relate to the here and now; He also promises you an eternal future.

> *Lord Jesus, I really want to walk on Your right path this year. Make me willing to submit my own will to Yours. Amen.*

# Stay on the right path

Whether you turn to the right or to the left, your ears will hear a voice behind you, saying, "This is the way; walk in it."

ISAIAH 30:21

In Matthew 7:13 Jesus warns that we should enter through the narrow gate, because the path that leads to destruction is broad, but the road that leads to life is narrow. If you want to get to heaven you should stay on the right path during the year ahead.

In the parsonage where we used to live there were two sets of steps to our front door. One set had broad steps that ascended gradually, while the other was narrow and steep with railings. We often asked our guests tongue-in-cheek whether they wanted to take the broad or the narrow path.

"This is the way, walk in it," writes the prophet Isaiah. In order to stay on the right path it is necessary that God Himself show you the right way. In Psalm 32:8 He undertakes to do precisely this: "I will instruct you and teach you in the way you should go."

According to another promise in Deuteronomy 31:8, you will not have to walk the path of the new year on your own. God promises to go ahead of you, to be with you, and not to forsake you.

It is frighteningly easy to take a wrong turn somewhere and to go astray: by befriending the wrong people, frequenting the wrong places, watching the wrong television programs or videos, or devouring the wrong kind of reading material. For God's children there is but one path. Make sure that you stay on it in the year ahead.

*Heavenly Father, please show me the right path for the new year, and warn me if I sometimes stray from Your path. Amen.*

# Travel with God

The LORD replied, "My Presence will go with you, and I will give you rest." Then Moses said to him, "If your Presence does not go with us, do not send us up from here."

EXODUS 33:14-15

This interchange between God and Moses was intended to test Moses. God wished to know whether His unfaithful people really wanted Him to accompany them on their journey through the wilderness. And Moses' response was unequivocal, "Lord, if You do not accompany us, do not let us continue our journey."

There is a vast difference between giving someone directions for a journey, and actually going with the person to show him the way. While His people were wandering in the desert, God was with them every day, showing them the right way with a pillar of cloud during the day and a pillar of fire at night. Because He Himself was present with them, they could embark on their journey through the desert with confidence.

In the coming year God not only wants to show you the right way; He wants to be an integral part of your life, accompanying you personally every day of the year ahead. And the guarantee that He gave Moses still holds true for you today: if you let Him accompany you on your journey through life, He will give you His peace.

God loves you very much and wants to be personally involved in your life. As your heavenly Father He wants to look after you every day. As your Shepherd He wants to guide you. As your King He wants to rule over every aspect of your life.

Will you allow Him to do this in the year ahead?

*Heavenly Father, I do not want to embark on the journey into the new year without You. Please accompany me and grant me Your peace. Amen.*

# When the road becomes dangerous

The LORD is a refuge for the oppressed, a stronghold in times of trouble. Those who know your name will trust in you, for you, LORD, have never forsaken those who seek you.

PSALM 9:9-10

We live in dangerous times. While I was writing today's devotion, the newspapers reported an incident of a mother and daughter who went fishing in the Eastern Cape and were brutally murdered.

Every day we read of people being attacked, assaulted, raped or murdered. We become so accustomed to these gruesome reports in the media that we are no longer even shocked or moved by them. And all these things turn us into fearful people; people who live with anxiety in our hearts behind heavy iron gates and complicated security systems.

Are you afraid that your journey through this year will take you into dangerous places? If so, you can depend on the Lord for protection. Of course, this does not mean that you will be exempted from all dangers, but it does mean that the Lord will always be with you, even in dangerous situations. He will be your stronghold in times of trouble, a refuge that will provide you with shelter.

Even though you might walk through the valley of the shadow of death you needn't be afraid, because God is with you, and in His hands you are safe (see Ps. 23:4).

*Heavenly Father, I pray for Your protection in the year ahead. Thank You that I needn't be afraid, because I am always safe in Your hands. Amen.*

# Light on an unfamiliar path

Your word is a lamp to my feet and a light for my path.

PSALM 119:105

While traveling the unfamiliar path into the new year we need a light to show us where the dangerous places are lurking. Marie Louise Haskins writes: "I asked the Man at the gateway of the new year, 'Give me a light so that I can walk safely through the unknown darkness.' And he told me: 'Go out in the darkness, and put your hand in the hand of God. This will be better than a light and safer than a familiar road.'"

God not only knows precisely what is waiting for you in the year ahead, but is also with you every day. He takes your hand and leads you from day to day.

But God does something even better: He not only firmly takes your hand, but also gives you a light to lead you along the unfamiliar path of the new year. This light is your Bible. When you are doubtful if something is right or wrong, you only need to consult your Bible, and light your lamp from God's light. God wants to speak to you from His Word every day.

If you want to hear His voice distinctly and clearly, you in turn need to be willing to spend some time in getting to know His Word. Make this one of your new year's resolutions right now!

*Lord Jesus, thank You for the assurance that You will be a light for me on the path through the new year. Help me to know Your Word so well that I will never have to walk in darkness. Amen.*

# Don't be afraid!

"Do not be afraid, Abram. I am your shield. " Abram believed the LORD.

GENESIS 15:1, 6

On the threshold of a new year there are always many things that fill us with apprehension, because a new year always brings with it new responsibilities. In this passage from Genesis Abram finds himself in something of a predicament: he has just returned from a war and is therefore acutely aware of how vulnerable he is. And on top of that, the Lord has not yet fulfilled His promise of giving him descendants.

The Lord knows full well what is going on in Abram's heart, and therefore He comforts Abram: "Abram, you needn't be afraid. I will protect you, and your descendants will be as numerous as the stars in the heavens." Even though Abram still has no proof, he believes that God's promise to him will be fulfilled. Faith always means that you trust in God for your future, despite the fact that the present seems rather dismal.

Here at the beginning of a new year it would be a good idea to borrow a page from Abram's book. As with Abram, the Lord also knows what is going on in *your* heart. Today He wants to offer His protection to you too, as He did to Abram. He undertakes to protect you in the year ahead and to fulfill every one of His promises.

Tell Him about all your fears and worries about the unknown. He wants to exchange them for His protection and peace, so that you can step into the new year with Him, filled with courage and hope.

*Heavenly Father, thank You that I needn't be afraid of the year ahead. Strengthen my faith so that I will trust steadfastly in You and in Your promises. Amen.*

# *Abram asks for proof*

But Abram said: "O Sovereign LORD, how can I know that I will gain possession of it?" On that day the LORD made a covenant with Abram.

GENESIS 15:8, 18

Abram believed in God, but he wanted proof too – much the same as we do. He wanted to know from the Lord how he could be sure that God's promise of offspring would be fulfilled. And then the Lord made a covenant with Abram. He undertook to be Abram's God if he and his descendants promised to be His people.

In those days a covenant between two parties was a very important matter. To seal the covenant animals were cut in half and the parties involved walked between the halves, arranged opposite each other. In doing so they committed themselves to honor the agreement and declared that the one who broke the agreement would also be cut to pieces, like the animals. But here God alone passes between the pieces of the animals. He knows that it will be impossible for Abram and his descendants to keep His covenant.

If you have been baptized you already share in God's covenant. If you break the covenant by committing sin, God promises to forgive you. He sent His Son to die in your place on the cross so that your sins may be forgiven once and for all. In the year ahead God wants to be the God of the Covenant to you. Are you willing to honor His covenant?

*Lord Jesus, I praise You for coming to fulfill every one of God's promises for me. Thank You for paying the debt of my sins on the cross.*

# Choose now!

Elijah went before the people and said, "How long will you waver between two opinions? If the Lord is God, follow him; but if Baal is God, follow him."

1 KINGS 18:21

In this Scripture passage Elijah presents the Israelites with a challenge. Decide once and for all: Is Baal God or is the Lord God?

You can no longer continue to sit on the fence. The time has come to make a choice. But the people still kept their silence. Before they answered Elijah's question they first wanted to see what was going to happen. Despite the fact that the Lord had helped them so many times in the past they still refused to choose Him alone as their God.

Perhaps we shouldn't be too quick to judge the Israelites. After all, none of us likes to be confronted directly by God. We too would prefer not to take sides, because in this way we can manage to be in the world and one of God's people.

It is natural for us to want to experience our religion in the most enjoyable way, in a way which is most convenient for us. If we seek something in our church and don't find it there, we easily wander from church to church.

If this is the case in your life, you should be confronted with this choice today: Do you choose God as your God, or are there other things that are more important to you?

*Heavenly Father, I want to choose You as the only God in my life. Show me if there are things in my life that I regard as more important than You, and help me to relinquish them. Amen.*

# The Lord will be with you

The Spirit of God came upon Azariah son of Obed. He went out to meet Asa and said to him, "Listen to me, Asa ... The LORD is with you when you are with him. If you seek him, he will be found by you."

2 CHRONICLES 15:1-2

King Asa was obedient to God's instructions and consequently the Lord blessed him and gave him the victory whenever he set forth to battle hostile nations. Azariah noticed this and under the guidance of the Holy Spirit gave King Asa the wonderful promise that still holds true for us today: If we are with the Lord, He will be with us. If we seek Him, He will be found by us.

King Asa listened to Azariah and had all the idols removed from the whole land of Judah and Benjamin. Together with his people he made a sacrifice to the Lord, and they promised to be obedient to the God of their ancestors.

In verse 15 this promise is described beautifully: All Judah rejoiced about the vow because they had sworn it whole-heartedly. They sought God eagerly, and He was found by them. So the Lord gave them rest on every side.

This peace and joy can become a reality in our country too if we are willing to obey God and to follow His commandments. If you remain with the Lord in the year ahead, He will also be with you. You can count on this promise!

*Heavenly Father, in the year ahead I want to grow closer to You. Thank You for Your promise that You will be with me if I seek You. Amen.*

# What are you thinking about?

Set your minds on things above, not on earthly things. For you died,
and your life is now hidden with Christ in God.

COLOSSIANS 3:2-3

What the heart is full of, the tongue speaks, as the well-known
saying goes. We cannot help speaking of the things that are
uppermost in our thoughts.

If one listens to the conversations of the average person it
would seem as if we do not in the least heed Paul's advice to
the church of Colosse. The things we talk about are usually
pessimistic. If our fellow Christians were to listen to us, they
would probably be unable to gather that we actually believe
that God will provide for us in the future.

Make a list of all the thoughts that crossed your mind today.
Very few of us actually think of the "things above." Children of
God not only ought to be new people, they should also learn
to think in new ways. If you want to see your life from God's
perspective, you have to be willing to fill your thoughts with
those things that Jesus came to teach us.

Wouldn't you like to start the new year by continually trying
to focus your thoughts on Christ? Truly strive to focus on His
Word, His promises and Second Coming, and contemplate what
these things mean for you personally. In doing so, you will find
that God is extremely close to you, and that His peace and joy
belong to you.

Heavenly Father, teach me to think the right kind of thoughts,
to focus on Your Word and Your promises, and to contemplate
Your Second Coming. Amen.

# Do you own the right shares?

His divine power has given us everything we need for life and godliness through our knowledge of him who called us by his own glory and goodness. Through these he has given us his very great and precious promises, so that through them you may participate in the divine nature.

2 PETER 1:3-4

"Every child of God shares in the godliness of Jesus," Peter writes. The Greek word that he uses here literally means "shareholders." Christians are shareholders in the godliness of Jesus.

Most of us know exactly what it means to be a shareholder, because we may own unit trusts or shares in some company. Unfortunately earthly shares, however coveted they are, will do us no good after death. The heavenly shares of which Peter writes offer much better dividends, because the shares that we own in God's kingdom also hold advantages for the life that is yet to come.

How do matters stand with your shares? Are you rich in earthly shares but poor in the heavenly ones? Then set about acquiring these shares of which Peter writes. Become a shareholder in Jesus' divine nature. Live as Jesus lived. Allow the Holy Spirit to take control of your life.

Only if you are this kind of shareholder will you be able to live like Jesus: as a new creation in the new year. Only then does the glorious promise of 2 Peter 1:11 also belong to you; only then will you too "receive a rich welcome" into Jesus' eternal kingdom.

*Lord Jesus, I want to share in Your divine nature. Please make it possible for me to become more and more like You every day. Amen.*

# Live like Jesus

Whoever claims to live in him must walk as Jesus did.

1 JOHN 2:6

There is a story about a young Japanese orange vendor who packed a pyramid of oranges on the stairs of the subway. In their rush to get to the train, the crowd of people coming down the stairs kicked over his little pile of oranges.

One man, however, turned around and helped the vendor to gather his oranges together and rebuild his pyramid. When they were done, the little boy tugged at the man's sleeve and asked him, "Is your name perhaps Jesus?"

This anecdote nicely illustrates exactly what John meant when he wrote that if we claim to live in Jesus, we should walk as He did and live in the same way that He did. To live like Jesus requires you to treat other people with the love of Jesus in your heart.

Every Christian should be a role model to others in his chosen sphere of life. Your behavior should clearly show unbelievers what the life of someone belonging to Jesus looks like. In your life they should be able to see what a vast difference He can make.

Martin Luther wrote that we should *be* a Jesus to other people. Some people wear bracelets with the letters WWJD inscribed on them. These letters stand for "What Would Jesus Do?" When you find yourself in a crisis situation, you would do well to ask yourself: What would Jesus do or say under these circumstances? How would He act? Consider this, and follow His example.

*Lord Jesus, You know that I love You and that I want to live in You. Please enable me to act as You would have done in every situation. Amen.*

# If it is the Lord's will ...

> Now listen, you who say, "Today or tomorrow we will go to this or that city, spend a year there, carry on business and make money." Why, you do not even know what will happen tomorrow ... Instead, you ought to say, "If it is the Lord's will, we will live and do this or that."
>
> JAMES 4:13-15

You probably have great plans for the new year. There are dreams to be fulfilled, ambitions to be realized, things that you have always wanted to do, goals to be accomplished ... Sometimes you are so busy planning for tomorrow that you forget about today. And actually today is the only time you really have at your disposal, because none of us knows what tomorrow holds for us.

Oswald Chambers writes that what we call *preparation*, God sometimes calls the *end*. And if you are focused on a particular goal, you may not be paying enough attention to the immediate present. Ask yourself whether what you are doing today is in line with God's will.

If you want to know what the Lord's will for you is, you will need to get to know the Bible better in the year ahead and you will conscientiously have to obey God's precepts, which are set out in it.

Perhaps you need to examine yourself carefully and once again become aware of your own insignificance. In reality you are nothing but mist that appears for a little while and then vanishes, as today's Scripture says. Admit your dependence on the Lord and use all the opportunities that He sends your way today.

*Heavenly Father, help me to seek Your will in everything that I say and do. Amen.*

# Are you doing the right things?

Anyone, then, who knows the good he ought to do and doesn't do it, sins.

JAMES 4:17

When God's children do the things that He asks of them, they experience a sense of self-confidence that fears nothing. However, "if you know the right thing to do and don't do it, that, for you, is evil" (*The Message*, p. 872).

It is important for Christians to do the right things. But sometimes it is so much more enjoyable to do those things that you know all too well are wrong.

If you know the good that you ought to do and choose not to do it, you are committing sin, James warns.

However, one can also sin by neglecting to do some of the things that God wants you to do. This is a somewhat difficult concept to grasp: You can actually sin by doing nothing at all. Sins of omission are those things that we so easily neglect to do.

God asks His children to love and serve other people, to help their neighbors, to pull their weight in the congregation, to be a witness for Jesus in their homes and in their places of work.

Be sure that you are not sinning by just sitting back with your arms back folded. Go ahead and check all the things mentioned above that you are not yet doing regularly, and immediately begin to do something!

*Lord, I am sorry that I sometimes sin by doing nothing. Make me a diligent servant of Your kingdom and show me what You want me to do. Amen.*

# All your ways are known to God

I obey your precepts and your statutes, for all my ways are known to you.

PSALM 119:168

You are probably wondering what surprises the new year has in store for you. But people cannot see into the future, despite the fact that so many have great faith in the weekly astrological predictions published in the majority of magazines. The new year is a new time in your life; it is completely unfamiliar and unknown to you.

We are usually afraid and unsure of the unknown, because we cannot see ahead of time what dangers and challenges lie in wait for us. For this reason we often tend to worry about thousands of things that are probably never even going to happen to us.

Standing on the threshold of an unfamiliar new year, it is a great comfort to know that God knows exactly how your life is going to develop in the future. All your ways are known to Him, writes the psalmist, and He will be there every day to help you, protect you, support you and guide you.

Even though you don't yet know what is going to happen to you in the year ahead, there is something that you can do to ensure that the new year will be a prosperous one: conscientiously obey God's precepts and statutes, which He gives to you in His Word.

God blesses those who keep His commandments: "Great peace have they who love Your law, and nothing can make them stumble," is the promise of Psalm 119:165.

*Heavenly Father, thank You for the assurance that You know exactly what is awaiting me in the new year. Please help me to obey Your Word and Your commandments. Amen.*

# When your strength wanes

O LORD, be gracious to us; we long for you. Be our strength every morning, our salvation in time of distress.

ISAIAH 33:2

Even though Israel so often abandoned their God for heathen idols, they knew very well that He alone was their strength and their salvation in times of distress. For this reason they were always very quick to run back to God whenever they found themselves in adverse circumstances. And because God is merciful and because He loved them, He was willing to help them, time and time again.

Jesus is still a tremendous source of strength for each of His children. Through the strength that He gives us we can accomplish anything, Paul writes to the church in Philippi (see Phil. 4:13).

In the new year there are likely to be many days when your own reserves will fail you; days when your batteries will be so flat that you won't be able to charge them yourself. Therefore, here at the beginning of the year, know that God's immeasurable source of power will always be at your disposal.

You will find the extent of this source of strength in Ephesians 1:19-20. You can draw on this strength throughout the year, but especially toward the end of the year when it feels as if your legs cannot carry you any further.

The Lord promises that He will renew the strength of those who are tired, that they will soar on wings like eagles and run without growing weary (see Is. 40:31). Feel free to draw on this strength in the year ahead!

*Heavenly Father, You know how little strength I have sometimes. Thank You for Your immeasurable strength, which You put at my disposal. Amen.*

# Rejoice in today

This is the day the LORD has made; let us rejoice and be glad in it.

PSALM 118:24

There are still about 350 days left of the new year. Perhaps you are dreaming so much about what you are going to do with them that you have forgotten how important today is. Or perhaps you wish that you could go back to yesterday and correct all the mistakes that you made. But yesterday has already passed and tomorrow is still in the future. Today is the only time that is truly yours.

*Carpe diem*, is an old and well-known Latin proverb. Seize the day! Stop dreaming about tomorrow and live today to the fullest. Every day is special, every day brings new opportunities to be explored, new lessons to be learned, new responsibilities to live up to. Utilize every hour at your disposal today to its full potential; it is irreplaceable.

Joni Eareckson Tada writes: "In God's economy it is today that is the most important. The way in which you hold on to Jesus today, the opportunities that you make use of today, or the things that you do today to help other people are the most critical and important activities of your entire life."

Forget about all the errors of the past and stop worrying about tomorrow. Live today to its full potential. It is a gift from the hand of God. There is a saying that summarizes it beautifully: Yesterday is history, tomorrow is a mystery, but today is a gift – that's why we call it the present!

Therefore, seize the day! God made it for you. Rejoice in it and utilize it to its full extent, all for His honor and glory.

*Heavenly Father, thank You for today. Help me to live each day to its full potential in Your honor. Amen.*

# Forgetting what is behind

But one thing I do: Forgetting what is behind and straining toward what is ahead, I press on toward the goal to win the prize for which God has called me heavenward in Christ Jesus.

PHILIPPIANS 3:13-14

Many people tend to cling to the past. They compare everything with the past: the price of houses, cars and food; they constantly complain that things back then were so much better, cheaper and safer than now. Others keep obsessing about the failures and mistakes of the past.

With this kind of attitude you won't get far. Rather be grateful that the failures are behind you, and focus on the future that beckons ahead. You can start anew, with the help of God's strength. If you want to be really happy and productive in the future, you must be willing to forget the past, and live today with all your might.

An athlete who runs the race while constantly looking back will not succeed. To be successful in a race you need to look ahead, to press on toward your goal of being the first to reach the finish.

The Message (p. 494) puts it very clearly: " I've got my eye on the goal, where God is beckoning us onward – to Jesus. I'm off and running and I'm not turning back. So let's keep focused on that goal, those of us who want everything God has for us."

Keep your eyes on Jesus and run the race of this year in such a way that you may win the prize for which God has called you heavenward in Christ Jesus.

*Lord Jesus, help me to run the race of life this year with my eyes focused on You, so that I may be assured of victory. Amen.*

# God wants to uphold you

"So do not fear, for I am with you; do not be dismayed, for I am your God. I will strengthen you and help you; I will uphold you with my righteous right hand."

ISAIAH 41:10

When a baby cries in the night, his crying immediately ceases when his mother picks him up and holds him. So too with a scared toddler, who is best comforted in his father's strong arms. To be held is to experience a sense of security and safety for which we all yearn. And Christians are people who can experience this sense of security every day, because we have a God who upholds us.

Therefore, when you start worrying about all the things that lie in wait for you in the year ahead, all the things that you don't really feel strong enough to face – remember that God upholds you. And because you are in His arms, you can safely relinquish all your worries about the future.

You can live today with confidence because you have the assurance that the God who upholds you will help and support you in the future. You can also encourage other people and tell them that God is completely in control of everything.

There is nothing new under the sun, says the teacher of Ecclesiastes. There have been dark times in the past, but God has always provided for His children. He will do the same for you in the year ahead.

*Heavenly Father, I praise You for the safety of Your arms. Thank You that I can always entrust all my fears and worries to You. Amen.*

# The right guidance

> Those who are led by the Spirit of God are sons of God. The Spirit himself testifies with our spirit that we are God's children.
>
> ROMANS 8:14, 16

We all make mistakes – mistakes that often have far-reaching consequences for our lives. Have you ever wished that you could always make the right decision and never do the wrong thing? This is actually possible, if you allow the Holy Spirit to lead you from day to day, if you are willing to listen carefully to His suggestions and do not insist on having your own way, come what may.

Those who are led by the Spirit are children of God, as Paul writes to the Christians in Rome. It is the Holy Spirit who makes us children of God. And children of God ought to live as God wants them to.

But who is the Holy Spirit? He is God Himself and He lives inside of you. He will give you advice for all your problems and solutions to all your questions. In this new year He wants to give you the guidance you need for every day.

The Spirit has renewed us completely (see *The Message*, p. 377). Therefore we should also allow Him to control our lives; we should keep in step with the Spirit at all times (see Gal. 5:25). Why not allow Him to give you the right guidance in the year ahead, and also to govern your behavior from day to day?

*Holy Spirit, I pray that You will help me to allow You to control my life every day. Please give me the right guidance in the year ahead. Amen.*

# God is who He is

God said to Moses, "I AM WHO I AM. This is what you are to say to the Israelites: 'I AM has sent me to you.'"

EXODUS 3:14

In Exodus 3 God first introduces Himself by this name to mankind. He tells Moses that His name is "I am who I am."

All too often we feel unable to face all the new challenges awaiting us in the new year. Today the Lord Himself wants to come and tell you who He is, just as He did so long ago with Moses. His Name is still "I am who I am." God is still the same God today as He was in Moses' time. He can still perform miracles and He can still redeem, help and guide His children.

With God at your side your own shortcomings no longer really matter, because you can appropriate His great strength for yourself to guide and support you in the future. Together with Him you are able to accomplish anything; together with Him you will be more than a conqueror in the new year. God's "I am" is so clear that you cannot hear your own "I can't" above it, according to a *Walk Thru the Bible* course.

If you undertake to trust in the Lord for the year ahead, He will in turn undertake to care for you as He cared for His people in Moses' time. And you can trust in Him, because you know from experience that He has always helped you in the past.

*Heavenly Father, I worship You as the God who is still exactly the same as in Moses' time. Thank You for promising to support me in the year ahead. Amen.*

# God will be with you

"May the LORD our God be with us as he was with our fathers; may he never leave us nor forsake us. May he turn our hearts to him, to walk in all his ways and to keep the commands, decrees and regulations he gave our fathers."

1 KINGS 8:57-58

Israel regarded the dedication of the temple as the sign that God had fulfilled His promises to David. Solomon prayed to God and asked Him to bless His people, to be with them always and to keep them faithful to Him. He also prayed that God would help His people to keep His commandments.

God also wants to be the God of the Covenant for you. But as with Israel there are certain conditions. You need to be faithful and obedient to His precepts as contained in His Word.

In Solomon's beautiful prayer we find four benedictions that you can carry with you into the new year and make your own:

- ❊ The Lord promises to be with you as He has always been with His children in the past.
- ❊ The Lord undertakes never to leave you or forsake you.
- ❊ He wants to make you willing to live according to His will every day.
- ❊ He Himself will help you to be obedient to His command-ments.

May each of these benedictions be a reality in your life in the year ahead.

*Lord, thank You for the assurance that You will be with me and that You will never abandon or forsake me. Make me willing to live according to Your will every day. Amen.*

# God keeps His promises

"Not one word has failed of all the good promises he gave through his servant Moses."

I KINGS 8:56

If there is one thing that history teaches us, it is that God is absolutely faithful. If He promises something, He does it, even though it sometimes takes a long time for His promises to be fulfilled.

God promised Abram that He would lead him to the Promised Land and cause a great nation to come forth from him. He promised Moses that He would help him to lead the people out of Egypt. He kept His promise by sending a series of miracles and plagues until Pharaoh agreed to let God's people leave. In this process all of Pharaoh's chariots and horsemen were destroyed.

In the desert God faithfully cared for His people. He provided them with manna, quail and water whenever they needed it. When the Promised Land at last became a reality He was still with them, helping them to conquer the land and battle hostile nations.

The Lord remains true to the promises contained in His Word to this very day. Go ahead and make a little list of your favorite promises from the Bible, and know that the Lord will fulfill each one of them at the appointed time.

You can also remind God of His promises: "You who call on the Lord, give yourself no rest, and give Him no rest" (Is. 62:6).

*Heavenly Father, I praise You for always keeping Your promises and because not one of the promises in Your Word has ever remained unfulfilled. Amen.*

# Seek first His kingdom

"But seek first his kingdom and his righteousness, and all these things will be given to you as well."

MATTHEW 6:33

There are many things that we want to have, and we are willing to toil day and night to obtain them. In His Sermon on the Mount, Jesus provides us with the secret of how to get the things that you want: First seek God's kingdom, and then He will give you all things as well.

God's children need to be willing to put God's kingdom above their own comfort and wealth. And it is by no means easy! In the year ahead this calling might demand that you deny yourself, take up your cross and follow Jesus without looking back at the past that seems to have been so much more comfortable.

Jesus' birth made an immense difference to the world: the oppressive darkness of sin gave way to His heavenly light. We, as His children, must be lights in a dark world, says Jesus. In the year ahead you too can make a difference in the world, country, neighborhood and house where you live by simply being a light for Him.

As a Christian, be sure to make a real difference in the lives of everyone you meet this year by living in such a way that everyone who looks at you will see God and give Him the honor that is due to Him.

Lord Jesus, I worship You as the Light of the world. Please let my light shine for You, and help me to put Your kingdom first in my life. Amen.

# Safe in an unsafe world

> In those days it was not safe to travel about, for all the inhabitants of the lands were in great turmoil.
>
> 2 CHRONICLES 15:5

During the reign of King Asa Israel was a very unsafe place. No one could travel about safely, and there was great turmoil in the land, as 2 Chronicles 15 tells us.

Today's verse reminds us of the situation in many countries today. Burglaries, hijacking and assaults place fear in many people. The current statistics on violent crimes are enough to discourage anyone. Considering all these things while standing on the threshold of this year, you may seriously doubt whether you will be able to survive an entire year of living surrounded by such negativity.

But in the very next chapter there is another verse that says exactly the opposite: "For the eyes of the LORD range throughout the earth to strengthen those whose hearts are fully committed to Him" (2 Chr. 16:9). God is watching over His world from above, so that He can see when and where His children need His help.

As in the time of King Asa, the Lord is still completely capable of helping and protecting you in the same way that He has always helped and protected His people. But then you have to cease being so negative and doubtful, and trust in Him completely. He knows what is best for you, and therefore you can confidently leave the problems of the new year in His hands.

*Heavenly Father, thank You for keeping Your eye on me to see when I might need Your help. Please keep me safe in this unsafe world. Amen.*

# You need a Shepherd

He tends his flock like a shepherd: He gathers the lambs in his arms and carries them close to his heart; he gently leads those that have young.

ISAIAH 40:11

"The Lord is my shepherd, I shall not be in want," David writes in Psalm twenty-three verse one. In the Bible the image of the shepherd is often used to illustrate God's caring love for His children. As a shepherd ensures that his sheep have sufficient grazing and water, as a shepherd leads his sheep and protects them from danger, so the Lord cares for and protects His children.

Today's Scripture verse provides us with a beautiful picture of a shepherd who truly cares for his flock. He gathers the weak ones and the lambs in his arms and carries them close to his heart; he gently leads those who have young.

The fact that you have the Lord as your shepherd is your guarantee that the Lord will look after you in the year ahead. Your shepherd loves you so much that He was even willing to sacrifice his life for you.

However, when Jesus describes Himself as the Good Shepherd in John 10, He also gives a condition that His sheep have to adhere to: "The sheep listen to His voice ... and His sheep follow Him because they know His voice" (Jn. 10:3-4).

If you want God as your Shepherd in this year, you must be willing to listen to His voice every day and to follow Him.

*Lord Jesus, I worship You as my Shepherd who cares for me every day. Make me willing to follow You and to listen to Your voice. Amen.*

# God will uphold you

The LORD upholds all those who fall and lifts up all who are bowed down. The eyes of all look to you, and you give them their food at the proper time. You open your hand and satisfy the desires of every living thing.

PSALM 145:14-16

Psalm 145 deals with the Lord's kingship. His kingship extends over everything and everyone. That is why His children should praise Him every day.

Today's Scripture verse contains many additional reasons why the Lord ought to be praised. The psalmist knows that the Lord is good, compassionate, merciful, loving, just, and always there to answer the prayers of those who venerate Him, if they faithfully plead for His help.

What beautiful verses these are, especially for those days when we feel slightly off kilter. When you stumble and fall, you can count on the Lord to uphold you. When you are discouraged and dejected, He will uplift you.

He will give you your food at the proper time, even if you are wondering how you are going to make ends meet when inflation continues to rise. He promises to open His hand to you and to satisfy all your desires in abundance.

Isn't this more than enough reason to praise and worship Him in the new year?

*Heavenly Father, how good You are to me! I praise You for upholding me when I fall, for uplifting me when I am dejected, for opening Your hand to me and satisfying all my desires. Amen.*

# God is faithful to His promises

Let us hold unswervingly to the hope we profess, for he who promised is faithful.

HEBREWS 10:23

Sometimes we hope that our dreams will come true, and then they don't. If this continues to happen you eventually forget how to dream and how to hope. Fortunately this will never be the case if you put your hope in God.

If there is one thing that you can steadfastly believe in, it is in God's complete integrity. He is the One in whom you can truly trust, as the prophet Isaiah writes (see Is. 33:6). When God gives you His promises in His Word, you can hold on to them in complete faith, even if it does not seem as if any of them will be fulfilled immediately. God always keeps His promises. But sometimes He expects His children to be willing to wait for the fulfillment of these promises.

Of course, God might also decide to give you things that are different from what you've asked for. You probably don't give your children everything that they ask for; it would simply not be good for them. However, you do provide them with the things they truly need.

This is God's promise to you, too: He will provide you with all those things that you need in the year ahead. He will keep all the promises He has made. And if His promises aren't fulfilled as quickly as you would like, wait for the Lord. He does not make mistakes. Whatever He decides to give you will always be the right thing.

*Lord, thank You that I can trust You completely and be assured that whatever You decide to give me will always be the best thing for me. Amen.*

# Wait for the Lord

I wait for the LORD, my soul waits, and in his word I put my hope. My soul waits for the Lord more than watchmen wait for the morning.

PSALM 130:5-6

The poet of Psalm 130 finds himself in a crisis situation. And from the depths of this crisis he calls upon the Lord. He confesses his sins and expresses his faith and trust in the Word of the Lord. He wants to restore his relationship with the Lord.

"Trust and dependence are cultivated in the crucible of life's dangers," Johan Smit writes in one of his devotionals. When things are going badly for you, you tend to pray more often than when the going is good.

It is only when you realize the inadequacy of your own strength in dealing with the crisis that you realize that only God can help you. And then you run into the open arms of the Lord.

Despite the fact that you should not seek the Lord only when you are in distress, He is always there for you.

But then you, like the psalmist, have to be willing to trust steadfastly in the Lord and to wait for His promises to be fulfilled. And don't be mistaken: sometimes the Lord will make you wait for a very long time, precisely because He wishes to test your faith.

If you currently find yourself in a waiting period, look at it as a test of the authenticity of your faith. Confess the sins that are still present in your life. And take the promise in verses 7 and 8 to heart: God will redeem you, for with Him is unfailing love and full redemption.

*Heavenly Father, thank You that I can also call upon You when I am in difficulty. I trust in You and know that You will redeem me. Amen.*

# Succor in times of need

"The Spirit of the Lord is on me, because he has anointed me to preach good news to the poor. He has sent me to proclaim freedom for the prisoners and recovery of sight for the blind, to release the oppressed, to proclaim the year of the Lord's favor."

LUKE 4:18-19

In this passage Jesus is preaching in the synagogue and reading from Isaiah 61, where the coming of the Messiah is prophesied. It was written while God's people were in exile. This prophecy was intended to tell them that they should not lose courage, but should rather look ahead to the time when the Messiah would come.

In Isaiah 61 the Messiah Himself is speaking. "The Spirit of the Lord is on me, because He has anointed me," He declares.

Jesus is speaking about Himself in this passage. Isaiah's prophecy was fulfilled with Jesus' birth. He is the King who came to earth to help people in their distress.

During His time on earth Jesus was always sensitive to others' needs. He gave food to those who were hungry, healed those who were ill, and restored the sight and hearing of the blind and the deaf.

If you want to follow in His footsteps, you will also have to develop a heart that is sensitive to people in need. There are so many of them all around you. Notice them. Reach out to them, open your wallet and your heart to them. Comfort those here on earth who are in need – as Jesus did during His earthly ministry.

*Lord Jesus, I pray that You will give me a sensitive and generous heart, and willing hands to help people who are in need. Make me a helper of people, as You were. Amen.*

# God's law

Heavenly Father,
Thank You for Your law;
the road map to my life that shows me
how to live joyfully in this confused world,
and how to eventually arrive at the right destination.
Thank You that Your law shows me the right course.
Help me to love You above all things
and to love my neighbor as I love myself.
Teach me to worship You alone,
not to have any idols, but to hallow Your Name;
to honor Your Sabbath and honor my parents;
not to take a life or commit adultery;
not to steal, tell lies
or covet the possessions of others.
Thank You for Your promise that I will be happy
if I undertake to follow this map closely.

_Amen._

# God's law shows me the right course

The law of the LORD is perfect, reviving the soul ... The precepts of the LORD are right, giving joy to the heart. The commands of the LORD are radiant, giving light to the eyes.

PSALM 19:7-8

The Torah had an entirely different meaning to the Jews in ancient times than the law of God has to us today. After all, a law usually supposes rules that must be obeyed; regulations that you must adhere to. And for that reason we are not always too keen on complying with God's law.

C. S. Lewis says that the law sometimes reminds us of a dentist's drill rather than the honey and gold that the Bible compares it to.

It should not be this way. God's commandments should be guideposts on our way, not chains on our hands and feet.

The Jews regarded their Torah or law as something positive: security in an uncertain world. The Jews of ancient times had far less security than we have today. Sound advice was therefore very important to them, particularly God's advice. And He recorded this advice for them in His law. The Lord still teaches His people through the Torah as He advises them how to live with joy.

"The precepts of the LORD are right," writes the psalmist, "giving joy to the heart" (Ps. 19:8). "Commandment rhymes with enjoyment," said a famous theologian.

To obey God's commandments should still be enjoyable to you, as it was to ancient Israel.

*Heavenly Father, I am sorry for so often thinking that Your law is a bunch of unnecessary rules. Make it a joy to me to comply with Your law. Amen.*

# The law is a school

The precepts of the LORD are right, giving joy to the heart. The commands of the LORD are radiant, giving light to the eyes. The fear of the LORD is pure, enduring forever. The ordinances of the LORD are sure and altogether righteous.

PSALM 19:8-9

The law teaches us the difference between right and wrong. It shows us how God wants us to live. Because we have the law, we know what sin is.

The Dutch theologian, van Ruler, says that there are three main reasons why the psalmist finds so much joy in the law:

☀ The law is the key to life for God's children. It is the instruction manual of the One who made everything. (The church organ in my home town broke years ago and no one could fix it. After a number of weeks the church council managed to get hold of an old man who managed to fix the organ as good as new. When the organist asked him how he managed to do it, he simply said: "I built the organ.")

🐚 The law introduces us to God. From the law we learn who God is and how He should be served. Every component of the law reveals an aspect of God to us. The more I obey the law, the bigger God becomes in my life.

🐚 The law also gives me the opportunity to be God's co-worker. If I obey it, I know that I act according to God's will. "To disobey the law is to sacrifice your freedom; it is a choice against God's authority, God's love," writes Johan Smit.

*Heavenly Father, make me willing to learn about Your law – show me where I am still sinful, and teach me to know You better. Amen.*

# The greatest commandment

"Teacher, which is the greatest commandment in the Law?" Jesus replied: "'Love the Lord your God with all your heart and with all your soul and with all your mind.' And the second is like it: 'Love your neighbor as yourself.'"

MATTHEW 22:36-37, 39

The Pharisees identified more than 600 laws from the Old Testament, which they strictly adhered to. They were also constantly distinguishing between which laws were more important than others.

A teacher of the law who wanted to trick Jesus once asked Him which of the Ten Commandments was the greatest. And then Jesus gave him the striking response in today's text. You must love God above everything and your neighbor as yourself. All the Law and the Prophets hang on these two commandments.

The actual meaning of Jesus' words is that when you truly love God and your fellowman, it will be easy to obey the whole law. After all, you do not worship other gods if you love God; neither will you rob your neighbor, cheat on your spouse, kill others and covet their possessions if you love them.

Therefore, you don't have to worry about all the things you are not allowed to do, as the Pharisees did in Jesus' time. Rather concentrate on the most important commandment, the commandment of love which Jesus identifies here. Do those things that prove your love for God and your neighbor.

*Heavenly Father, please help me to love You above everything else and my neighbor as myself. Show me the things I can do to prove my love for You and my neighbor. Amen.*

# God above everything

"The most important one," answered Jesus, "is this: 'Hear, O Israel, the Lord our God, the Lord is one. Love the Lord your God with all your heart and with all your soul and with all your mind and with all your strength.'"

MARK 12:29-30

The teachers of the law understood the answer Jesus gave them perfectly well. They knew that the law required them to love God and to worship Him as the one Lord. But their definition of "love" differed vastly from Jesus' definition. To Jesus, love is always a verb.

If you want to love God with all your heart and with all your soul and with all your mind and with all your strength, you have to prove it with your life – this is what He was actually telling the teachers of the law.

You can obey the laws of the world without loving the people who made those laws, but it is different with God's law. You can never fully obey His law without loving Him.

Johan Smit writes: "God's law is a law that can function meaningfully only in the context of a love affair. You obey the law because you love the Legislator. And this love is a love that is concerned with life."

In other words, God's love for you means that He makes eternal life possible for you. And your love for Him should mean that you are willing to surrender your life to Him. It must be an all-encompassing love that comes from your heart, soul and mind. That is how God loves you. Do you love Him like this?

*Heavenly Father, thank You for Your love for me. Teach me to love You above all things and to prove that love with my life. Amen.*

# Your neighbor as yourself

"The second is this: 'Love your neighbor as yourself.' There is no commandment greater than these."

MARK 12:31

It is interesting to note that Jesus says here that you must love your neighbor as yourself. We all know what this means because most of our lives are centered mainly around ourselves. There are very few people who are as important to you as yourself. Don't you first attempt to make sure that you're all right in everything you do? Don't you first try to get to the top before you think of helping others?

It is good to love yourself, because you were created in the image of God and you are His representative here on earth. Therefore you are not to regard yourself as inferior; you should love yourself, but in the right way.

If you love yourself in the right way, you will know precisely how you should love your neighbor.

Loving yourself in the right way also means that you should not think more of yourself than is appropriate, and that you should esteem all other people as highly as yourself. This sounds impossible, doesn't it? And so it is, but God can help you to achieve it through the strength of His Holy Spirit who lives in you.

Jesus concludes by saying that these two laws – to love God and your neighbor – summarize the rest of the law. No other commandment is greater than these two.

*Lord, I am sorry if I sometimes love myself more than I love others. Teach me to love other people as much as I love myself, and You above all. Amen.*

# The Ten Commandments

"I am the LORD your God, who brought you out of Egypt, out of the land of slavery."

EXODUS 20:2

In the Ten Commandments, God explains to His people that they are not allowed to live as they please, but that they should obey the rules of His covenant if they want to be truly happy.

The law of the Ten Commandments is recorded for us in Exodus 20 and Deuteronomy 5. The first four commandments deal with our love for God and the last six with our love for our neighbor.

It is significant that God begins His Ten Commandments with a declaration of love to the people He chose for Himself above all other peoples: "I am the LORD your God, who brought you out of Egypt, out of the land of slavery."

The Israelites were used to many gods; the heathens worshiped various idols, but the God who is speaking here is the God of the Covenant, the God of Abraham, Isaac and Jacob; the God who loved His people, and who freed them from Egyptian slavery.

This God has never changed. He is the same God as He was in the time of Moses. He still loves His children and wants to care for them and protect them.

So great is His love that He sent His Son to the world so that you can also be counted as one of His people if you believe in Him. He is still committed to freeing you from the yoke of sin that weighs you down. When you consider the Ten Commandments, first understand who it is that presents this law to you.

*Lord, thank You that I can consider Your law in the certain knowledge that You love me and that You want to free me from sin. Amen.*

# No other gods

"You shall have no other gods before me."

Exodus 20:3

The Israelites were used to the fact that the heathen nations they came into contact with worshiped dozens of idols.

These nations, who did not know the God of Israel, saw nothing wrong with worshiping a variety of gods. The Egyptians even added the sun, the moon, the stars and the Nile to their long list of gods.

This multitude of gods posed quite a temptation to the Israelites, because the worship of heathen gods was usually accompanied by enticing rituals. And Israel did stray from the only God many times to get a taste of what it was like to worship such a heathen god.

But the God of Israel is different. He is the only Lord. He is a jealous God who demands undivided faithfulness from His children. It would serve no purpose for His people to obey His law strictly if they did not worship Him as the only God. That is why He punished them severely when they did stray from Him.

Today we no longer worship idols of wood and stone, but there are still many things that could become as important as our God if we are not careful. Sex, power, money and security are only a few of these.

Even good things such as your spouse, children or grandchildren can take God's rightful place in your life. And this must not be. God asks your undivided heart: you may have no other gods besides Him.

*Heavenly Father, help me to identify all the idols that may be in my life and to relinquish them so that I can worship You alone. Amen.*

# Beware of idols

"You shall not make for yourself an idol in the form of anything in heaven above or on the earth beneath or in the waters below."

EXODUS 20:4

In the time when the commandments were recorded, people often made idols from wood or stone that they could carry with them. Even religious Israelites kept such talisman-idols which served as proof that they had their god with them.

When God forbade idols He wanted to teach His people that they could not make a likeness of Him. God is so holy that no one has ever seen Him. Therefore it is impossible to make an idol or likeness of God. God is omnipresent; He is with His children every day, but He cannot be contained in a manmade idol. He is also a jealous God who demands absolute faithfulness from His children (see Deut. 5:15).

We are still in danger of attempting to confine God to one place. We put Sundays aside for God as the one day on which we go to church. We regard the church as the house of God where we meet Him.

But this is not true: God is everywhere and we are His house. Our bodies are temples that God inhabits through His Holy Spirit. Through His Holy Spirit, God is therefore with each of His children every moment of every day, not only on Sundays.

We are also in danger of making "idols" of people or of issues if sport or politics become more important to us than God.

*Heavenly Father, I praise You for being with me always; for living in me through Your Holy Spirit. Make me absolutely faithful to You. Amen.*

# *Undivided faithfulness*

"You shall not bow down to them or worship them; for I, the LORD your God, am a jealous God."

Exodus 20:5

The heathen nations with whom the Israelites were in contact had the habit of kneeling before their idols and worshiping them. And God refused to tolerate this behavior from the people He chose for Himself.

Our God is a jealous God. He demands undivided faithfulness from His people. He does not share His children with anyone or anything. If they obey Him, He promises that they will always be prosperous and that He will keep His promises to them. Unfortunately Israel repeatedly exchanged their God for idols, and were punished accordingly.

If you undertake to love God above everything else, so that He becomes the single most important thing in your life, you will not run the risk of bestowing this loyalty, which is due to God alone, on other people or things. No person or thing may take God's rightful place in your life. He asks you to love and serve Him with all your heart and all your soul and with all your strength.

Consider carefully whether there are things in your life to which you devote more time, money and effort than to the things of God. If this is the case, you are worshiping an idol. Then God no longer has your undivided faithfulness.

*Heavenly Father, I come to confess that there are still so many matters in my life that consume too much of my money, time and attention. Help me from now on to serve You with undivided faithfulness. Amen.*

# God's name is sacred

---

"You shall not misuse the name of the LORD your God, for the LORD will not hold anyone guiltless who misuses his name."

EXODUS 20:7

---

Recently we were blessed with a new grandchild, and I was so pleased that she was given my name that it made me consider the importance of a name again.

After all, everyone's name is important to him, and God's Name, so the Bible teaches us, is His honor. God first revealed to Moses what His proper Name was when He said: "I AM WHO I AM. This is what you are to say to the Israelites: 'I AM HAS SENT me to you'" (Ex. 3:14).

The name *Yahweh* was so sacred to the Jews that they did not speak it out loud. God's Name assures His children that the living God is truly present with His children.

When you hear God's Name, you think about His Person, who He is: holy, almighty, all-knowing, omnipresent. Because God is holy, His Name is also holy and His children are never to use it without respect and reverence.

"Hallowed be Your name," Jesus teaches us to pray in the Lord's Prayer. Even when you pray, you must honor God's Name and not use it as a filler. And when people around you use His Name in vain by cursing – as so often happens these days in movies, books and conversations – it is your duty to protest and defend His name.

*Lord, I pray that You will help me to honor Your Name in everything that I say and do. Help me to see to it that everyone around me does the same. Amen.*

# The day of the Lord

"Remember the Sabbath day by keeping it holy. Six days you shall labor and do all your work, but the seventh day is a Sabbath to the LORD your God. On it you shall not do any work."

ExoDUS 20:8-10

The Sabbath day is a day of rest instituted by God Himself: "For in six days the LORD made the heavens and the earth, the sea and all that is in them, but He rested on the seventh day. Therefore the LORD blessed the Sabbath day and made it holy" (Ex. 20:11).

The Israelites' Sabbath day fell on our Saturday, but because Jesus rose from the dead, we now put aside Sundays as the Lord's day. The Lord's day is special to His children, and there are therefore special conditions about how we should spend this day.

Sunday is the one day on which you need not attend to those things that make demands on you during the rest of the week. It is the one day on which you have time to spend on the matters of the Lord. You can use it to go to church and read spiritual books; you can make time to talk to God and make extra time for Bible study.

How do you spend Sundays? Do you celebrate the day of the Lord as the fourth commandment instructs you to? Or do you use it mainly for your own relaxation: to work in your garden or to go to the beach?

The Sabbath day should not only be a rest day for the children of God, but also a day of celebration; a day on which the Lord must be honored and praised and served.

*Lord, please teach me to spend my Sundays as a day of rest and celebration in Your honor. Amen.*

# Honor your father and your mother

> "Honor your father and your mother, so that you may live long in the land the LORD your God is giving you."
>
> EXODUS 20:12

The fifth commandment is the beginning of the second table of the law, which not only teaches us to live in the correct relationship with God, but also with our fellowman.

In this commandment the relationship between parents and children is discussed. In Israel the father's authority over the family was absolute. The parents were God's representatives in the lives of their children. And God wanted this authority to be recognized. It was so important to Him that He made this the only commandment that comes with a promise.

Today it seems as if children no longer really value the biblical structure of authority. They want to do their own thing in their own way. They want to do as their friends do. To them, mother and father are sometimes rather old-fashioned. But these words of authority were instituted by God Himself: He is the one who appoints parents over their children and it is His will that children honor and obey their parents. If they fail to do this, it is unlikely that they will have respect for God and for other people.

God appoints you over your children. Make sure that you maintain the necessary discipline in your family so that your children will honor you and acknowledge your authority. God makes a beautiful promise to those children who acknowledge the authority of their parents: "so that you may live long in the land the LORD your God is giving you" (Ex. 20:12).

*Heavenly Father, thank You for appointing me over my children to bring them up for You. Help them to obey Your commandment. Amen.*

# Life is precious

"You shall not murder."

EXODUS 20:13

If we look at television and the newspapers it would seem that life has become cheap. People are murdered left, right and center. And it seems as if the murderers get off scot-free. Many of them get reduced sentences and others are simply released when the evidence against them is insufficient. It seems as if we no longer have respect for human life.

In Old Testament times there was just as much bloodshed. And this was as intolerable then as it is now. God is the only One who can give life. And life is precious to Him. He forbids man to take a life because man has no authority over life and death.

Perhaps the sixth commandment does not bother you because you have never even considered taking someone else's life. But you could be guilty of "murder" if, for example, you drive recklessly and consequently put the lives of other people at risk; if you decide to have an abortion, or if you are in favor of euthanasia.

Even if you watch television programmes that propagate violence or if you endanger your own life through recklessness, you are guilty of murder. The Bible even says that if you curse someone you are guilty of murder (see Mt. 5:22).

Every person is precious to God. God wants you to regard the lives of others as just as precious as your own life, and not to deny the human dignity of other people.

*Heavenly Father, I realize that I am sometimes guilty of murder. Please forgive me and help me never to injure other people's human dignity. Amen.*

# Protect your marriage

"You shall not commit adultery."

EXODUS 20:14

God instituted marriage. "Therefore what God has joined together, let man not separate," Jesus Himself says in Mark ten verse nine.

Unfortunately divorce has become ridiculously easy nowadays. Simply not getting along with each other is regarded as reason enough for divorce.

This is not what God intended marriage to be. A marriage consists of two people God personally chose to complement each other and to be a help to each other. His will is for two people who are married to remain faithful to each other forever.

Never degrade your marriage by sinful sexual desires. The cheap pornography that floods our stores is one of the things that threatens marriages.

Marriage is the sphere created by God Himself where two people can exercise their love for each other. And sexual love is God's gift to two people who love each other, a gift that can be properly enjoyed within the space of marriage.

Love your spouse. The warning lights of your marriage should begin flashing if another man or woman even quickens your pulse.

Simply looking at another man or woman with desire means that you have already committed adultery, as Jesus Himself says in His Sermon on the Mount (see Mt. 5:27). God requires you to be absolutely faithful to your spouse and you can only do this if your relationship with God is right.

*Lord, thank You for the marriage partner You personally selected for me. Help us to be absolutely faithful to You and to each other. Amen.*

# Don't steal

"You shall not steal."

EXODUS 20:15

To steal, according to the dictionary, is to take something that does not belong to you. Our possessions are a gift from God and it is not right to take things that belong to someone else. None of us would simply break into somebody's house or business and steal things. But there are other ways in which the eighth commandment can be broken.

Some individuals and businesses go so far in evading taxes that it could certainly be termed stealing. You can even steal with your eyes by appropriating someone else's ideas as your own.

You can also steal from God by failing to give Him the rightful part of your income. Everything you have, comes from God and therefore it actually belongs to Him. Even your abilities and gifts were given to you by Him. By abusing them, you also steal from God.

There is yet another way in which you can transgress this commandment. If you see people who are in need and refuse to help them, your Christian testimony lacks power.

Remember that everything you are and possess is pure grace from the hand of God, and it is fitting that you praise and honor Him for it.

Treat other people as you would like to be treated and you will have no trouble with the eighth commandment.

*Lord, thank You for everything that I receive so undeservedly from Your hand. Help me never to take others' possessions for myself or be tempted to steal from You. Amen.*

# Tell the truth

> "You shall not give false testimony against your neighbor."
>
> EXODUS 20:16

I recently watched an amusing movie called *Liar, Liar* in which a young boy wishes that his dishonest lawyer father would not tell a lie for one full day. His wish is granted, with hilarious consequences.

While I was watching the movie I started thinking of how easily even Christians twist the truth, or add a little detail here or there, thinking that it isn't really a lie. We often tell white lies to soothe people and not to hurt them unnecessarily. We also twist others' words without really giving the matter any serious thought.

Tell the whole truth and nothing but the truth, the ninth commandment orders us. Don't harm the good name of another by saying questionable things about him. Women are particularly guilty of this. We like gossiping about other people and then we justify ourselves by thinking that there's nothing wrong with it as long as these stories are true.

But this unnecessary gossiping compromises the good name of our neighbor. Furthermore, we even transgress the ninth commandment if we hear somebody else slandering our neighbor and fail to defend him.

Before saying something about someone else again, make sure that it is both true and friendly. The Lord wants you to regard the name and reputation of other people as just as important as your own.

*Heavenly Father, please forgive me for all those times that I harmed someone else's reputation – consciously or unknowingly. Help me to always tell the truth in future. Amen.*

# Don't covet

"You shall not covet."

EXODUS 20:17

The tenth commandment has always been particularly difficult for me. Every single one of us must at some stage have wanted something that belongs to someone else.

Think, for example, of the exceptional painting, the lovely house, the brand-new car your friends recently bought and which you can only look at with longing and wish that it could have been yours.

Fortunately the tenth commandment doesn't say that you are not allowed to want certain things, but rather that you are not allowed to harm your neighbor in order to satisfy your desires. You are not to be envious of someone because they own something you would like to have.

In other words, this commandment is not so much concerned with desire as such, but rather with the things that belong to your neighbor.

To desire another man's wife or possessions to such an extent that you would kill for it as David and Ahab did, is obviously a sin. Then you are transgressing the tenth commandment. You are, however, allowed to admire your neighbor's lovely house and truly desire your friends' new car, but not if this wish would be at their expense.

Be satisfied with the things the Lord gives you rather than sulking about other people's possessions and envying those who have more than you. Don't begrudge your neighbor what he has, rather wish him the joy of owning it.

*Lord, please forgive me for so often being dissatisfied with what You give me, and for then desiring other people's possessions. Take away my envy and fill my heart with love. Amen.*

# Where sin begins

Above all else, guard your heart, for it is the wellspring of life.

PROVERBS 4:23

Sin usually originates in our hearts and in our thoughts. Children of God should be able to control their negative emotions and should be able to focus on those things that are good and right in the eyes of God. Make sure that your emotions guide you in the right direction.

Before actually doing something wrong, before transgressing God's law, the wrongful deed you want to commit takes shape in your mind. You consider the sin before committing it. Through the things you think about you can get a pretty good picture of what you look like: "As water reflects a face, so a man's heart reflects the man" (Prov. 27:19).

Even more importantly, your thoughts have an immense power in your life. "Man is what he thinks," an eastern philosopher said thousands of years ago. God can renew your mind. He can teach you to think in a new way.

God can turn negative, despondent people into cheerful, positive people: "Be transformed by the renewing of your mind. Then you will be able to test and approve what God's will is – his good, pleasing and perfect will," Paul writes to the Christians in Rome (Rom. 12:2).

Pray every day that you will not be tempted to transgress God's law.

Lord, I pray that You will renew my mind so that I will know what Your will is for my life, and so that I will be able to obey Your commandments. Amen.

# Use your road map

How can a young man keep his way pure? By living according to your word. I seek you with all my heart; do not let me stray from your commands.

Psalm 119:9-10

This verse does not apply only to young people, but has relevance for all people. The only way in which we can truly keep our lives free of sin is by obeying God's Word. And to obey that Word it is essential to know it.

The Ten Commandments are repeatedly explained to us in different phrases in the Bible. They show us how the Lord wants His children to live and obeying them is the only way in which we can achieve true happiness. We should not view God's commandments as a constraint. Do not let them simply become a list of may-nots and must-nots.

However, they do provide a clear road map that directs God's children the right way. Although this route is not always followed by the world, it is the only correct way for those who know and love the Lord.

Reread all Ten Commandments in Exodus 20 carefully. Is there any commandment that you still at times tend to transgress? If this is the case, ask the Lord to help you to obey each commandment fully. You cannot do this by yourself, but the Holy Spirit can make it possible for you.

And remember, God's way is always the best way for you. Therefore, consult your road map every day of your life.

*Heavenly Father, thank You for Your commandments that serve as a map to guide me. Help me by the power of Your Spirit to keep my life pure by obeying Your Word. Amen.*

# On the right path

Trust in the LORD with all your heart and lean not on your own understanding; in all your ways acknowledge him, and he will make your paths straight.

PROVERBS 3:5-6

It serves no purpose to have the right map but still to be on the wrong path. It is essential for God's children to acknowledge Him in everything they say and do. Only then can they be sure that He will guide them along the right path.

God has a plan for each of His children. This master plan of God may differ vastly from our own selfish little plans. Sometimes we grow impatient for God's plan with our lives to be fulfilled and then we do things in our own way to help His plan along as Sarah did when Abraham's promised heir did not arrive soon enough for her liking. But when people interfere with God's plans things go terribly wrong, as we learn from the story of Sarah.

Before beginning to make your own plans, first consider the advice offered in Proverbs and acknowledge God in all your ways. Only then can you be sure that you are on the right path.

Study your Bible when you have doubts and when you are not quite clear on what the right thing to do would be. In His Word God shows you the right path time and again.

His Word is the light on your path. Therefore, first ask before you do something. If you pray first and then act, you will not easily make a mistake.

*Heavenly Father, thank You for Your Word in which You show me the right way time and again. Make me willing to walk Your path. Amen.*

# Stay on God's path

Walk in all the way that the LORD your God has commanded you, so that you may live and prosper and prolong your days in the land that you will possess.

DEUTERONOMY 5:33

Israel often strayed; they simply couldn't seem to manage staying on God's path. Time after time they forsook their God for heathen idols. Even when Moses was on the mountain to receive God's law, they convinced Aaron to make them a golden calf which they worshiped fervently.

But before we condemn Israel we have to ask ourselves whether we are still on the right path. We all have our personal "idols" for which we care a great deal. Calvin said that the heart of every person is a factory of idols.

Verse 32 clearly refers to the law: "So be careful to do what the Lord your God has commanded you; do not turn aside to the right or to the left." Like Israel of old we too tend to adjust God's law slightly; we tend to do as we please as long as we remain roughly true to what God asks. Unfortunately this is not good enough.

God asks His children to obey His law in absolute detail; He requires you not to deviate from it even slightly. Only by doing this will you be able to remain on His path and to avoid the many trails that lead away from it.

*Heavenly Father, please make it possible for me to obey Your law in minute detail and not to interpret it as I please. Amen.*

# God's law brings joy

Direct me in the path of your commands, for there I find delight.

PSALM 119:35

God's law is not only intended as your road map through life, but it also shows you the way to happiness. If you follow this map you will discover that living according to these particular instructions that God gives you in His Word will make you extremely happy.

After all, this is why you were created: to do His will and to honor Him. So, when you obey His law, joy will automatically follow because you will know that you are fulfilling His purpose for your life.

The psalmist has firsthand knowledge of this joy. The entire Psalm 119 is an extended song of joy about the law of God, "Your statutes are my heritage forever; they are the joy of my heart. I long for Your salvation, O LORD, and Your law is my delight" (Ps. 119:111, 174). Paul, too, knows this joy that comes to those who obey God's law: For in my inner being I delight in God's law (Rom. 7:22).

Because God loves you, His law gives you clear guidelines for living each day with joy. If you undertake to obey the law you will truly be able to testify with the psalmist: "I rejoice in following Your statutes as one rejoices in great riches" (Ps. 119:14).

Then you will also be able to make the beautiful promise of Psalm 112:1 your own: "Blessed is the man who fears the LORD, who finds great delight in His commands."

*Heavenly Father, I praise You for the joy that comes into my life when I obey Your law. Amen.*

# Tell your children

These commandments ... are to be upon your hearts. Impress them on your children. Talk about them when you sit at home and when you walk along the road, when you lie down and when you get up.

DEUTERONOMY 6:6-7

It is not sufficient for parents who know and love the Lord simply to comply with the Ten Commandments themselves.

The Lord also requires them to discuss these commandments with their children. Religion was an integral part of the lives of God's people. From an early age children were taught their history and God's law. Their religion was directed toward practical application and not merely towards theoretical knowledge.

If you want your children to know and love the Lord you will have to teach them from an early age in a simple and understandable way to love and serve God and to obey His commandments.

To achieve this you will have to live your faith in practice; you will have to show your children through your life what you believe. It serves no purpose to say one thing and do something completely different.

A certain theologian once said that faith is not a set of rigid rules that should be presented to your children, it is a Person, Jesus Christ, who should be revealed to them in your life.

If you obey God's commandment in Deuteronomy 6:6 you will be able to make the beautiful promise in verse 3 your own, "Hear, O Israel, and be careful to obey so that it may go well with you."

*Heavenly Father, help me to teach my children in such a way that they will also serve and love You and obey Your commandments. Amen.*

# God wants to give you insight

Give me understanding, and I will keep your law and obey it with all my heart.

PSALM 119:34

The fact that different scholars interpret the Bible in so many different ways can be rather confusing. At times you no longer know whom you should believe.

Pray before you read the Bible. When you are busy with God's Word and law, ask God continually to give you the necessary insight in His Word to be able to obey His law and keep His commandments with all your heart. Also ask God for wisdom so that you will be able to interpret His Word, His message to you, correctly.

Bible study is extremely important for God's children. Keep a Bible commentary or concordance at hand that can explain the Word to you when you read your Bible. Paul writes to Timothy, "Every part of Scripture is God-breathed and useful one way or another – showing us truth, exposing our rebellion, correcting our mistakes, training us to live God's way.

Through the Word we are put together and shaped up for the tasks God has for us" (*The Message*, p. 530).

Ask God to give you insight into His Word so that you will be able to obey His commandments and keep them with all your heart.

*Lord, I pray that You will give me insight into Your Word; that You will personally explain the Word to me so that I can keep Your commandments with all my heart. Amen.*

# Obedience out of love

"If you love me, you will obey what I command. Whoever has my commands and obeys them, he is the one who loves me ... and I too will love him and show myself to him."

JOHN 14:15, 21

The Lord expects His children to obey His law. He asks us to keep the commandments that He gives us in His Word, not because we have to, but because we truly love Him.

If you truly love someone, you like doing those things he wants you to do. Therefore you should also like obeying God's commandments precisely because they provide you with a way to express your love for God.

Your obedience to God's law is the visible proof of your love for Him. If other people can see from your life that you do what the Bible asks of you, they will also be able to see that you truly serve and love the Lord.

Love is always more than pretty words and solemn vows. It requires you to live a life devoted to God, and to keep His commandments.

And the single biggest thing God asks of you is to love God above all things and your neighbor as yourself. To truly know God is to experience Him every day through love. If you exercise this unselfish love in the world, God Himself can be seen in the world.

Can you do this?

Heavenly Father, I pray that You will make it possible for me to obey Your commandments in the smallest detail because I love You. Help me to make You visible to others in this way. Amen.

# Jesus comes to fulfill the law

"Do not think that I have come to abolish the Law or the Prophets; I have not come to abolish them but to fulfill them."

MATTHEW 5:17

In the Old Testament God gave His laws to His people so that they could serve and love Him all their lives. Unfortunately Israel frequently broke these laws or applied them incorrectly.

The teachers of the law in the time of Jesus went even further: they turned these laws into a profusion of confusing rules that were practically impossible to keep.

They obeyed these rules slavishly while their hearts remained unchanged. And this was never God's intention. He looks at our hearts. That is why He sent His Son to the world to fulfill His law.

Jesus Himself sums up the way in which He came to do this, "A new command I give you: Love one another. As I have loved you, so you must love one another. By this all men will know that you are My disciples, if you love one another" (Jn. 13:34-35).

To keep God's commandments means that we will change our hearts, that we will make God's love visible in a world devoid of love.

Jesus is our living example of God's love. To keep the commandments therefore means that we will become more like Him every day. If you truly love Him and follow His example, it will not be difficult for you to obey God's law.

Are you a living example of God's love?

*Lord Jesus, please help me to love other people with the same love with which I love You. Make me a living example of Your love. Amen.*

# *The law can't save you*

Therefore no one will be declared righteous in his sight by observing the law; rather, through the law we become conscious of sin.

ROMANS 3:20

Shortly after my fiftieth birthday I made a fairly unpleasant discovery: my eyes had grown increasingly weaker. Before I knew it, I could no longer read without my glasses or look up a telephone number or consult a recipe book. People whose eyesight is failing need glasses. Similarly, God's law is a pair of glasses: it makes it possible for you to clearly see right from wrong. If you know the law well, you will also know what God regards as sinful.

Still, it will do you no good merely to follow every single one of the Ten Commandments slavishly. The law has no power to save you from sin. God does not forgive your sins because you obey His law.

The law, somebody once said, is simply a finger pointing to Jesus. To keep the commandments to the letter cannot guarantee you a place in heaven. Only Jesus can do that: "I am the way and the truth and the life" He tells Thomas. "No one comes to the Father except through Me" (Jn. 14:6).

Jesus is the only door to heaven. Through His death on the cross He created a bridge spanning the distance between heaven and earth. Through His atoning sacrifice He made it possible for sinners to become holy children of God.

*Lord Jesus, I see now that it will do me no good to keep Your commandments if I do not believe in You. Thank You for making it possible for me to be God's child. Amen.*

# Love is the fulfillment of the law

Love does no harm to its neighbor. Therefore love is the fulfillment of the law.

ROMANS 13:10

All the commandments – do not commit adultery, do not murder, do not steal, do not covet, and whatever other commandment there may be – are summed up in this single rule: "love your neighbor as yourself," Paul writes to the Christians in Rome (see Rom. 13:9). If we love each other with the same love with which we love God, it means that we are keeping the entire law of God.

It sounds like fun to toss aside the law and only to love one another, but actually this is terribly hard to do. In fact, for most people it is entirely impossible.

The love Paul speaks about here is an unselfish love, a love that is prepared to forgive and forget, a love that says "others first." And this kind of love never comes naturally because every person is inherently sinful and selfish.

It is not possible for any of us to love like that. But we owe each other this love (see Rom. 13:8). Jesus wants to make it possible for you to do this, to pay your debt of love to your fellowman in full.

By making your will subservient to His, and through the power of His Spirit that lives in you, it will be possible for you to love others like this.

Ask Him to do this for you.

*Lord Jesus, I try so hard to love other people but I constantly fail. Please make it possible for me to keep Your commandments through my love for others. Amen.*

# God's love burns fiercely

"How can I give you up, Ephraim? How can I hand you over, Israel? My heart is changed within me; all my compassion is aroused."

HOSEA 11:8

Even though no one can keep God's commandments in his or her own strength, God loves us and does not condemn us. Hosea 11 is the story of a trial. Israel repeatedly responded to God's love and faithfulness with rejection and unfaithfulness.

As a father teaches his child to walk, so in the desert the Lord taught Israel the first steps of what it means to His people. He protected them and cared for them. Teaching a baby to walk requires a lot of patience, love and support. God treated His unfaithful people just as lovingly. And still they acted as if they did not know Him. Clearly Israel was guilty and deserved the death penalty.

But before God sentenced them to death, He hesitated. He could not leave them to their own devices, because His love for them was too strong. If Israel did not want to turn back, God would turn back and reconsider His decision; He would once again forgive their unfaithfulness.

Since Jesus came to the earth, everyone who believes in Him becomes a member of His family. We too are often disobedient and we too deserve to be abandoned by God.

But His love is much too strong for this to happen. He sent His Son to the world so that the price for our debt of sin could be paid in full. Jesus died so that you can live. God still wants to cover you with His loving touch.

*Heavenly Father, please forgive me for not being able to keep Your commandments. Thank You that Your love for me is so strong. Amen.*

# Faith

Many definitions of faith have been formulated. In my opinion, William Hendrikson is the author of one of the best:

Faith is the window of the soul through which the love of God flows into our lives; faith is the open hand with which man reaches out to God, the Giver of everything; faith is the coupling which joins man's train to God's engine; faith is the trunk of the tree of redemption of which the roots are grace and the fruit good works.

Faith is always a gift of grace, because it is impossible to believe by ourselves; God alone through His Holy Spirit can bring about faith in the heart of a human being.

This month we are not only going to learn more about faith, but we are also going to seek inspiration from the courage of the champions of faith in the Bible.

# *You need faith*

And without faith it is impossible to please God, because anyone who comes to him must believe that he exists and that he rewards those who earnestly seek him.

HEBREWS 11:6

The gallery presented to us in Hebrews 11 is God's photo album of men and women of faith. We are not all equally fond of browsing through photo albums. To tell the truth, the photo albums of people who have toured foreign countries are very boring for visitors, while they evoke wonderful memories in the travelers.

The difference is in the experience; for the people who experienced the events and places depicted in the photographs, looking at them again means something quite different from what it means for the people who have never been there. Thus believers read Hebrews 11 in quite a different way from unbelievers.

Faith is a gift, a present that only God can give you. Just as you cannot obey God's law on your own, you will not be able to believe in God by yourself. It is God who places faith in your heart by His Holy Spirit. You cannot earn it, but you can stretch out your hands to God and take it for yourself. However, it is not enough just to believe that God exists.

True faith requires a personal relationship with God. Do you believe that Jesus died on the cross for you and that He is your only Lord and Redeemer? Only then can you be sure that you are living in line with God's will.

*Holy Spirit, thank You very much for working faith in my heart and that I can take this gift and embrace it as my own. Amen.*

# *What is faith?*

Now faith is being sure of what we hope for and certain of what we do not see.

HEBREWS 11:1

We like saying that "seeing is believing." However, faith is being certain of what we cannot see. It is the guarantee of the Christian's faith that every one of the promises of God in the Bible will be fulfilled.

The world is still of the opinion that seeing is believing: the negative facts of declining currencies, rising interest rates, spiraling violence cannot be reasoned away. We feel these realities personally. We believe what we experience.

Believing in God, however, puts you in another dimension. It radically changes your way of living. The letter to the Hebrews was actually written to suffering people. Its message is that one's faith is the guarantee that what one cannot yet see will become a reality. Thus, one may cling to God's promises even though they have not yet been realized in one's life.

Our eldest son likes bungee jumping. You need faith to take a jump like that: that the harness will be able to carry your weight and that the rope is not so long that you will crash at the bottom.

In the first instance faith is trust. Faith is to be able to look into the dark and see God there, to know that God is there, whatever your circumstances may be, to accept that God will look after you and provide for your needs.

*Lord Jesus, thank You that I may be sure of the things that I hope for. Thank You for a faith grounded in You and in the promises of Your Word. Amen.*

# Abraham obeyed God's command

By faith Abraham, when called to go to a place he would later receive as his inheritance, obeyed and went, even though he did not know where he was going.

HEBREWS 11:8

Abraham was a very rich and influential man. Nevertheless, he was immediately willing to obey God's command and cut himself free from everything that was dear and familiar to him. He was immediately willing to move from his country and familiar surroundings to the unknown land to which God would direct him, even though he didn't know where exactly he was going.

God set Abraham a difficult test in faith. Abraham could pass this examination of faith only because he could see the invisible God. He could see more than what people only perceive with their eyes because he had an unshakeable trust in God.

Believers are people who believe in what they cannot see, as well as in what is beyond what they can see.

Believers are people who dare to step out into the dark, because they trust in God. They are people who see the One who cannot be seen so clearly that they have no doubt about Him.

Abraham was willing to leave the familiar for a city with steadfast foundations that he could not see yet. He tackled the unknown because he believed.

Would you be willing to do the same?

*Heavenly Father, please make it possible for me to trust You completely as Abraham did, so that I would also be willing to venture a step in the dark should You expect it from me. Amen.*

# *Abraham believed in the impossible*

By faith Abraham, even though he was past age – and Sarah herself was barren – was enabled to become a father because he considered him faithful who had made the promise.

HEBREWS 11:11

When Abraham obeyed God and moved from his country, God made a covenant with him. Although Abraham and his wife were childless, God promised them descendants as numerous as the stars and as countless as the sand on the seashore. Abraham firmly persevered in believing God's promises of many descendants, even after it had become humanly impossible for Sarah and him ever to have children.

While his wife was making her own clever little plans to help God's plan along a little, Abraham continued firmly to believe in God. His faith makes our understanding reel!

God remained true to His promises. Isaac was born when Abraham was a hundred and Sarah ninety years old. God always keeps His promises if we are willing to keep on believing in Him.

By means of Abraham's story of faithful trust God wants to say to you today: even though your own circumstances seem hopeless to you at present, even though you fear that God's promises will never come to pass in your life, you need not be discouraged. Keep on believing!

Like Abraham you may cling to God's promises. God always rewards a faith like Abraham's. If you keep on believing in Him to the end He will fulfill every one of His promises to you.

*Heavenly Father, please give me faith like Abraham's, so that I can cling to Your promises, even though it seems humanly impossible to me that they will ever become true in my life. Amen.*

# When faith wanes

Abraham and Sarah were already old and well advanced in years, and Sarah was past the age of childbearing. So Sarah laughed to herself as she thought, "After I am worn out and my master is old, will I now have this pleasure?"

GENESIS 18:11-12

Unfortunately Sarah didn't have the same strength of faith as her husband. At times her faith waned. Even when God Himself announced that she would have a son in a year's time, she decided that this thing God had promised was totally impossible. She actually laughed when she received the news that she would bear a child.

Perhaps we shouldn't blame Sarah too much for her laughter. By this time it was really humanly impossible for her to fall pregnant.

It is truly difficult to keep on believing when time passes and those things that you are praying for, those things you believe God will give you, do not happen. It is usually not crises that are our greatest problems, but the waiting time before God's promises are fulfilled.

George Müller was once asked whether the Lord had ever refrained from answering one of his prayers. He answered: "Never, but I have been praying for 17 years for the son of my neighbor to be converted."

Sarah's laugh of unbelief changed into a laugh of joy with the birth of Isaac. Perhaps you are finding it hard to believe at the moment. Just keep on believing. For God nothing is impossible. He will fulfill His promises at the right time for you.

*Heavenly Father, thank You for the assurance that nothing is impossible for You. Help me to wait patiently for the fulfillment of Your promises. Amen.*

# The testing of Abraham's faith

> By faith Abraham, when God tested him, offered Isaac as a sacrifice. Abraham reasoned that God could raise the dead.
>
> HEBREWS 11:17, 19

Abraham was God's friend: And the Scripture was fulfilled that says, "Abraham believed God, and it was credited to him as righteousness," and he was called God's friend (Jas. 2:23). Nevertheless, God did an almost unbelievable thing to His friend, Abraham.

God said, "Abraham, take the fruit of your faith, your only child for whom you waited such a long time and sacrifice him to Me as a burnt offering."

Not once do we hear Abraham protesting. He did exactly what God demanded of him. Early the next morning he took Isaac and left for Moriah to sacrifice him as God requested. Only when Abraham had already bound Isaac on the altar and taken the knife to slaughter him did God intervene by providing a ram in Isaac's place.

With this incredible command God wanted to test Abraham's faith. Abraham passed the test with flying colors: "Now I know that you fear God, because you have not withheld from Me your son, your only son," God told Abraham (Gen. 22:12).

God gave a ram in Isaac's place, but when His own Son had to die on the cross He did not let the cup of suffering pass Him by. Abraham's son was spared, but God's Son had to die so that you and I can live.

*Heavenly Father, make it possible for me to also pass the test like Abraham did when You test my faith. Amen.*

# Because Noah believed ...

By faith Noah, when warned about things not yet seen, in holy fear built an ark to save his family.

HEBREWS 11:7

Like us, Noah lived in a world full of violence, sin and corruption. God gave the righteous Noah a strange command.

He was going to annihilate all the sinful people on earth, but Noah and his family would be saved. Therefore, Noah was instructed to build an ark on dry ground, and in addition see to it that there would be pairs of all the kinds of animals on earth in the ark, because the earth would shortly be flooded.

Because Noah believed, he obeyed God's strange and humanly impossible command: He built an ark on dry ground, very far away from any water. In addition he undertook to get all the animals into the ark.

The building of the ark is Noah's testimony of the fact that he had faith in God. The ark became the gateway to new life for him and his family. The people of his time, however, thought it was sheer madness. Surely his neighbors laughed at him and his family was probably ashamed of him.

But Noah did not care. He continued believing and he reverently obeyed God: "By his faith he condemned the world and became heir of the righteousness that comes by faith" (Heb. 11:7).

Noah's faith contrasts strongly with the unbelief of the people of his time. Because he believed, God redeemed him and his family.

*Heavenly Father, I pray for a faith that will always hold fast to You and keep on trusting You under all circumstances. Amen.*

# Faith makes a road through the sea

By faith the people passed through the Red Sea as on dry land; but
when the Egyptians tried to do so, they were drowned.

HEBREWS 11:29

At the time described in this verse things were rather grim for
the Israelites. After Pharaoh had at last consented to give them
their freedom, he regretted it and pursued them with his whole
army. They had no defense against these superior numbers.
They were trapped between the devil and the deep blue sea.
But their God is omnipotent, He can do anything if the faith of
His children is strong enough.

God commanded Moses to stretch out his hand over the
sea and the water was driven back by a strong east wind. The
Israelites could then pass through the sea on dry land (see Ex.
14:22).

When the Egyptians wanted to do the same, however, the
Lord first made the wheels of their chariots come off and then
commanded Moses again to stretch his hand out over the sea.
At daybreak the sea returned to its place, so that all the Egyptians drowned. Not one of them survived.

This miracle was a confirmation of Israel's faith: "When the
Israelites saw the great power the LORD displayed against the
Egyptians, the people feared the LORD and put their trust in
Him" (Ex. 14:31).

God is the same today as He was in the time of Moses. He
can work miracles in your life too if you are willing to believe
in Him unconditionally.

*Heavenly Father, how great and wonderful You are! Thank You
for still working wonders today if the faith of Your children is
strong enough. Amen.*

# Faith cancels debt

By faith the prostitute Rahab, because she welcomed the spies, was not killed with those who were disobedient.

HEBREWS 11:31

When Rahab, a prostitute of Jericho, first hid the Israelite spies under the stalks of flax on her roof and later helped them to flee through the window, she proved that she believed in the God of Israel. "Our hearts melted and everyone's courage failed because of you, for the Lord your God is God in heaven above and on the earth below," she told Joshua (Josh. 2:11).

Rahab's faith made her reckless in a way: she was willing to betray the people of her city for two foreigners. In doing so she chose for God against her own people.

As a result of this act of faith she and her whole family were saved when the Israelites conquered Jericho and killed the rest of the inhabitants.

Through her act of faith Rahab was also counted as one of God's people. Her son, Boaz, later married Ruth and they became the grandparents of Israel's most excellent king, David. She even earned a place for herself among the great people of faith in Hebrews and in the family tree of Jesus.

There were probably many people who looked down upon Rahab because of her doubtful "career." However, God looks deeper: He saw the faithful heart of this woman.

Perhaps your past is like Rahab's, also not without blemish. If you believe in God, He will acquit you as He did Rahab. Indeed it is for this reason that Jesus came to the earth, to save sinners.

*Lord Jesus, You know me so well. You know that I still have many sins counting against me. Thank You that my faith in You can eradicate every one of them. Amen.*

# Train yourself in faith

"Lord, if it's you," Peter replied, "tell me to come to you on the water." But when he saw the wind, he was afraid and, beginning to sink, cried out, "Lord, save me!"

MATTHEW 14:28, 30

By faith Peter succeeded in achieving the impossible: he walked on the water toward Jesus. However, the moment Peter took his eyes off of Jesus and evaluated his circumstances realistically, he started to fear the power of the wind and he began to sink.

Perhaps you, like Peter, sometimes also swing your feet carefully over the side of the boat; perhaps you do indeed believe that you are capable of everything in the power of Jesus. However, as soon as you see your negative circumstances, you take your eyes off Jesus, and you are then doomed to sink.

C. S. Lewis wrote that we need to train ourselves in the habit of faith. The first step is to realize that you are not going to feel the same every day. We all have times when we start to doubt our faith, times when the wind becomes too strong for us and we start to sink like Peter.

For that reason Lewis is of the opinion that daily prayer, reading the Bible and other spiritual books and church attendance are necessary parts of the Christian life. You have to be reminded continually of your faith.

Your faith in God will not remain alive automatically; it has to be nourished. Faith is a growing process: it demands that you get to know God better and love Him more day by day.

Lord Jesus, I want to get to know You better every day so that my faith can be nourished. Please help me to succeed. Amen.

# *Reaching out in faith*

But when he saw the wind, he was afraid and, beginning to sink, cried out, "Lord, save me!" Immediately Jesus reached out his hand and caught him. "You of little faith," he said, "why did you doubt?"

MATTHEW 14:30-31

Fortunately Peter did not become flustered: when he saw that he was sinking, he stretched out his hand to Jesus. He called out, "Lord, save me!" Immediately Jesus was there for Peter: He took hold of the hand stretched out toward Him and saved him. "You of little faith, why did you doubt?" He asked.

Peter's story is a beautiful demonstration of courageous faith. Because he believed, he succeeded in the humanly impossible: he walked on the water. But when he looked away and started to sink, Peter experienced his faith a little differently. He reached out his hand toward Jesus.

His call to Jesus became his redemption. Only when he realized that he was fully dependent on the saving hand of Jesus, did he distinguish himself as a believer.

This is the primary expression of our relationship with God: two pairs of hands. Mine, dependent; God's, saving. This is the only way in which you can truly walk on the water: next to God with your hand in His.

The children of God need never doubt. He is there for you when you find yourself in a crisis. The only thing you have to do is reach out your hand in faith toward Him.

*Lord Jesus, thank You for the assurance that I can simply reach out my hand to You in times of crisis in the certain knowledge that You will always be there to help and save me. Amen.*

# Faith and deeds

> What good is it, my brothers, if a man claims to have faith but has no deeds? Can such faith save him? ... faith by itself, if it is not accompanied by action, is dead.
>
> JAMES 2:14, 17

C. S. Lewis points out that Christians often argue about what will get us into heaven: our faith or our good works. He comes to the conclusion, "To me it seems like arguing about which of the two blades of a pair of scissors is essential."

It is a fact that you cannot earn your redemption with good works. But you can also not declare that you believe in Christ without faith becoming visible in your life.

Faith and works cannot be separated. They are two sides of the same coin. If you say you believe, but other people cannot see it in the things you do and say (and don't do and say!) your faith is worthless. Faith must be seen.

James goes even further when he says that faith that does not express itself in deeds is dead (see Jas. 2:26).

How are things with you? Can total strangers who watch you see that you really believe in Jesus, because you truly care about other people and love them with the same love with which Jesus loves you? That is the only way in which people will be able to see that your life underscores your faith.

*Lord Jesus, You know that I believe in You. Help me to live in such a way that I will testify to my faith by the things I do. Amen.*

# Faith and your self-image

Know that the LORD is God. It is he who made us, and we are his;
we are his people.

PSALM 100:3

Many people suffer unnecessarily from inferiority complexes.
We have not yet learned that faith has a lot to do with the way
you see yourself. Although we are small and insignificant when
measured against the magnificence of God, He created us. We
are people created in His image and we belong to Him.

Women who believe in God need never suffer from an inferiority complex. You are special because God "doesn't make
no junk", somebody once rightly said.

You are special to God. In the whole world there is not a
single other person just like you. What God thinks of you is
more important than what you think of yourself, not so?

To know how highly God thinks of you, you can just go and
read your Bible. It is written that you are the apple of His eye,
that He knows you by name, that you are precious to Him,
that He looks after you, helps you and protects you, that He
promises to be with you always. You are indeed created in His
image and are His representative here on earth.

However, we also read in the Bible that we must love other
people just as much as we love ourselves.

Thus, God wants you to love yourself, to feel good about
yourself. Whenever you feel inferior again, think about how
positively and highly God regards you.

*Heavenly Father, it is wonderful to realize that I have been cre-
ated in Your image and that You love me. Thank You that I need
never feel inferior again. Amen.*

# Faith is to look at God

Let us run with perseverance the race marked out for us. Let us fix our eyes on Jesus, the author and perfecter of our faith ... Consider him ... so that you will not grow weary and lose heart.

HEBREWS 12:1-3

The life of a Christian on earth is like a race. On the pavilion there is a crowd encouraging the Christian athlete to persevere to the end.

An athlete will never win a race if he continually looks back, nor if he is not willing to persevere to the end. In the same way our life race can be completed successfully only if we fix our eyes on Jesus and concentrate on Him. He is the Author and Perfecter of our faith.

Learn to focus on Jesus in your personal race of faith. Always be willing to do your best, to give everything, and do not keep looking at the circumstances surrounding you. You must also not lose heart and throw in the towel. When you look at Jesus, you will never tire or fall out of the race.

Furthermore, an athlete wearing a coat will also never win a race. The second requirement if you want to win this race of life is that you need to discard those things that hinder you from running. Everything that is more important than Jesus is an encumbrance to you.

Do you not know that in a race all the runners run, but only one gets the prize? Run in such a way as to get the prize, Paul writes to the church of Corinth (1 Cor. 9:24).

Make it your motto today!

Lord Jesus, I want to run my race today with my eyes fixed on You. Make it possible for me to complete this race in a positive spirit. Amen.

# Only faith is necessary

But whatever was to my profit I now consider loss for the sake of Christ. What is more, I consider everything a loss compared to the surpassing greatness of knowing Christ Jesus my Lord.

PHILIPPIANS 3:7-8

In Philippians 3 Paul provides an impressive summary of his religious history: he was of the people of Israel, of the tribe of Benjamin, he was circumcised on the eighth day, he was also a Pharisee and so serious about his Jewish religion that he had previously zealously persecuted the church of Jesus. According to Jewish law, he had not set a foot wrong.

Today such an excellent CV would definitely ensure him of a very important career.

Nevertheless, Paul came to the conclusion that all these things of which he could justifiably be proud in the eyes of the world, didn't mean much to him.

One thing was important to him: to know Jesus. All his previous accomplishments were worthless to him in comparison with his faith in Christ.

God does not ask you to achieve certain things to become His child. The only thing that is necessary is faith. Only faith is of any importance to Him; all other matters are worthless in the end.

What is your spiritual CV like? Not as good as Paul's? It doesn't matter to God. What does matter is whether you believe in Jesus Christ. You don't need to earn anything. You have already gained everything in Christ that you need to get to heaven one day.

Lord Jesus, my spiritual CV is not all that impressive. Thank You for the assurance that I need only faith to be Your child and to be able to know You. Amen.

# Faith is to know Jesus

I want to know Christ and the power of his resurrection and the fellowship of sharing in his sufferings, becoming like him in his death.

PHILIPPIANS 3:10

$P$aul gave up everything in order to know Christ and the power of His resurrection. Every believer has access to this know-ledge and power. The Danish theologian, Kierkegaard, wrote that there were three groups of people that followed Jesus when He was on earth:

※ The first group were the admirers of Jesus: those people who followed Him around and hung on His words, people who were truly amazed at the things He did and taught. These people liked what He said and they enjoyed quoting Him.

※ The second group were the pupils of Jesus: they were somewhat nearer to Jesus than the first group. They pondered what Jesus said and studied His doctrines. They even taught other people.

※ The third group was nearest to Jesus: His disciples. They were not only excited about what Jesus said and did, but they followed Him, they knew Him personally, their lives were inextricably bound to His.

Faith means that you should know Jesus personally. In which of the above-mentioned categories do you fall? How well do you know Jesus? Is knowing Him your highest priority? Just remember that knowing Jesus does not come at the snap of a finger: it requires a daily process of growth. It is a road that you must walk with Him.

*Lord Jesus, I do want to get to know You as personally as Your disciples did. Help me to follow You, to walk along life's way with You every day. Amen.*

# Elijah listened for the rain

And Elijah said to Ahab, "Go, eat and drink, for there is the sound of a heavy rain."

I KINGS 18:41

Faith is not only to see what you are actually unable to see, it is also to hear what you are not really able to hear. In this passage of Scripture Elijah promised Ahab that it would rain. Then he sent his servant to see if there were any signs of rain in the sky. Only the seventh time did he see a cloud as small as a man's hand rising up from the sea.

However, Elijah didn't care about the clouds, he listened for the sound of the rain. He was hearing the roaring of water while there were still only the signs of a taxing drought to be seen.

God did not disappoint Elijah's faith, "Meanwhile, the sky grew black with clouds, the wind rose, a heavy rain came on" (1 Kgs. 18:45).

Today, faith works in exactly the same way. Are you still not able to see any of God's promises being fulfilled in your life? Look again! To see what people ordinarily cannot see, that is true faith.

Perhaps it is difficult for you to believe as steadfastly as Elijah did because you are still prone to allowing yourself to be led by negative circumstances.

For once, look away from your circumstances! Listen for the rain! God will fulfill His promises in your life if you keep on believing as steadfastly as Elijah did.

*Lord, make it possible for me to hear the rain while there is still no cloud in the sky. Thank You that I can know that You always keep Your promises. Amen.*

# Elijah under the broom tree

> He came to a broom tree, sat down under it and prayed that he might die. "I have had enough, LORD," he said. "Take my life; I am no better than my ancestors."
>
> 1 KINGS 19:4

After periods of unfailing faith there often come "broom tree times" in the lives of God's children, times when we are only ordinary people who have questions and doubts, even though we believe and have ourselves experienced God's omnipotence and power to work miracles.

On Carmel Elijah had convinced the people that the Lord is God. He had prayed to God with unfailing faith to consume the offering with fire from heaven, and everything had happened as he had asked. The Lord had also sent rain in answer to Elijah's prayer of faith.

However, instead of Elijah persevering in faith like Abraham did, he ended up sitting under a broom tree, wishing that he could die.

Elijah was deeply disappointed when he had to flee again, when his people forgot their declaration of faith on Carmel so soon and started following Queen Jezebel again.

Nevertheless, God did not forget Elijah. He sent an angel to refresh him with bread and wine (see 1 Kgs. 19:6).

After a powerful experience of faith we also often discover that our faith is not as strong as we thought, that we are also weak and fallible.

Perhaps today is one of your broom tree days. Take heart, God knows you and He wants to strengthen you as He did Elijah.

*Heavenly Father, thank You so much that You know exactly when I am discouraged. Strengthen me please, and encourage me again as You did Elijah under the broom tree. Amen.*

# Faith is to keep on calling

Those who led the way rebuked him and told him to be quiet, but he shouted all the more, "Son of David, have mercy on me!"

LUKE 18:39

The blind man at Jericho had a problem with which only Jesus could help him. In those days blind people had no dignity, they were dependent on the favor of other people, their future was grim. The blind man in our story had nothing to look forward to, but he had a great need in his heart.

When he heard Jesus passing him, he kept on calling to Jesus to have mercy on him. The people tried to keep him out of Jesus' way, but his faith was so strong that he did not give up, but kept on calling until Jesus heard.

The Greek word translated here as "mercy" is noteworthy. It does not only mean to "feel sorry," but also to make the impossible possible.

The blind man asked Jesus to do something for him, to become involved with him. Jesus could help, because the blind man truly believed in Him. "Receive your sight; your faith has healed you," He told him (Lk. 18:42).

If you can succeed in persevering in faith in Jesus like this man did, to tell Him without hesitation what you want Him to do for you, Jesus will also make the impossible possible for you.

If you have the same steadfast faith as the blind man, He will hear each one of your prayers.

*Lord Jesus, I pray that You will have mercy on me, that You will also solve my problems like those of the blind man. Please strengthen my weak faith. Amen.*

# The faith of a woman

A Canaanite woman from that vicinity came to him, crying out, "Lord, Son of David, have mercy on me! My daughter is suffering terribly from demon-possession."

MATTHEW 15:22

Unexpectedly a gentile woman came to Jesus asking Him to heal her child who was possessed by demons. Jesus responded quite differently from how He usually did. At first He kept quiet so that His disciples asked Him to send the woman away. When she kept on asking, He, who had healed so many people, told this anxious mother that He had come to this world for the Israelites.

However, the Canaanite woman kept on pleading. She knelt before Jesus and asked again, "Lord, help me!" Then Jesus said something that sounds quite unsympathetic to us, "It is not right to take the children's bread and toss it to their dogs" (Mt. 15:26).

However, the faith of the woman was so great that she refused to give up. She answered Jesus in the same vein, "But even the dogs eat the crumbs that fall from their masters' table" (Mt. 15:27). This time Jesus responded. The woman's faith touched Him so deeply that He healed her child. "Woman," Jesus said to her, "you have great faith! Your request is granted" (Mt. 15:28).

"She transforms impending defeat into jubilant victory," W. Hendriksen said of this woman's faith. What is the state of your faith? Do you really believe that God can do everything? Then it is possible for you to change the impending defeats in your life into victories.

*Lord Jesus, thank You that You can fulfill desires when the faith of people is great enough. Help me where my faith is still too weak. Amen.*

# Faith is a gift

For it is by grace you have been saved, through faith – and this not from yourselves, it is the gift of God.

ЕPHESIANS 2:8

In 1998 a well-known author admitted in a Christian women's magazine that she could not believe in God; not because she did not want to, but because she could not. As a result of this confession a virtual literary storm broke out around her. Among other things, a prize for literature that she had won shortly before, was withdrawn.

I sincerely wished that I could have a conversation with her and tell her that faith is not something that we do, it is a gift. It comes from God. We cannot earn it; we can only gratefully accept it because Jesus earned it for us on the cross. He makes it possible for us to believe, because He has fully paid the price of our debt of sin.

C. S. Lewis explains it beautifully: When we speak about somebody who does something for God or gives something to God, it is like a little child going to his father, saying, "Daddy, give me some money to buy you a gift for your birthday." Of course the father does so and he takes pleasure in the gift his child gives him. However, Lewis concludes, it is only an idiot who would think that the transaction brought any profit into the pocket of the father!

If you believe in God, it is never something you have achieved for yourself. Be sure to thank God for the precious gift of faith with which He has entrusted to you.

Heavenly Father, thank You very much for enabling me to believe in Jesus. Thank You for the gift of faith in my life. Amen.

# Faith is to look through the cross

God is love. Whoever lives in love lives in God ... And he has given us this command: Whoever loves God must also love his brother.

1 JOHN 4:16, 21

"Faith," my husband once said in one of his sermons, "is to look at other people as God looks at them. The only possible way in which we can love our brother is if we learn to look at him through the cross of Jesus."

After this sermon a member of the congregation, who does beautiful woodwork, brought my husband a cross with a round hole in it. It hangs against the wall of his study and every time I enter the study, this cross reminds me that I must look at other people as God looks at them: through the cross of His Son.

When one looks at other people through the cross of Jesus, the values of this world become quite different than they are for people who do not yet know God.

For somebody who looks through the cross of Jesus, God is the most important. Such a person sees life differently. God was willing to sacrifice His Son so that every person could be saved. Every person (even those who deserve it least of all) is so valuable to Him that He was willing offer Jesus for him.

How do you look at the world? Are there still many other things more important to you than your faith? And how do you look at other people? With condemnation, or through the cross of Jesus?

*Heavenly Father, I confess that so often I still condemn other people and act unsympathetically toward them. Please help me to look at them through the cross of Your Son. Amen.*

# God is in control

These were all commended for their faith, yet none of them received what had been promised. God had planned something better for us so that only together with us would they be made perfect.

HEBREWS 11:39-40

The people about whom the author of the book of Hebrews writes here never experienced the fulfillment of God's promises. They were cruelly persecuted and had to suffer terribly. All of them died before the Second Coming of Jesus. Nevertheless, every one of them had met the invisible God.

Faith always means to look away from your circumstances and to hold on to God's promises, even if they have still not come to pass in your life. Faith is lived out when you grapple with the relentless realities of your life and still know: God is here. He can still achieve positive results in my life through this suffering.

People who believe know with certainty that God is always in control, He is King, whatever my circumstances may be. He will teach me to see the invisible like the champions of faith did in Hebrews 11.

Is it possible for you to look away from newspapers and television newscasts about riots and violence and to hold on to God's promises? Even though God's promises of peace have not yet been realized for us, we know that He is completely in control. Learn to "see" God in spite of external circumstances. Only then will you start to experience faith.

Heavenly Father, thank You that I can ignore all the negative things here on earth and can look up to You in the sure knowledge that You are still in control and that everything will end well. Amen.

# Faith is contagious

We do not want you to become lazy, but to imitate those who through faith and patience inherit what has been promised.

HEBREWS 6:12

Imitate what the Christians before you have done, the author of the letter to the Hebrews says. They inherited what God had promised because they were patient and always trusted God. As believers we must be willing to imitate the example of those who received what had been promised through their faith and patience.

Faith should be contagious. When we use the word "contagious" we usually think of diseases. When you come into contact with a person who has a contagious disease you have no control over the process. Contact with the germs infects you too, without any effort on your part.

When other people are confronted with your Christianity it should be just as contagious. Other people should be infected by you because you are overflowing with Jesus.

As a disease makes you feverish, your heart must pound warmly for the kingdom so that the hearts of other people can also be touched.

You must not be like the lukewarm people of Laodicea. If you are, God will also spit you out of His mouth (see Rev. 3:16).

Are you willing to be a spiritual mentor for other people as the champions of faith in the Bible are for you?

The closer you live to Jesus, the more you will become like Him, act like Him and think like Him.

*Lord Jesus, help me to inspire other people by the way in which I live out my Christianity. Amen.*

# Faith focuses on the future

Instead, they were longing for a better country – a heavenly one. Therefore God is not ashamed to be called their God, for he has prepared a city for them.

HEBREWS 11:16

The champions of faith discussed in the letter to the Hebrews understood well that this world was not their true home.

They looked forward to their real home, a heavenly city, prepared for them by God Himself.

Faith is mainly concerned with the future. The world and the things of the world (including the suffering that is inextricably part of it) are of little importance when weighed against the eternal glory awaiting us in heaven.

For this reason Christians are able to deal with suffering much better than unbelievers. Children of the Lord are also not afraid of death. We know for certain that dying is just a passing on into eternal life.

Faith makes it possible for you to have true insight into the things of God's kingdom. Faith empowers you to see in your heart those things that you cannot yet see in the physical world. You know there is an invisible God behind the visible things.

Peter wrote that we have a living hope in an inheritance that can never perish, spoil or fade, kept in heaven for us (see 1 Pet. 1:4-5). Because you believe, you are shielded by God's power until the coming of the glory that is ready to be revealed to you at the right time.

Lord Jesus, thank You for the inheritance in heaven that You are keeping safe for me, which I can now already take into my possession by faith. Amen.

# *Persevere in faith*

> So do not throw away your confidence; it will be richly rewarded.
> You need to persevere so that when you have done the will of God,
> you will receive what he has promised.
>
> HEBREWS 10:35-36

If you really take God's promises seriously, you will have to be willing to persevere in your faith. Paul warned that believers should not shrink back, "But you need to stick it out, staying with God's plan so you'll be there for the promised completion," (*The Message*, p. 556).

I once read that the start and the finish of a race are not its most difficult parts. At the start you are still full of courage; you can still manage what lies ahead.

At the end the winning-post is in sight and the crowd of spectators are encouraging you enthusiastically to persevere until you break the ribbon. However, it is the part in the middle that is the most difficult. If you are already very tired but cannot yet see the winning-post, it is easy to be disheartened and to quit.

At the time of your conversion it is also easy to believe. Your faith is still a new experience to you. However, as time passes and the temptations increase, your faith sometimes decreases.

If things are going badly for you at the moment, just keep on believing, keep on trusting God. God Himself will empower you to persevere in your faith, until each one of His promises has been fulfilled in your life.

> *Lord, You know when my faith is dangerously low. At such times help me to keep on believing and to do Your will. Amen.*

# Extremely expensive faith

He sacrificed for their sins once for all when he offered himself.

HEBREWS 7:27

There is a story about a Welsh miner who could not believe because faith sounded too easy for him. To simply get to heaven by believing in Jesus did not involve enough effort and exertion for him.

One day, one of his Christian friends asked him how he had come out of the mine the previous day. "With the lift, of course," the surprised miner said. "Well, what did you pay for it?" the friend wanted to know. "Nothing," was the answer. "Don't you think it was too cheap?" his friend asked. "Well," the miner replied, "it was free for me, but it cost the mining company thousands."

"Precisely," his friend said, "the faith that sounds so cheap to you, cost God His Son and Jesus His life." After this the unbelieving miner was powerfully converted. For the first time he realized that faith is not cheap, but actually extremely expensive.

To make it possible for you to be able to believe cost Jesus His life. He sacrificed Himself on the cross so that the ransom for each of your sins could be paid. God gave the life of His Son – out of love for you – so that you can believe in Him. Nothing is needed from your side. The only thing you have to do to receive eternal life is to believe in Jesus.

Never forget how extremely expensive faith is!

*Heavenly Father, I praise You because You were willing to give up Your Son so that I can believe in You. Lord Jesus, thank You that You died so that I can live. Amen.*

# The reason for our humanity

For we are God's workmanship, created in Christ Jesus to do good works, which God prepared in advance for us to do.

EPHESIANS 2:10

In this passage of Scripture Paul writes that the believers who were previously dead as a result of their sins, were recreated by Jesus to do good works, which God prepared in advance for us to do.

By now you know already that faith is completely free. Your faith and redemption are a gift from God, because there is no way in which you can earn it. However, now that you are saved your life ought to change radically. Your sinful nature is no longer your master, you are no longer the slave of sin. Now you can begin to fulfill your purpose as a child of God. Prove your gratitude and joy by being obedient to God.

Your good works should, however, always be motivated by gratitude and not compulsion.

You do not do good deeds so that you may be saved; you are already a child of God. God saved you because He wanted to do it. However, He does have a purpose with your redemption. He wants you to give your whole heart to doing the good works that He has ordained for you to do.

You do not work for a reward. On the contrary, you received a gift (your redemption) and now you do good works because you are grateful for the gift you received.

Heavenly Father, thank You very much that You saved me because You love me. Help me now to do the good works for which You made me. Amen.

# *Believe in your Redeemer!*

I myself will see him with my own eyes – I, and not another. How my heart yearns within me!

JOB 19:27

Job dearly wanted to see God and this hope caused him to cling to God long after he had lost the material possessions on which he could set his hope. He clung to God even though everything around him had collapsed; even though he had lost everything: his health, his wealth, his children; and even his wife had turned against him.

Even though poor Job had practically nothing left, a flicker of hope that refused to be extinguished remained alive inside him.

The reason for this is found in verse 25. Job knew and believed that his Redeemer lived and that he would therefore eventually triumph. He also knew that he would one day see God with his own eyes. (In Job's days a redeemer was somebody who paid so that a slave could go free, or somebody who looked after for a widow.)

Job had great faith even though he lived before the cross. We who live on this side of the cross have a much greater reason to believe in God. We have come to know Jesus, our true Redeemer, and we know that one day He will come again to fetch His children. Every child of God can cling to this glorious hope, even though his circumstances are exceedingly difficult.

Are you suffering at present? Then cling like Job to the hope that your Redeemer lives and that you will one day see Him with your own eyes.

*Lord Jesus, I praise You because You are my Redeemer, and because I can know for certain that I will see You with my own eyes one day when You come again. Amen.*

# Keep your eyes on Jesus

Let us run with perseverance the race marked out for us. Let us fix our eyes on Jesus ... who for the joy set before him endured the cross, scorning its shame, and sat down at the right hand of the throne of God.

HEBREWS 12:1-2

The last portrait that the author of Hebrews displays in the gallery of the faithful is that of Jesus Himself. He came to show us through His life the exact meaning of faith. If we steadfastly trust in Him we will be able to complete the race.

Jesus is not only the Author and Perfecter of our faith, He is also the only Source of it. He is the Instructor who shows His children here on earth how to run the race.

Jesus was absolutely obedient to the will of His Father. This obedience caused much suffering: He had to give up heaven and come to earth as an ordinary human being. Moreover, He had to be willing to die the most cruel death imaginable.

Your faith is also going to place demands on you. Faith always has a price.

When you begin to get weary and you want to drop out of the race, remember to look at the portrait of Jesus. You can only persevere in faith if you cling to Him. He makes it possible for you to keep on running and not to fall back.

In your turn you can inspire other people to greater trust. By persevering in the race of faith you can help others to reach heaven.

*Lord Jesus, please help me to run my race of faith with my eyes fixed on You. Thank You that You encourage me to persevere and to complete the race. Amen.*

# Strangers on earth

All these people were still living by faith when they died. They did not receive the things promised; they only saw them and welcomed them from a distance. And they admitted that they were aliens and strangers on earth.

HEBREWS 11:13

The heroes of faith mentioned in Hebrews 11 all died without experiencing the fulfillment of God's promises. But they did realize that their lives on earth were only temporary.

At the moment God's children are nothing but strangers and aliens here on earth; we are only residing here temporarily. In reality we are citizens of heaven, because that is the destination to which we are all headed. Here on earth we are only preparing ourselves for heaven.

Even though we are mere strangers and aliens on earth, we should still live according to God's will. "Here on earth Christians do not have permanent residence, only a temporary residential permit," says Johan Smit. "But we must keep in mind that we also have a work permit."

The place where you live is also the place where you should work as a witness for God. You are part of God's task team here on earth, and you are able to do your job through the strength of the Holy Spirit who resides in you.

However, you must constantly be on your guard not to become too attached to this world. Rather store up for yourself treasures in heaven, where moth and rust cannot destroy it, says Jesus in the Sermon on the Mount, because "where your treasure is, there your heart will be also" (Mt. 6:21).

Lord Jesus, help me to live in such a way that I will prepare myself for my final destination: the heaven that awaits me. Amen.

# *J*esus suffers for you

Lord Jesus,
In this month I want to walk the Way of the Cross with You,
and contemplate the meaning of Your suffering.
Once again I want to think about how much You had to
suffer so that I could be saved.
When I pause to think about the people surrounding Your
cross, teach me the same lessons that they learned.
Grant that I will never deny You,
that I will always be willing to put myself last,
that I will follow You unconditionally.
Thank You that You were forsaken by God
so that I will never have to live without Him.
This is also the month in which I want to rejoice
over Your resurrection;
in which I want to celebrate because You have conquered
Satan and death for all eternity
so that I can now be a conqueror with You.
Make it possible for me to live as a conqueror
from day to day, because I can do anything in the strength
that You give me.

*A*men.

# Not me, Lord!

But Peter declared, "Even if I have to die with you, I will never disown you." And all the other disciples said the same.

MATTHEW 26:35

Jesus was distressed about the suffering that was awaiting Him, and He was upset because He knew that His disciples were all going to forsake Him. The impetuous Peter unequivocally declared his faithfulness to Jesus. After all, he was Peter, the rock upon which Jesus would build His church.

Peter was willing to relinquish everything for Jesus' sake when Jesus called him. And Peter did truly love Jesus, but Jesus knew him better than he knew himself. He knew all too well that in a crisis Peter's human nature would get the upper hand over his faith.

According to the dictionary, to disown someone means to refuse to accept something or someone as one's own, or to say that one has no connection with something or someone. Peter is the last person who would have admitted that he, of all people, would disown Jesus. And so he vehemently denies that he, Peter, will disown Him, "Even if all fall away on account of You, I never will" (Mt. 26:33).

But the real picture looks very different. Peter denied Jesus three times. Only when he heard the rooster crowing did he remember Jesus' words.

Have you perhaps, like Peter, been denying your culpability, saying, "Not me, Lord!" while knowing all too well that you have failed Jesus in the things you have said and done?

Lord Jesus, I want to confess that I have disowned You so many times through my words and actions. Please forgive me and help me not to do it again. Amen.

# Peter in a corner

Then he began to call down curses on himself and he swore to them, "I don't know the man!" Immediately a rooster crowed. Then Peter remembered the word Jesus had spoken.

MATTHEW 26:74-75

Matters take an entirely different course from what Peter imagined. Jesus was arrested, and until the very last moment Peter tried to come to His aid. Peter even cut off the ear of the servant Malchus, but then Jesus actually healed the man! Peter did not quite understand what was going on: Jesus was acting so differently from what he expected.

Despite everything, Peter followed Jesus at a distance, right into the courtyard of the high priest. It was here where his faith finally foundered and where he disowned Jesus. Only when he heard the rooster crow did he remember the words Jesus had spoken earlier. At this moment he was filled with remorse over his betrayal.

Peter collapsed when he was put to the test. He denied being a follower of Christ. How about you? Would you be able to continue following Jesus, even if your decision were to have negative consequences for yourself? It requires self-denial to accomplish this.

Jesus Himself said, "If anyone would come after Me, he must deny himself and take up his cross and follow Me" (Mt. 16:24). Following Jesus demands commitment, dedication and complete surrender. Are you up to it?

This Easter you will once again have to choose between yourself and Jesus.

Lord Jesus, I want to renew my commitment to You this Easter, even if it means that I will have to follow You while carrying my cross. Amen.

# The new Peter

But Peter and John replied, "Judge for yourself whether it is right in God's sight to obey you rather than God. For we cannot help speaking about what we have seen and heard."

ACTS 4:19-20

Fortunately Peter's story does not end in the courtyard of the high priest. When we read of Peter again, in the beginning of Acts, we encounter an altogether different Peter. His inspiring sermon on the day of Pentecost caused three thousand people to come to repentance. Afterwards, when the Sanhedrin commanded Peter and John not to speak or teach at all in the Name of Jesus, he declared in no uncertain terms that they could not keep quiet about what they had seen and heard.

What happened to bring about this profound change in Peter? The Holy Spirit was poured out, and the Holy Spirit always brings about a radical change in peoples' lives. He transforms a scared disciple into a witness for Christ, filled with conviction.

All Christians have the Holy Spirit in their lives, but the Holy Spirit does not yet possess all Christians. How much of yourself you surrender to the Holy Spirit depends entirely on your personal decision. If your own self is still firmly ensconced on the throne of your life, the Holy Spirit will not be able to accomplish much of anything with your life.

Only when you are willing to entrust the control of your entire life to Him, only when you agree to submit your everything to His sovereignty, can He change you as He changed Peter.

*Holy Spirit, I want to fully surrender my life to You. Please change me as You changed Peter, and make me a radiant witness for You. Amen.*

# The best seats, please!

> Then James and John came to him. "Teacher," they said, "we want you to do for us whatever we ask." "What do you want me to do for you?" he asked. They replied, "Let one of us sit at your right and the other at your left in your glory."
>
> MARK 10:35-37

Toward the end of His life on earth Jesus continuously implored His disciples to be humble and subservient. In the passage just preceding this one Jesus predicted His death for the third time. And yet the disciples did not quite yet get it. They were still concerned about worldly matters. And to make matters worse, it was James and John, two of Jesus' star disciples, who piously asked Him whether they might have the best places at His right and left hands when He reigned as King.

Jesus was probably deeply hurt by His disciples' behavior and attitude. It must have been extremely difficult for Him to accept that this group of people, who had lived with Him for three years and received all the in-service training they could possibly have needed, could still be this self-centered.

Self-fulfillment remains an important motivating factor in our lives. All of us want to get ahead in life. But Jesus is still seeking people who are willing to follow in His footsteps. You will only manage to do this if you admit that you can do nothing in your own strength.

Perhaps you should use this Easter time to ponder your own attitude. What are the motivating factors in your life? Are you willing to put your own interests last and others' first?

*Lord Jesus, forgive me for living such a self-centered life; for regarding myself as the most important thing in life. Make me willing to put my own interests last and others' first. Amen.*

# Beyond the cross

> This is how we know what love is: Jesus Christ laid down his life for us. And we ought to lay down our lives for our brothers. If anyone has material possessions and sees his brother in need but has no pity on him, how can the love of God be in him?
>
> 1 JOHN 3:16-17

John – the same John who so desperately wanted to sit at the left or right of the Lord in His glory, who was so concerned with his own self-importance – has drastically altered his tune. Christians should be willing to lay down their lives for the benefit of their fellow believers. If we ignore the needs of other people and refuse to help them, it can mean only one thing: we do not have the love of Christ in our lives.

After Jesus' crucifixion John made an important discovery: he realized that fulfillment can only come about through self-denial. Self-denial means becoming the person God wants you to be: humble and subservient to others, and with an open hand and heart for the needs of your fellow believers.

If you really want to serve God this Easter, you would do well to take a page from John's book. It means that you will also have to be willing to look around you, notice the needs of the people around you and do something about it.

True love is not merely an attractive idea, but it always involves action. You too should be willing to show your love for God in the good deeds you do for others. Will you make a commitment to do so?

> Lord Jesus, teach me how to transform my love for You into good deeds, so that I can provide for other people's needs. Amen.

# The triumphal entry into Jerusalem

The crowds shouted, "Hosanna to the Son of David! Blessed is he who comes in the name of the Lord!"

MATTHEW 21:9

At Easter we are often asked to renew our commitment to Christ. The people who were present when Jesus entered Jerusalem were under tremendous group pressure. They acknowledged Jesus as King, not because they really believed this, but rather because the expectation of the Messiah was an inherent part of Jewish history.

When Jesus rode into Jerusalem on a donkey, they remembered Zechariah's prophecy that the long-awaited King would enter Jerusalem riding on a donkey.

They were therefore not true believers, but really only a group of people who wanted the Man on the donkey to help them personally. To them Jesus was nothing more than the symbol of a national dream: the Messiah who had come to free them from their Roman oppressors.

Many people today still decide to follow Jesus for entirely the wrong reasons. Singing hosanna does not necessarily mean that this King is truly the Ruler of your life. It is infinitely more difficult to actually walk the road to the cross with Him.

When God becomes a symbol that represents the fulfillment of your self-centered dreams, things are taking a wrong turn. It is all too easy to get caught up in group excitement, but the Lord expects you to make a personal commitment of faith. This Easter be sure to not merely be swept up by the excitement of the crowd, but surrender yourself completely to Jesus as the King of your life.

Lord Jesus, I confess that I too sometimes follow You for the wrong reasons. I pray that You will truly be the King of my life this Easter, and in all the days to follow. Amen.

# Jesus weeps for Jerusalem

As he approached Jerusalem and saw the city, he wept over it and said, "If you, even you, had only known on this day what would bring you peace – but now it is hidden from your eyes."

Luke 19:41-42

While riding into Jerusalem Jesus was all too aware of the fact that the hearts of the cheering people did not belong to Him. When He saw the city lying before Him, He was deeply moved. He wept, and His tears were not tears of joy because the people were honoring Him as King.

Rather, He was weeping for the people who were thinking only of themselves and the future of their country. He wept for people who were not yet ready for a cross. He wept because they did not really understand that He was the Messiah, but saw Him only as the fulfillment of their religious prophecies. He wept because He knew that soon after, these people would renounce and crucify Him.

Does Jesus perhaps have reason to weep for you? Perhaps not because you haven't yet chosen Him as Lord of your life, but because you still cling to an illusionary concept of Jesus, one in which you regard Him as someone who has to serve you, answer your prayers and help you.

Are you still struggling to take up your cross and follow Him? And yet Jesus wants to offer you the gift of His grace and grant you His peace. But then you have to acknowledge Him as the King of your life. This Easter, ask Him to help you completely devote yourself to Him.

*Lord Jesus, thank You that You offer me an opportunity to choose You as the Lord of my life. Help me to serve You devoutly. Amen.*

# Would you like to meet Jesus?

Now there were some Greeks among those who went up to worship at the Feast. They came to Philip ... with a request. "Sir," they said, "we would like to see Jesus."

JOHN 12:20-21

In Jesus' time there was a marked division between Israel and the rest of the world, because the Israelites were God's chosen people. No other nation had such access to God. Jesus' miracles caused the people to wonder whether He wasn't perhaps the Messiah who had been promised to them. However, Jesus had no interest in an earthly kingdom, while the Jews only wanted Him to free them from the yoke of Roman oppression.

The Jews would also never have approved of Jesus mingling with gentiles like the Greeks. However, these Greeks had heard of Jesus and approached Philip, saying that they would very much like to meet this exceptional man. (It is interesting to note that they probably chose to approach Philip because he had a Greek name.)

When Jesus heard that the gentiles also wished to meet Him, He realized that the hour of His glorification had arrived. He had to die, so that the harvest of God would become visible in the world, so that other peoples who believe in Him could also become children of God.

Because Jesus gave His life on the cross it is possible for you too to meet Him, to believe in Him, and to become a child of God. Have you responded to His offer of grace yet? There is no better time to get to know Jesus than right now, during Easter.

Lord Jesus, thank You that I can meet You once again during this time when we remember Your crucifixion and resurrection. Make me a witness for You, so that I can bring the message of Your gospel to those who don't yet know You. Amen.

# Lose your life to gain it

I tell you the truth, unless a kernel of wheat falls to the ground and dies, it remains only a single seed. But if it dies, it produces many seeds.

JOHN 12:24

In this Scripture passage Jesus explains to His disciples how important His death is to the world. *The Message* (p. 255) translates this verse as follows: "Unless a grain of wheat is buried in the ground, dead to the world, it is never any more than a grain of wheat. But if it is buried, it sprouts and reproduces itself many times over."

A kernel of wheat must die before it can live, Jesus declares. In the same way He too had to die so that we might live. If you want to follow Him, you must undertake to follow His example. If you are willing to put other people's interests above your own you might also perhaps lose your life, as He did, but ultimately you will gain everything, because God guarantees you eternal life.

You have to die to be able to truly live. You can gain life only by losing it. This does not sound very exciting to us. It also held no obvious benefits for Jesus' disciples. Perhaps you also feel that it won't benefit you to follow Him.

When Jesus includes the Greeks and other heathen peoples in His plan of redemption, He breaks down existing boundaries and unites people who would ordinarily have nothing in common. But in doing so He ensures a bountiful harvest for God's kingdom.

Are you ready to be part of that harvest?

*Lord Jesus, help me to walk in Your footsteps, to be willing to let my own self die, so that I may one day have eternal life. Amen.*

# On the Way with Jesus

---

Now learn this lesson from the fig tree: As soon as its twigs get tender and its leaves come out, you know that summer is near. Even so, when you see these things happening, you know that it is near, right at the door.

MARK 13:28-29

---

You can experience the story of the Passion in two ways: you can be a spectator of events, like someone watching a Passion play, or you can decide to put yourself in the midst of the action. The events of the last week before Jesus' crucifixion are clearly recorded in the Bible.

Jesus' triumphal entry into Jerusalem was on the Sunday; on the Monday He cursed the barren fig tree and purified the temple; on the Tuesday the fig tree withered; and Thursday was the day of the Lord's Supper, when Jesus also prayed in Gethsemane and Judas betrayed Him. On the Friday Jesus was accused, condemned, crucified and buried. The whole of Saturday He spent in the tomb, and on the Sunday He rose from the dead and appeared to His disciples.

With every Easter that comes around, we are faced with a new challenge: How are you going to experience the events of Easter this year? As spectator or as participant? You are responsible for making this choice. You can choose the crucified Christ by living for Him and testifying about Him. You can walk the Way of the Cross step by step with Jesus. You can truly realize what suffering Jesus was willing to go through in your place. During this Easter, you can discover the magnitude of God's love for you by walking in Jesus' footsteps during His last week on earth.

*Lord Jesus, this Easter I want to walk the Way of the Cross with You, step by step. Help me to truly experience the events of Easter this year. Amen.*

# Make disciples!

"Therefore go and make disciples of all nations, baptizing them in the name of the Father and of the Son and of the Holy Spirit, and teaching them to obey everything I have commanded you."

MATTHEW 28:19-20

Before His ascension Jesus' last commission to His disciples was to go into the world and to make disciples of all nations.

The disciples fulfilled their commission exceptionally well, contrary to expectations.

According to an old legend, after His ascension to heaven the angels wanted to know from Jesus where His army was. In answer to their question He pointed to the small group of people standing on the Mount of Olives.

I am sure that His little band of followers seemed rather feeble to the angels. The Bible also does not paint a very positive picture of the disciples. After all, in Jesus' inner circle one disciple betrayed Him, one disowned Him and the rest ... deserted Him and fled (Mt. 26:56).

It appears as if they weren't really the best team for carrying the gospel into a depraved world. And yet this apparently feeble army – with the help and support of Jesus, of course – spread His message to the known world as He asked of them.

You too are a member of Jesus' army here in this world. What are you doing to spread the good news of His wonderful salvation? Jesus promises to be with you if you are willing to tell others about Him. With His help and strength your testimony can be just as powerful as the testimony of His first disciples.

*Lord Jesus, I want to spread Your gospel and make people Your disciples. Thank You for being with me and helping me. Amen.*

# From disciple to traitor

> Then Judas Iscariot, one of the Twelve, went to the chief priests to betray Jesus to them. They were delighted to hear this ... So he watched for an opportunity to hand him over.
>
> MARK 14:10-11

Three times in the Gospel of Mark Judas is referred to as "one of the Twelve." It is clear, therefore, that it wasn't just some ordinary person who betrayed Jesus; it was a disciple, someone who was part of Jesus' inner circle. He was specially chosen by Jesus Himself. For three years He walked with Jesus every day, listened to His words, saw His miracles first hand. Why would Judas betray the Lord he was supposed to love?

The reason for Judas's betrayal is probably found in the surmise that Jesus failed to live up to Judas's human expectations of Him. Judas wanted Him to end the Roman oppression and reinstate Israel as a sovereign nation with Himself as Messiah-King. Judas was focused on his immediate material world, and he did not have an inkling of what Jesus' kingdom was really about. Therefore he nurtured completely misplaced expectations of Jesus.

None of us really has any sympathy with Judas, and yet we perhaps condemn him too easily. The story of the Passion always places a choice before people. It was Judas's choice to betray Jesus. This Easter, perhaps you should ask yourself whether Jesus always lives up to your expectations. Why do you have faith? Do you have faith for the sake of the expansion of His kingdom or merely for the sake of possible gains for yourself? Are you too betraying Jesus in the things that you think and do, as Judas did?

*Lord Jesus, forgive me for still sometimes cherishing misplaced expectations of You. This Easter, help me to choose You as the Lord of my life. Amen.*

# Your testimonial

People will be lovers of themselves, lovers of money, boastful, proud, abusive, disobedient to their parents, ungrateful, unholy ... treacherous.

2 Timothy 3:2-4

In this passage Paul is providing Timothy with a rather dismal testimonial of the people who will live in the last days. And what is more, the people Paul is speaking about are people of the church, believers – but yet people who have repudiated the power of Christ as a result of their own selfishness.

Actually this list of characteristics reminds one very much of Judas. "Are you perhaps like Judas?" is the question that yesterday's devotion posed to you. Perhaps you should take the time to contemplate this matter carefully.

What would your testimonial look like should the Lord have to write one for you? What characteristics do other people see when scrutinizing your life? Would they catch glimpses of the selfishness, avarice, conceit and lovelessness of which Paul speaks? Is your love of pleasure still greater than your love for God? Is Jesus truly your King, or are there a couple of other little kings before whom you kneel? Do you possibly have the external appearance of faith without the substance and strength of faith?

God must never become an instrument to serve your own interests. Make doubly sure that you are willing to deny yourself, to take up your cross and to follow Jesus every day. Or are you still betraying Him like a Judas?

*Heavenly Father, I must confess that I still notice many of the negative characteristics that Paul describes in my own life. Please forgive me and help me to become more Christlike. Amen.*

# Jesus and the women

Some women were watching from a distance. Among them were Mary Magdalene, Mary the mother of James the younger and Joses, and Salome.

MARK 15:40

Throughout His ministry Jesus had a special relationship with women. We read that a group of women cared for Jesus: In Galilee these women had followed Him and cared for His needs (Mk. 15:41). It was women like Mary and Martha who invited Jesus to eat with them.

Mary even anointed Him with precious oils, washed His feet with her tears and dried them with her hair. The women sincerely loved Jesus and cared for His needs. This group of faithful women also followed Jesus at a distance on the day of His crucifixion.

These women must have found it extremely difficult to see Jesus dying on the cross. Even in the hour of His bitterest suffering Jesus noticed these women. He asked John to take His mother into his home and care for her.

After Jesus' crucifixion it was once again a group of women who went to the tomb to anoint His body. And the first person to whom Jesus appeared after His resurrection was also a woman, Mary Magdalene.

Unlike most men of His time, Jesus did not regard women as inferior beings. He recognized women as people in their own right. In His kingdom women have their own special place.

You too are important to Jesus. He loves you, and has a special place and task for you in His kingdom.

*Lord Jesus, thank You for not regarding me as somehow inferior to men. Thank You for loving me and using me in Your service. Amen.*

# The centurion at the cross

And when the centurion, who stood there in front of Jesus, heard his cry and saw how he died, he said, "Surely this man was the Son of God!"

MARK 15:39

Throughout the Bible we find a contrast between Jesus' own people who rejected Him, and the gentiles and foreigners who worshiped Him and acknowledged Him as the Messiah. His own townspeople refused to listen to Him, while a Roman officer and his entire family had faith in Him.

The Jewish elders, teachers of the law and the scribes of Jesus' time took no notice of His teachings, while sinners and publicans were converted when He spoke to them. Pilate unequivocally declared that he found no guilt in Jesus, while the Jewish leaders insisted on having Him crucified. While Jesus was hanging on the cross the Jews mocked Him and told Him to save Himself, but one of the thieves crucified next to Him begged Him for mercy.

It is then also not surprising that the Jews completely failed to notice the unusual events that took place during Jesus' crucifixion: the darkness and the tearing of the temple curtain. But an unknown Roman soldier who was in command of the events at the cross noticed these events and testified that Jesus must surely be the Son of God.

Who is Jesus to you? Is He just a historical figure that you read of in your Bible, or can you testify from your heart that He is truly the crucified, resurrected Savior, the Son of God who came to sacrifice His life to atone for your sins?

*Lord Jesus, thank You that I may be assured that You are truly the Son of God, and that You earned me the gift of eternal life through Your death on the cross. Amen.*

# Only one sacrifice is necessary

Such a high priest meets our need – one who is holy, blameless, pure, set apart from sinners, exalted above the heavens. Unlike the other high priests, he does not need to offer sacrifices day after day, first for his own sins, and then for the sins of the people. He sacrificed for their sins once and for all when he offered himself.

HEBREWS 7:26-27

When Jesus died on the cross and sacrificed Himself for our sins, He made the perfect offering. This sacrifice, Jesus Himself, will never have to be repeated. Through Jesus' atoning death we who believe in Him are redeemed once and for all. Jesus died for the sins that you have already committed as well as the sins that you are still going to commit in the future. No further sacrifice is necessary.

Jesus sacrificed His life as an atonement for your sins. God willingly paid a costly price for your sins to be forgiven. You have to do nothing on your part to earn atonement through Jesus' sacrifice.

However, you can and must have an answer to His sacrifice. I recently saw a striking poster of Jesus on the cross. Underneath was written: "It's your move." In dying on the cross Jesus did everything in His power; there is nothing left that He can do.

But what about you? Have you accepted His offering yet? Have you made it your own and asked Him to forgive your sins? It is indeed your move.

This Easter, decide for yourself what you are going to do with the sacrifice that Jesus made for your sake.

*Lord Jesus, how could I possibly thank You for such a great sacrifice? I accept it with all my heart. Please forgive all my sins and help me to live as Your child from now on. Amen.*

# Crucified with Jesus

For we know that our old self was crucified with him so that the body of sin might be done away with, that we should no longer be slaves to sin – because anyone who has died has been freed from sin.

ROMANS 6:6-7

Walking the Way of the Cross together with Jesus this Easter makes us part of everything that happened to Jesus on the cross. It is once again a demonstration of God's grace and love for us. You can do one of two things with God's grace: you can either underestimate it or overestimate it.

You can try to earn God's grace by keeping His commandments, or you can scorn His grace by continuing to sin, because after all God will just have to forgive you. Unfortunately there are very few Christians who regard sin as seriously as they ought to.

It is crucial for you to understand God's grace correctly: Jesus died in your place on the cross, but you too must be willing to die with Him. Your sinful human nature should have died with Him on the cross.

You should be willing to get rid of every sin that is still present in your life. Every time when you are tempted to commit a sin, remind yourself that you are dead to your sinful nature, and resist sinning through Jesus' strength!

If your sinful nature has been crucified, it also means that you will live for Christ from now on. He has made you a new creation; live as God wants you to live.

*Lord Jesus, I am sorry that my old sinful nature resurfaces so forcefully every now and again. Help me to truly crucify my sinful nature, so that I can live only for You from now on. Amen.*

# Reconciled with God

For if, when we were God's enemies, we were reconciled to him through the death of his Son, how much more, having been reconciled, shall we be saved through his life!

ROMANS 5:10

*The Message* translates this verse as follows: "If, when we were at our worst, we were put on friendly terms with God by the sacrificial death of His Son, now that we're at our best, just think of how our lives will expand and deepen by means of His resurrection life!" (p. 371).

Jesus sacrificed His life so that you could return to God, and so that sinful people and a holy God could be reconciled. When He died, the curtain of the temple was torn in two. Jesus' sacrificial death not only broke down the walls between God and sinful people, but also the walls that people build between one another.

If you are to participate in Jesus' act of reconciliation, you ought to be able to testify that you live in a close relationship with God. Furthermore, your relationship with your neighbor should be indicative of this reconciliation.

If this is not yet the case, confess the sins that are marring your relationship with God, and restore the relationships between you and the people close to you.

Always remember that Christ is one with your fellow believers, regardless of the differences that may exist between you and them.

*Lord Jesus, I praise You for enabling me to live in peace with God and my neighbor through Your death on the cross. Amen.*

# Reconciliation and redemption

But now that you have been set free from sin and have become slaves to God, the benefit you reap leads to holiness and the result is eternal life.

ROMANS 6:22

Reconciliation and redemption go hand in hand. The wages of sin may be death, but God grants us eternal life because Jesus has earned it for us on the cross.

Ever since the Fall man has been living in a prison – every human being has original sin in his blood. We have all already been condemned to death. But when the shadow of Jesus' cross falls on the door of your prison it is unlocked. Jesus frees you from the power of sin. *The Message* puts it like this: "Those who enter into Christ's being-here-for-us no longer live under a continuous, low-lying black cloud ... The Spirit of life in Christ, like a strong wind, has magnificently cleared the air, freeing you from a fated lifetime of brutal tyranny at the hands of sin and death" (p. 376).

If you profess your belief that Jesus has freed you, the door of your prison cell has been opened, but you might still be trapped in the death cell. You may be a new creation, but you will also have to learn to live like a new creation. If you have been crucified with Christ, you are now in the service of God.

In Romans 6 Paul tells you how you can accomplish this: "That means you must not give sin a vote in the way you conduct your lives ... Throw yourselves wholeheartedly and full-time ... into God's way of doing things" (*The Message*, p. 373).

Will you meet this challenge with all your heart?

*Lord Jesus, would You please keep sin from ever having a hold over me again? Help me to live only for You from now on. Amen.*

# Jesus becomes human

Your attitude should be same as that of Christ Jesus: Who ... made himself nothing, taking the very nature of a servant, being made in human likeness.

PHILIPPIANS 2:5-7

When we talk of Jesus' suffering on earth we usually refer to the time and events surrounding His crucifixion. We often forget that Jesus' suffering started with His birth. Jesus, the Son of God, left heaven of His own free will and became an ordinary human being, just like us.

It must have been a terrible humiliation, and yet He did not recoil from it for even one moment. The Bible tells us that we should have exactly the same attitude as He did.

The movie *The Horse Whisperer* is based on the true story of Monty Roberts, a legendary American horse-breeder. Monty had the extraordinary ability to become one with his horses, to speak their language, as it were. He knew his horses so well that he knew exactly what they were thinking. Because of this gift he was able to tame even the wildest horse simply by talking to it.

Jesus became a human being for us, a human being like us. Therefore He understands us completely. He was willing to sacrifice all His rights and to become a servant. And you and I must, in turn, be willing to become like Him. Martin Luther writes that one's attitude is proved only when it is transformed into deeds. What does your attitude look like? Are you able to live, act and serve as Jesus did?

*Lord Jesus, You know me inside and out, because You were a human being just like me. Make me humble and willing to be a servant, as You were. Amen.*

# Prepared to suffer

For it has been granted to you on behalf of Christ not only to believe on him, but also to suffer for him.

PHILIPPIANS 1:29

It would be fitting for God's children to keep in mind this Easter that suffering is inevitable in the Christian life. It is part and parcel of human life. But because we don't ordinarily regard suffering as a privilege, Paul's choice of words in this passage seems rather odd. People always find suffering difficult. It is not something that we would willingly choose and we would definitely not regard it as a privilege. But when your suffering is the consequence of the fact that you are a Christian who serves God faithfully, you know that God is using you positively by allowing you to suffer for His sake.

The apostles left the Sanhedrin, rejoicing because they had been counted worthy of suffering disgrace for the Name, Luke reports in Acts 5:41. This kind of suffering – for the sake of your faith – shows other people that you are faithful to God. There are essentially four positive things about this kind of suffering:

☀ It provides you with the correct perspective on earthly comforts.
🥀 It brings to light the true colors of those who are Christians in name only.
🌼 It strengthens the faith of those who persevere.
🌸 It serves as a powerful example for potential followers.

Jesus showed His obedience by suffering for your sake. Are you willing to do the same for Him?

Lord Jesus, You know that I easily recoil from suffering. Please make me willing to suffer for Your sake. Amen.

# The meaning of Jesus' suffering

About the ninth hour Jesus cried out in a loud voice: *"Eloi, Eloi, lama sabachthani?"* – which means, "My God, my God, why have you forsaken me?"

MATTHEW 27:46

Because we celebrate Easter every year, it is all too easy to become blasé about the facts of Jesus' suffering on the cross. But Jesus' suffering must never become commonplace to us. We think of His suffering in human terms, focusing on the physical pain that He suffered.

But Jesus' mental anguish was much worse than the physical punishment that He had to endure. On the cross Jesus bore the full brunt of God's wrath against sin. And He did it without the assistance of His Father.

When you know that God is with you, it is possible to endure suffering and yet to remain hopeful, but without Him it is altogether impossible.

The worst suffering that a Christian can possibly undergo is to be forsaken by God. On the cross Jesus experienced the worst conceivable suffering on earth when His Father forsook Him, particularly because He was used to living close to His Father and being one with God.

The intensity of His suffering culminates in His cry: "My God, My God, why have You forsaken Me?"

Jesus suffered because of God's wrath against sin. He bore it in our place so that you and I will never have to experience that wrath again. Through His suffering Jesus earned God's absolution for you. He lost His life so that yours could be saved; He died so that you may have eternal life.

*Lord Jesus, thank You that You bore God's wrath against sin in my place, and in so doing earned me eternal life. Amen.*

# Obedient unto death

Although he was a son, he learned obedience from what he suffered and, once made perfect, he became the source of eternal salvation for all who obey him.

HEBREWS 5:8-9

During His life on earth, Jesus often endured physical, human suffering. He lived the life of a vagrant, He often experienced discomfort, and had no home or possessions of His own. He also knew that tremendous suffering awaited Him at the end of His life.

In the Garden of Gethsemane He implored His Father to take the cup of suffering from Him, but ultimately He resigned Himself to God's will.

Through His suffering on earth and on the cross Jesus taught us what true obedience to the Father means. Because He was willing to be obedient to this extent, He is now our source of eternal salvation. His obedience makes it possible for us to be God's children.

God asks the same kind of obedience from us. And through His Holy Spirit He enables us to walk in the footsteps of Christ.

Are you prepared to yield your will to the will of God? Are you willing to be truly obedient to all His commands, even if that were to cause you suffering and pain?

If you are not yet absolutely obedient to God, perhaps this Easter is a good time to say *yes* to God's commands.

*Lord Jesus, it is so difficult for me to be as obedient as You were, especially when the cost is high. Thank You for helping me to be more obedient every day. Amen.*

# God gives His Son

> "For God so loved the world that he gave his one and only Son, that whoever believes in him shall not perish but have eternal life."
>
> JOHN 3:16

It is no coincidence that John 3:16 is one of the best known verses in the Bible, because it summarizes God's love for His people in a nutshell: He loved us so much that He sacrificed His Son's life so that we may have eternal life.

With each Easter we are amazed once more by the extent of God's love for His sinful human children. We once again rejoice over the wonder of Jesus' willingness to leave heaven, to come to earth as an ordinary man, and to be crucified so that our sins could be forgiven.

God is love, and we should carefully consider what this means. God loved us so much that He sent His Son to redeem us from our sins.

This is God's most important and salient quality: He is love. You only have to consider Jesus' death on the cross to realize the extent of God's love for you personally. God loves the world so much, God loves *you* so much that He sacrificed His only Son so that you may have life.

If you are going to accept His offer of grace, it is essential for you to believe in Jesus: "Whoever does not believe stands condemned already because he has not believed in the name of God's one and only Son" (Jn. 3:18).

Be sure to use this Easter to reaffirm your faith in Jesus.

*Lord Jesus, I believe in You. Thank You for the assurance that I will not perish, but that I already have eternal life. Amen.*

# The meaning of Jesus' resurrection

And if Christ has not been raised, your faith is futile; you are still in your sins. If only for this life we have hope in Christ, we are to be pitied more than all men.

1 Corinthians 15:17, 19

Jesus' resurrection confirms everything He told His disciples. It irrevocably establishes the fact that He redeemed us from our sins. It also confirms the fact that we who believe in Him will one day rise from the dead just as He did.

According to the Heidelberg Catechism Jesus' resurrection means three things to me:

- ☀ It fulfills the promise of Good Friday. Jesus died on the cross precisely so that we should have life. We can put a tick behind our names: Jesus has paid all the debt of our sins, and we have been justified by faith. Because of Jesus, God forgives your sin. When God looks at you, He sees you through the cross of His Son.
- ✿ The resurrection also has a bearing on the way in which you live now. God's children ought to live in this world with the power of the resurrection in them. They are, after all, people who daily experience Jesus' peace in their lives.
- ◉ The resurrection compels us to look ahead toward the unknown that awaits us: death is inevitable. But for Christians Jesus has removed death's sting. Through His crucifixion He conquered death, and His resurrection brings you the message that you too will one day rise from death into a new life.

*Lord Jesus, thank You that You not only died for me, but also rose from the dead so that I will one day have eternal life with You. Amen.*

# Live in reverence before God

Since you call on a Father who judges each man's work impartially, live your lives as strangers here in reverent fear.

1 Peter 1:17

Although we are here on earth temporarily, God still expects His children to live in a distinctive way, revering God. To have reverence for someone means that you hold that person in high esteem and respect him. If you revere your parents you will be obedient to them. The same is true of Christians: we show our reverence for God by obeying His Word.

In the Sermon on the Mount Jesus gives a detailed description of what the citizens of heaven should be like. They are people who are salt and light, who love their enemies, and who choose God rather than Mammon. The ultimate requirement for people who revere God is contained in Jesus' summary of the commandments: they should love God above all and their neighbor as they love themselves.

Most of us feel at home here on earth. We so easily become accustomed to the fact that the world doesn't really have much reverence for God and His commandments. We therefore try to live like people who hold two passports: one for heaven and one for the world.

Unfortunately it doesn't work this way. You will have to choose which one is more important to you, and you will have to be willing to live in such a way that the world will hear your testimony loudly and clearly.

*Lord Jesus, help me to live my life here on earth in reverence for You, so that other people will be able to see You in my life. Amen.*

# Love one another

> For you know that it was not with perishable things such as silver or gold that you were redeemed ... but with the precious blood of Christ ... Now that you have purified yourselves by obeying the truth ... love one another deeply, from the heart.
>
> 1 PETER 1:18-19, 22

God hates sin and can never leave it unpunished. The wages of sin are always death. But through His death on the cross Jesus redeemed us of the punishment for sin, and therefore we should love one another from the heart in obedience to Him, as Peter writes. Jesus is the power behind our obedience. His death on the cross freed us from the tyranny of our sinful human nature and redeemed us from our sins, so that we could be God's children.

This month we walked the Way of the Cross with Jesus. We contemplated the fact that Jesus was crucified for our sakes, that He rose from the grave and conquered death. And because He did this, heaven is our destiny. His crucifixion and resurrection make eternal life possible for us. God redeemed us from sin through the death of His Son. Jesus earned our heavenly citizenship for us; all we have to do to receive it is to believe in Him.

Therefore you can live your earthly life in the assurance that heaven awaits you. This fact bestows on you a different value, makes you different from the rest of the world. From now on you should live and behave in such a way that other people will notice this difference in you.

*Lord Jesus, thank You for earning a place in heaven for me through Your death on the cross. Help me to live as Your child by loving other people. Amen.*

# What does God ask of you?

Now that you have purified yourselves by obeying the truth so that you have sincere love for your brothers, love one another deeply, from the heart.

1 PETER 1:22

How should we live? What exactly does God ask of us? What is His purpose with us? The Bible clearly shows us God's purpose and direction: we should purify ourselves by obeying the truth, and love one another sincerely, as brothers.

God expects us to love one another, Love one another, for he who loves his fellowman has fulfilled the law (Rom. 13:8). This commandment sums up all of the other commandments.

When we consider what exactly this biblical love looks like, we always fall far short of the ideal. The love that God requires of us is self-sacrificing and unselfish. It does not seek its own best interests, but always puts the interests of other people first. It does not exist because our fellow human beings deserve it, but rather flourishes despite all the shortcomings and faults of our neighbors. This is the way in which Jesus loved.

And now God asks you to love others in the same way that Jesus loves you. It sounds impossible, and so it is. In your own strength you will never accomplish this, but God can make it possible through His Holy Spirit who lives in you. Ask Him right now to help you.

*Lord, when it comes to love I always fall short of Your ideals. You know that I still love myself better than I do others. Please forgive me, and enable me to love my neighbor in the same way that You love me. Amen.*

# Arise in a new life!

Now if we died with Christ, we believe that we will also live with him. In the same way, count yourselves dead to sin but alive to God in Christ Jesus.

ROMANS 6:8, 11

To have been crucified with Jesus means to be dead to sin. All the wrong you did before should now be something of the past. Your old nature and love for sin died with Christ. As Paul testifies in Galatians 2:20, "I have been crucified with Christ and I no longer live, but Christ lives in me." That is why you should not get bogged down in the thought of Jesus' death on the cross, but should rather concentrate on the fact that He lives and that you live with Him.

You now share in His resurrection life and have an intimate Father-child relationship with God. As a brand-new person, you should now live every day to the utmost, and to the glory of God.

Unfortunately all of this does not mean that you will be completely free of sin from now on. But you are no longer the slave of sin. Sin is no longer your master. When you commit a sin, you know that you are doing wrong and you can immediately make a U-turn back to God. He is willing to forgive your sin every time, and will always accept you with open arms.

*Lord Jesus, I praise You for the wonder of being crucified with You and now living my life to the fullest for You. Show me when I do wrong and help me to be willing to leave my sins behind me. Amen.*

# Eternal life

---

Jesus said to her: "I am the resurrection and the life. He who believes in me will live, even though he dies; and whoever lives and believes in me will never die."

JOHN 11:25-26

---

None of us likes to talk about death. Besides the fact that such talk spoils our appetite for life, death also remains a largely unknown territory to us. We don't quite know what to make of death. What we are sure of is that it awaits all of us. No one can escape death. Actually, death provides us with irrefutable proof of the reality of the Fall. We carry its seed in us from the day of our birth.

Death also awaits Christians. The Bible says that our lives are brief and transient, like the flowers of the field.

But Jesus also promised Martha that everyone who believes in Him will live, even though he dies. Because Jesus died and rose from the dead, He has made eternal life possible for us. It is impossible for us to grasp this fact with our limited understanding, but we can believe it, because Jesus has made it a reality for us through His death on the cross.

You therefore need not only place your hope in Him for this life: you can know for certain that heaven awaits you. At Easter the orthodox Greeks greet each other with a traditional Easter greeting: Jesus has truly risen!

If you do not yet believe this with all your heart, you are standing on the threshold of heaven – but still outside.

---

*Lord Jesus, I praise You as the risen Savior who came to make life after death a reality for me. Amen.*

# God is with you

Heavenly Father,
It is so wonderful to know that You are always there for me,
that You love me and know my name,
that I am the apple of Your eye,
that I can talk to You any time of the day or night,
because You neither slumber nor sleep.
Thank You for Your continued presence in my life,
for the fact that You care for me,
and give me Your peace in my life.
With You at my side,
I know that there is nothing that I need fear,
that I am able to accomplish anything
because You give me the strength.
That I can face every challenge that comes my way
in complete confidence,
because I know that I will be able to handle it
with Your help.
Thank You that I can be more than a conqueror
because You live in me.
I praise You because I can step joyfully into each new day,
for I know that You will let all things work for my good.

*Amen.*

# With God at your side

Shout aloud and sing for joy, people of Zion, for great is the Holy One of Israel among you.

ISAIAH 12:6

The fact that the Israelites worshiped a God who was with them, set them apart from all other nations. Because God was with them, they managed to defeat armies stronger than them time and again, and things always seemed to turn out well for them. The Israelite leaders were all too aware of this fact. When the Lord refused to accompany His people any further because of their sins, Moses said unequivocally: "How will anyone know that You are pleased with ... Your people unless You go with us? What else will distinguish ... Your people from all the other people on the face of the earth?" (Ex. 33:16).

You too can face life fearlessly if you are sure that you have God with you. With God at your side you can be assured that everything is all right, even though things may seem to be terribly wrong.

If you have God at your side you can know for certain that He will provide a way out of your troubles, even in times of intense suffering. Therefore you need not fear anything. You can depend on God, not only for enough strength to face every day, but also for the fulfillment of all your needs in the year ahead.

Are you ready to testify that God is your strength, your protector and your Savior? If you ever doubt God's omnipotence, take a look at His creation. This wonderful God wants to walk with you every day of your journey through life. Will you allow Him to?

*Heavenly Father, how great You are! Thank You for the assurance that You are with me, and that You walk with me every day on my journey through life. Amen.*

# God wants to take care of you

Blessed are those you choose and bring near to live in your courts!
We are filled with the good things of your house, of your holy temple.

PSALM 65:4

God reveals Himself in nature as well as in the history of His people. He always cared for them and looked after their interests. This beautiful psalm is a song of praise for God's goodness and His caring love for His people.

Unfortunately His people time and time again allowed sin to separate them from God. Before God's praises could be sung properly His people needed to confess their sins and ask God to forgive them.

The temple in Jerusalem was the place where the people went to meet the Lord. It was also the place where they confessed their sins and made sacrifices for atonement. As the psalmist writes in verses two and three: "To You all men will come. When we were overwhelmed by sin You forgave our transgressions."

You and I also need to take stock of our sins before we start to praise the Lord for loving us and caring for us. The church, the house of the Lord, is still the place where we go to meet God.

Be sure to make time in your busy schedule to visit the house of the Lord. Once you have done so you are allowed to praise Him, because you will know that He will look after you every day of your life.

Heavenly Father, please forgive my sins. Thank You that I can praise You, because I experience Your love and care daily. Amen.

# God cares for our country

You care for the land and water it; you enrich it abundantly. The streams of God are filled with water to provide the people with grain, for so you have ordained it.

PSALM 65:9

The Lord not only cares for you; His power encompasses the whole earth. When the Lord loves people and adopts them as His own, He also cares for the country in which they live. And when the Lord provides, He always does so in abundance. As the psalmist says in verse 11, "You crown the year with Your bounty, and Your carts overflow with abundance." Israel believed that God's abundant blessings in nature were proof of His love for them.

Despite the sinful condition of the world, God still cares for people everywhere. The abundance in nature is a gift from God.

It is He who gives us rain and who ensures that the soil brings forth fruit. He crowns the year with His bounty, writes the psalmist. He promises His children abundant blessings.

God is not only willing to look after His creation, but He also wants to provide for the needs of the people He created. Everything is the work of His hands. And in the abundance of nature you can also see His love for you.

Be sure to praise Him for this every day of your life, as the psalmist did.

*Lord, I praise You for Your goodness! Thank You for abundantly providing for all my needs, and for caring for our country. Amen.*

# Only God can give peace

The LORD replied, "My Presence will go with you, and I will give you rest."

EXODUS 33:14

If you have God in your life, He gives you His peace, even in the midst of unrest and strife, because the peace of God does not depend on external circumstances, but rather comes from within. When Jesus promises this peace to His disciples, He says, "Peace I leave with you; My peace I give you. I do not give to you as the world gives. Do not let your hearts be troubled and do not be afraid" (Jn. 14:27).

At the moment our country is experiencing unprecedented levels of violence. If we are honest, we would have to admit that we are often disturbed and afraid. We all long for peace. We pray that the prevailing violence will come to an end, so that we can have peace and calm once again. We long simply to feel completely safe in our homes, in the streets and in the areas where we live.

The peace that the Bible speaks of, which can only be given by God, means precisely this: to heal, to make whole. It encompasses much more than just the cessation of violence. The Bible's peace always involves relationships: God first wants to restore His relationship with you and then your relationships with the people around you.

When this has been accomplished, peace will once more reign supreme in your life: the kind of peace that only God can give.

Ask God right now to bestow this peace not only on your life, but also on your country.

*Heavenly Father, I pray that You will be with me every day and grant me Your peace, in my life as well as in my country. Amen.*

# The apple of His eye

In a desert land he found him, in a barren and howling waste. He shielded him and cared for him; he guarded him as the apple of his eye.

DEUTERONOMY 32:10

There are few places in the Bible where God's caring love for His children is expressed as clearly and lucidly as in this chapter of Deuteronomy. Here Moses gives a short overview of the history of Israel, continually emphasizing the way in which the Lord always provided and cared for His people.

While His people were wandering in the wilderness, the Lord was with them every day, in the form of a cloud and a pillar of fire. As today's Scripture puts it, the Lord shielded His people, cared for them and guarded them as the apple of His eye. This image reminds one of a mother playing with her baby. In the next verse (v. 11) God assures His people that He will carry them from day to day as an eagle carries its young on its wings.

These two beautiful promises still hold true for us today. We can carry them with us every day of our lives.

Even in times of hardship we only have to think back on how the Lord helped us repeatedly in the past, and trust Him to do the same for us now.

Always remember that you are precious to God, that you are the apple of His eye. You never have to doubt His love and care for you.

*Heavenly Father, thank You for the loving way in which You care for me from day to day. Thank You that I am precious to You and that You love me. Amen.*

# Keep your eyes on God

But my eyes are fixed on you, O Sovereign Lord; in you I take refuge – do not give me over to death.

PSALM 141:8

To get through any situation, keep focused on God and not on what is happening around you. The person who keeps his eyes fixed on the Lord, who never looks away from Him for even a second or loses sight of His will, will walk through life confidently.

Many people (like Peter at the Sea of Galilee) have experienced that looking away from God causes the water to give way under you.

Our experience today is often similar to Peter's: as soon as you look away from God for a moment and come face to face with your own problems, those problems threaten to overwhelm you as the high swells threatened to overwhelm Peter on the Sea of Galilee. And then you will begin to sink.

Fortunately we know that when we undertake to keep our eyes fixed on God, when we vow to keep His law and be obedient to His commands, He promises to be with us always. And if at times you still feel that you are overwhelmed by life, you only have to reach out your hand to Him. He is always there to take your hand and rescue you from your difficulties, as He did with Peter.

All you have to remember is not to lose sight of Him.

*Lord, You know that I have often felt as if I were drowning in the crises surrounding me. Please help me to keep my eyes fixed on You alone, in the steadfast knowledge that You are always there to help me. Amen.*

# All's well that ends well

---

The LORD will fulfill his purpose for me; your love, O LORD, endures forever – do not abandon the works of your hands.

PSALM 138:8

---

In Psalm 138 the psalmist praises the Lord because He has redeemed him and repeatedly rescued him from adversity.

Finally, he emphasizes the fact that the Lord's love for His children endures forever and that He will fulfill His purposes for them.

It is inevitable that God's children will experience crisis situations. Being a Christian does not safeguard us from pain and suffering, just as God's Son was not safeguarded from it.

Perhaps you have also had to cope with problems and crises during the course of the year. When you feel overwhelmed by your problems, just remember the testimony in verse 7 of this psalm, "Though I walk in the midst of trouble, You preserve my life; You stretch out Your hand ... with Your right hand You save me."

No crisis is so great and no disaster so overwhelming that God isn't able to help you through it or grant you enough strength to be able to carry it.

And you as a Christian have a further assurance: this God who protects you against harm and danger will also fulfill His purpose for you, making sure that everything ends well for you. All's well that ends well, says the proverb. God will cause even the negative things in His children's lives work out positively. Remember this the next time life seems overwhelmingly bleak to you.

---

*Heavenly Father, thank You for all the times in the past that You have helped and protected me. Thank You for the knowledge that You will work everything for my good. Amen.*

# God's level ground

Answer me quickly, O LORD; my spirit fails. Teach me to do your will, for you are my God; may your good Spirit lead me on level ground.

PSALM 143:7, 10

When David wrote this psalm he was undoubtedly extremely discouraged. "My spirit fails," he says to the Lord. But then David remembers everything that the Lord has done for him in the past, all His deeds that reveal His omnipotence, and David once again reaches out his hands to God and confirms his trust in Him: "Let the morning bring me word of Your unfailing love, for I have put my trust in You. Show me the way I should go, for to You I lift up my soul" (Ps. 143:8).

If you are willing to do God's will, He Himself will show you the right way. You can know God's will by studying His Word and by listening to His Spirit.

If you are willing to do this in the year ahead, you can take the promise in verse 10 to heart: the Holy Spirit will lead you on level ground in the times ahead. Every morning of your life you can awaken with the assurance of God's love and care, provided that you are willing to trust in Him completely.

The word here translated as "trust" actually means to tie yourself to someone. Tie yourself to God for the rest of your life, especially in those times when your path may become uneven. If you do so, the Lord will undertake to lead you on level ground.

*Heavenly Father, thank You for the unfailing knowledge that I can steadfastly trust in You every day. Please lead me on Your level ground. Amen.*

# *Belonging to the Lord*

"One will say, 'I belong to the LORD'; another will call himself by the name of Jacob; still another will write on his hand, 'The LORD's,' and will take the name Israel."

ISAIAH 44:5

Here the prophet Isaiah is describing the unique relationship between God and Israel. God created and chose Israel above all the other nations to be His special people.

Despite the fact that the Israelites repeatedly turned their back on God and consequently were sent into exile, the Lord was willing to start anew with them and to acknowledge them as His people. He intervened in their circumstances and changed their fate. He undertook to pour out His blessing on them so that they would grow up like poplar trees by flowing streams.

When Jesus came into the world He made it possible for you to be counted as one of God's people. If you believe in Him, you too belong to the Lord: He has made you and redeemed you.

If you make something with your own hands it belongs to you exclusively. One of the members of our congregation made a beautiful wooden go-cart for a church bazaar and then bought it back for his grandchild. In truth, this go-cart belonged to him twice over. He made it and bought it.

The same is true of God's children. He not only made you, but also paid the price for your sin on the cross. You therefore belong to Him twice over. Like Israel you too can write on your hand: the Lord's.

*Lord Jesus, I praise You for not only making me, but also for redeeming me from my sin, so that I now belong to You over and again. Amen.*

# God calls you

> "Before I formed you in the womb I knew you, before you were born I set you apart; I appointed you as a prophet to the nations."
>
> JEREMIAH 1:5

Despite the fact that the prophet Jeremiah was still very young, the Lord had chosen and set him apart for the Lord's service. Jeremiah was a prophet during a very difficult time in Israel's history. But Jeremiah could stand strong and preach God's message despite the opposition of the rest of the prophets, because He knew that God had planned a particular course for His people.

The Lord knows everything about you too: He knows every one of His children through and through. If you love Him, He chose you to be His child even before you were born. He chose you to be a witness for Him in this world and to spread His message.

The fact that God chose Jeremiah as His prophet does not mean that Jeremiah was without sin, but rather that God set Jeremiah aside for His service. Even though Jeremiah was a sinful human being, God called him to His service. And Jeremiah was willing to obey despite his youth.

If you belong to God, He calls you too. Are you willing to say yes to God, as Jeremiah did? Or are you still looking for excuses about why you can't be His witness? If you say yes to God He will put His words in your mouth and help you to fulfill the task that He has chosen for you.

*Heavenly Father, I am filled with wonder at the thought that You chose me to be Your child so long ago. Make me willing to be Your witness in this world. Amen.*

# God works for your good

And we know that in all things God works for the good of those who love him, who have been called according to his purpose.

ROMANS 8:28

"That's why we can be so sure that every detail in our lives of love for God is worked into something good" (*The Message*, p. 378).

It is a wonderful comfort to know that God will use everything, absolutely everything that happens to you to your advantage, even those things that seem difficult, unacceptable and incomprehensible to you. But there is a condition: you have to love God.

A Christian does not believe in the existence of anything like fate or Lady Luck. Nothing in our lives happens by coincidence: everything is part of God's master plan for our lives. So next time something incomprehensible happens in your life, don't ask "why," rather ask "where to," as Dr. Daniël Louw says. The Lord uses crises and times of suffering to teach you some of His most valuable life's lessons.

It is precisely in times of suffering that we live closest to Him.

The next time you have to face one of life's crises, entrust its outcome to the Lord and ask Him to transform this crisis into something beneficial. As Psalm 55:22 says: "Cast your cares on the LORD and He will sustain you; He will never let the righteous fall."

*H eavenly Father, thank You that You work everything for my good, even the difficulties of my life. Amen.*

# God is my joy

You, who through faith are shielded by God's power until the coming of the salvation that is ready to be revealed in the last time. In this you greatly rejoice, though now for a little while you may have had to suffer grief in all kinds of trials.

1 PETER 1:4-6

God, not your external circumstances, is your source of joy. Because you love Him, you are able to be patient in suffering and grateful in prosperity. It also enables you to look forward to the future with confidence. Christians are people who ought to live joyfully.

*The Message* translates this passage as follows: "We've been given a brand-new life and have everything to live for, including a future in heaven – and the future starts now ... I know how great this makes you feel, even though you have to put up with every kind of aggravation in the meantime" (p. 575).

When crises come into our lives, we always want to feel that we are in control, and the feeling of losing control is one of the greatest causes of stress. When the carpet is pulled from under your feet and you suddenly fear that you will no longer be able to provide for your own needs, hold on to God's promise that He is in control.

Rather learn to be patient in times of crisis. Biblical patience is an active word: it implies that you surrender the control of your life to the Lord.

Ask the Lord to give you His joy, not only when all is sunshine in your life, but also when the storms start brewing.

*Heavenly Father, I praise You because You are the source of my joy. Help me to be happy, even in times of suffering, because it will prove the genuineness of my faith. Amen.*

# Be grateful!

However many years a man may live, let him enjoy them all ... Follow the ways of your heart and whatever your eyes see.

ECCLESIASTES 11:8-9

When things are going well for us we often forget to be grateful. The theologian Veldkamp says that while God is pampering us with so many blessings, we often have a lot of petty objections. We are never completely satisfied; there are always more things that we would like to have.

Do you perhaps recognize yourself in this description? Are you truly grateful and satisfied with the things that the Lord gives to you, or are you often to be found complaining that life is so unfair, because there are so many people who have more than you do?

To be truly grateful means to have open and willing hands to serve others. You show your gratitude for God's grace by being prepared to serve others. Everything that God gives you is pure undeserved grace and grace should always be shared. Because God gives you things that you do not deserve, you, in turn, should be willing to give to others what they do not deserve.

When the quadruplets of a married couple in our congregation were seriously injured in a car accident, they testified that God used this experience to teach them gratitude and to give them a new vision of who He truly is. They had a firsthand experience of other people coming to share God's love with them.

Don't wait a minute longer to transform your gratitude to the Lord into good deeds for other people.

*Heavenly Father, forgive me for still living with so much ingratitude in my heart. Help me to show my gratitude to You by serving others. Amen.*

# Keep yourself in God's love

Keep yourselves in God's love as you wait for the mercy of our Lord Jesus Christ to bring you to eternal life.

JUDE 21

Christians need not fear the future, because they are people who live with hope in their hearts, people who are sure that God loves them, people who have guarantees for the way ahead. God sent Jesus to the world precisely because He wants to give His children hope and wants to assure them of His unchanging love for them.

Your faith does not prevent storms from coming into your life. And if you take your eyes off God, you, like Peter, will start sinking because you fear the intensity of the storm. However, God can guarantee you peace and calm in the midst of the storms of life. These storms may hurt you badly, but they do not have the last say in your life. Even in the midst of life's storms you can still remain in God's love.

If you belong to God, you are guaranteed that nothing and no one can ever separate you from God's love. God has His hands around you, and He will carry you when you are no longer able to walk by yourself.

What's more, He will also help you to carry others and to share His love with them. You can feel God's hands around you in the hands of other believers reaching out to you. You can be God's hands by reaching out to others in their times of suffering.

*Heavenly Father, thank You for keeping Your hands around me when life becomes difficult. Help me to reach out my hands to other people, and to share Your love with them. Amen.*

# Only one solution

Then Peter began to speak: "I now realize how true it is that God does not show favoritism but accepts men from every nation who fear him and do what is right."

ACTS 10:34-35

The Israelites looked down on other nations who did not know God, and regarded them as unclean. In Acts 10 God teaches Peter a visual lesson about His grace. In a vision God orders Peter to eat unclean animals. When Peter refuses God shows Him that it is wrong to call anything impure that God has made clean. To Him all people are equally important, regardless of their descent or their race, as long as they fear Him and do what is right.

Many South Africans, especially of the older generation, often find it difficult to accept circumstances in the new South Africa. If we are honest with ourselves, we would have to admit that many of us still carry around quite a bit of racism within us.

Perhaps we need to learn the same lesson Peter did: God loves all people equally. And the only solution for the current problems in our country is for every citizen truly to believe in God.

It is essential that we forget the bitterness of the past and take each other's hands. Take the trouble of getting to know people of other races, and reach out to them. If you are a Christian you are also God's representative in your country. He is the only Factor that will finally really bring us together.

Lord Jesus, I know all too well that You are the only solution to our country's problems. I pray that You will start with me and help me to reach out to other people and bring them to You. Amen.

# There is only one God

For who is God besides the LORD? And who is the Rock except our God?

PSALM 18:31

It seems these days that religion is pandering more and more to the wishes of people. The New Age movement is gaining more and more ground. We hear more and more voices pleading for a greater tolerance toward other religions. Some theologians even believe that we should give recognition to the gods of other religions.

Fortunately the Bible knows better. In the Scriptures the fact is repeatedly and indisputably stated: the Lord is God and there is no other. "Before Me no god was formed, nor will there be one after Me. I, even I, am the LORD, and apart from Me there is no savior," as God Himself says through the prophet Isaiah (Is. 43:10-11).

Isaiah 45:14 says: "'Surely God is with you, and there is no other; there is no other god.'" This could not be stated any clearer! This is why God repeatedly punished His people when they abandoned Him for pagan gods.

There is also no way to enter heaven other than through the propitiatory sacrifice of Jesus. Are you still wavering and wondering whether Allah is perhaps just the same as God? After today you can be sure that there is only one God, and He is the God of the Bible, the triune God who is God the Father, the Almighty, the Creator of heaven and earth, Jesus Christ His Son, and the Holy Spirit.

*Lord, I worship You as the only God, as Father, Son and Holy Spirit. Thank You for being present in my life. Amen.*

# The Lord lives!

The LORD lives! Praise be to my Rock! Exalted be God my Savior!

PSALM 18:46

There is one fact that the psalmist is completely sure of: the God that He worships is a living God. He is mighty to help his children and to give them the victory over their enemies. He is the rock where we can find shelter when things seem to be falling apart in our lives. David in his own life repeatedly experienced God with him, and through the strength that God gave him, he was able to accomplish the apparently impossible.

Nietzsche's proposition that "God is dead" has managed to unnerve many people. Those who have always had doubts about the existence of God especially wonder: Can there really be a God if things around us seem to be so wrong and if it is impossible to see Him in the chaos around us? Why would a loving God allow things like violence and suffering in the world?

Unfortunately there are no easy answers to these questions, but of one thing we can be sure: our God is not dead; the Lord lives! Every child of God can testify to this from firsthand experience, because He supports us every day and we experience His love and grace in our lives every single day.

Even amidst the storms of your life God still remains the Rock to which you can cling. He is completely able to help you in every crisis, to save you from every dangerous situation, just as He did for His people in the past.

*Heavenly Father, thank You that I can know and experience Your living presence in my life every day. I know that You can help and deliver me just as You did in the past. Amen.*

# *Praise the Lord!*

The mountains and hills will burst into song before you, and all the trees of the field will clap their hands.

ISAIAH 55:12

The beautiful tiny garden of our townhouse gives us endless joy. The gardener who lived here before us had a masterful hand with a garden. Our garden is filled with pink, white and light blue flowers and there isn't a time of the year when at least a few kinds of flowers or shrubs aren't in bloom. The birds have also discovered this paradise and our garden is alive with birds and butterflies.

When I see all the different kinds of flowers, it seems to me that every flower, bird and butterfly is praising the Lord for His greatness.

Have you ever experienced the feeling that nature around you is praising the Lord? The early-morning birds, the first roses of spring, a sunset over the sea? Martin Buber wrote that he walked to a little pond close to his house every morning at sunrise so that he could learn the song the little frogs sing to praise the Lord.

The Bible often uses images from nature, like mountains and trees, to sing the praises of the Lord: "Let everything that has breath praise the Lord" (Ps. 150:6). The purpose of this is to glorify the Lord: "This will be for the Lord's renown, for an everlasting sign, which will not be destroyed" (Is. 55:13).

Everything that God has created praises Him. Today look around you at the beauty of nature, and praise God for all the beautiful things that He gives to you.

*Heavenly Father, how great and wonderful You are for creating a world so exquisitely beautiful. For this I want to praise and worship You every day of my life. Amen.*

# Give in the right spirit

"Everything comes from you, and we have given you only what comes from your hand. I know, my God, that you test the heart and are pleased with integrity."

I CHRONICLES 29:14, 17

Most of us have heard many sermons on this Scripture passage, especially during fundraising drives for the benefit of the church. The entire issue of tithes and offerings is very controversial. Can anyone really still afford it? And should I calculate my tithe based on my gross or my net income?

Before you give your offering of thanks, there are only two things you need to clarify:

☀ You ought to realize that everything that you own actually belongs to God.

🌿 You should also know that God is not interested in your money if your heart and your attitude are not right. God does not really need your small contribution; every animal of the forest and the cattle on a thousand hills all belong to Him (see Ps. 50:10). If you are, first and foremost, willing to give your heart to Him, then you will also know exactly how much money to give.

This year, first make sure that your heart is right before you decide on the amount of money to give. And what you do give, give with sincerity. This year, make your offering of thanks a matter of the heart, and not a matter of your wallet.

Lord, when I think that everything I have actually comes from You, I am ashamed at the insignificance of my offering of thanks. I want to give my heart to You right now, and leave the rest to You. Amen.

# The fragrance of Christ

But thanks be to God, who ... through us spreads everywhere the fragrance of the knowledge of him. For we are to God the aroma of Christ among those who are being saved ...

2 Corinthians 2:14-15

I find it very difficult to decide which is my favorite flower – roses, gardenias, sweet peas or daffodils – but I think that the rose with its wonderful fragrance will win by a small margin. The incredible fragrance of "Peace" can give me goosebumps of delight.

In some eastern languages the words for a woman and a rose are exactly the same. And, after all, being a woman is synonymous with sweet-smelling fragrances. I don't think there is a woman who does not adore a particular perfume. As a woman you can spread your fragrance like a rose in the lives of your husband and children and friends.

It is even more important that you will be a woman who spreads the fragrance of Christ. As *The Message* puts it: "Everywhere we go, people breathe in the exquisite fragrance. Because of Christ, we give off a sweet scent rising to God, which is recognized by those on the way to salvation – an aroma redolent with life" (p. 441).

Can you testify that everyone who knows you is aware of this fragrance of Christ in your life? The next time you put on your favorite perfume, ask the Lord to help you to spread the knowledge of Christ like a pleasant fragrance around you every day.

*Lord Jesus, I love to be the carrier of Your fragrance. Help me to be a woman who will spread the wonderful fragrance of Jesus to other people. Amen.*

# God's abundance

The grace of our Lord was poured out on me abundantly, along with the faith and love that are in Christ Jesus.

I TIMOTHY 1:14

I have to confess that I haven't always felt like performing as a public speaker. I even once asked the Lord to point out a specific text to me if He wanted me to do it. I found it difficult to reconcile myself to the fact that this responsibility fell on my shoulders, especially since public speaking isn't one of my talents.

It was while I was complaining about this again that the Lord gave me this verse from Timothy 1:14, "The grace of our Lord was poured out on me abundantly, along with the faith and love that are in Christ Jesus." I was ashamed since this is indeed true of my life.

Every day God pours out His love on me; every day I experience the abundance of His grace in my life. This verse reminded me of the painting of the crucified Jesus, under which is written: "I did this for you, what are you doing for Me?"

When God gives, He doesn't give just enough, He always gives in abundance. He spoils us by literally saturating our lives with good things. Won't you use this opportunity to make a decision with me to do more in the future? Let's do more in God's kingdom, because we are grateful for the abundant love, grace and faith that God pours out on His children day after day.

*Heavenly Father, I praise You for the abundance of Your love and grace in my life. Please make me willing to give more of myself and my talents in Your service. Amen.*

# Continue doing good

> To those who by persistence in doing good seek glory, honor and immortality, he will give eternal life. For God does not show favoritism.
>
> ROMANS 2:7, 11

I recently read an interesting little story about a wise man who was asked by a group of people: "How can we know when the darkness disappears and the day breaks? Is it when we see a tree in the distance and know that it is an oak tree and not a willow? Or is it when we see an animal and know that it is a fox and not a wolf?"

"No," the wise man answered, "those things won't help you at all. We know that the darkness is disappearing when we see a fellow human being and know that it is our brother or sister. Otherwise, regardless of what the time is, we are still living in darkness."

Paul says that eternal life belongs to everyone who does God's will. This does not contradict the statement that we can only gain eternal life through faith. What Paul is emphasizing here is that those who have been saved will want to live according to God's will, because they love Him and because He redeemed them. Your good deeds are therefore a grateful response to God's grace and not a prerequisite for earning His grace.

And what God wants most is for you to love other people, and regard every other person as your brother or sister. Are you living up to this ideal yet?

*Heavenly Father, thank You for showing no favoritism, but loving each of Your children equally. Make it possible for me to do the same. Amen.*

# Choose today!

But if serving the LORD seems undesirable to you, then choose for yourselves this day whom you will serve ... But as for me and my household, we will serve the LORD.

JOSHUA 24:15

At Shechem Joshua taught all the tribes of Israel a history lesson. He told them about their forefathers and of the great things that the Lord had done for them as a nation in the past. Then he presented them with a choice: "Choose for yourselves this day whom you will serve ... But as for me and my household, we will serve the LORD."

In response the people immediately declared themselves willing to follow Joshua's example, "We will serve the LORD our God and obey Him" (Josh. 24:24).

We are all faced with a multitude of choices every day of our lives. Some of these are fairly insignificant: how you are going to wear your hair today or what clothes you are going to put on. Others are a great deal more important: what career you are going to follow or whom you are going to choose as a marriage partner.

But the most crucial choice that any person can face is the one that Joshua puts to the Israelites: Are you going to choose Jesus? He has already invited you to be His child. But the final choice is always yours. Only you can answer God's invitation.

Have you made a conscious decision to follow the Lord for the rest of your life, like Joshua and his family did? If not, don't postpone it any longer!

Lord, thank You for choosing me to be Your child. Today I want to choose You. Thank You that I can now be sure that I belong to You. Amen.

# Remember to praise God

I will exalt you, O Lord, for you lifted me out of the depths ... that my heart may sing to you and not be silent. O Lord my God, I will give you thanks forever.

PSALM 30:1, 12

The whole of Psalm 30 is a song of praise honoring God. David praised the Lord because He intervened in his life and redeemed him. He praised God for His benevolence, that lasts forever.

When God created man He ordained his entire life to be a song of praise honoring his Creator. "The essence of life is to be found in rejoicing, in human joy over all the things of life. Because in doing so we praise the Creator, and He finds glory in it," writes, van Ruler.

Sometimes we, like David in Psalm 30, need some anguish in our lives to help us realize the importance of joy. All too often it is only when we lose the things we take for granted that we really become grateful, that we truly discover how much goodness God bestowed upon us in the past. It was only after my husband had a serious heart attack that both of us discovered how wonderful it is to be healthy.

The next time troubles cross your path, cling to David's words, "God's anger lasts only a moment, but His favor lasts a lifetime" (Ps. 30:5). Even though you have to live with your tears at the moment, the Lord will soon deliver you from your troubles. In the midst of your suffering you may even learn to praise God more, because your suffering provides you with a new perspective on God's grace.

*Heavenly Father, thank You for always being there when crises come across my path. I praise You for Your goodness which endures forever. Amen.*

# Together with Jesus

> For you died, and your life is now hidden with Christ in God. When Christ, who is your life, appears, then you will also appear with him in glory.
>
> COLOSSIANS 3:3-4

You have been raised from the dead with Christ, reads the first verse of today's Scripture passage. Paul expresses what God has done for His children by saying that we are now "hidden with Christ." Jesus died on the cross for your sake. Actually His cross on Golgotha is your tombstone. Not only were you buried there, but you were also resurrected there so that you can now live for Jesus.

Christians are bound to God through Jesus. Just as an unborn child can only live because he is connected to his mother by the umbilical cord, so you can only be alive in Christ if you are connected to God through Him.

He is the lifeline that ties you to God. He wants you to live in such a way that He will be pleased with your lifestyle and all the things that you think and do. He wants the temporary, earthly things that were so important to you before, to become less important in your life.

Through His death on the cross Jesus made a new life possible for you. Make sure that you are dead to sin, and alive in and for Him every day of your life. Then you can also be assured that you will share in His glory when He appears again.

*Lord Jesus, thank You for making it possible for me to be dead to sin and to be resurrected in a new life with You. Amen.*

# Repent!

And so John came, baptizing in the desert region and preaching a baptism of repentance for the forgiveness of sins.

Mark 1:4

John began his ministry with an inaugural sermon that has retained its great significance to this day. He told the people coming to him in the desert to repent and be baptized, so that God could forgive their sins. And the people listened to John: the inhabitants of Jerusalem streamed to him to confess their sins, and he baptized them in the Jordan River, as Mark tells us.

Before you can reach God, you need to repent. Repentance requires you to accept Jesus as your personal Savior and Redeemer. You have to turn your back on sin and turn to face Jesus.

Repentance demands a change of lifestyle. Before your conversion you lived in the darkness of sin, but now you live in the light of God.

Many people tend to over-spiritualize conversion, but it really means that our lives should change, that we should think and act differently. Conversion has nothing to do with the way in which you intend to be someday, but it focuses on the way in which you live here and now.

Don't you want to turn to Jesus and try to live as He did, from now on? Only then will your repentance and conversion become practical, only then will it be more than lip service.

Turn to Jesus right now. Look at the world and the people around you through His eyes. God can only reach and help them through you.

Lord Jesus, I want to turn to You right now, so that my entire way of life will become different. Help me to look at the world through Your eyes. Amen.

# The recipe for happiness

But you must return to your God; maintain love and justice, and wait for your God always.

HOSEA 12:6

Despite the fact that Israel repeatedly strayed from God, He was always willing to accept them back again.

In this Scripture passage the prophet Hosea implores the people to repent; to return to God. But he also makes it clear that if they decide to do so their lives will have to undergo a radical change.

Yesterday we spoke about repentance and conversion. But repentance alone is not sufficient. People who repent need three things to be happy, according to the prophet Hosea: firstly, they have to be willing to return to God; secondly, they should love Him and obey His commands, and thirdly, they should always wait for Him and put their faith in Him.

If you have turned to the Lord, you will also have to be willing to allow Him to change your life. You need to love Him and to do the things that He asks of you in His Word. You must also put your hope and trust in Him: this means that you will have positive prospects for tomorrow and the day after, because you belong to God.

Do you want to choose today to follow Hosea's recipe for happiness? Look at the Lord with new eyes, realize how great His love for you is, make sure of what the Lord asks of you in His commandments, and put your hope in Him.

Lord, I want to make a U-turn back to You. Help me to love You, to be obedient to You, and to put my hope in You. Amen.

# God calls you by name

But now, this is what the LORD says – he who created you, O Jacob, he who formed you, O Israel: "Fear not, for I have redeemed you; I have summoned you by name; you are mine."

ISAIAH 43:1

Here Isaiah is talking to God's people during their time in exile. He assures these exiles that they belong to God and therefore need not fear, because their redemption is assured.

This message is directed not only at Israel, but at every child of God. And the Lord is not using the plural, but the singular. He wants to say to you today: "I have summoned *you* by name; *you* are Mine."

Even though there are millions and millions of people on this planet, God knows your name. And God's knowledge of you is not incidental or superficial, but profound and thorough. The Hebrew word that is translated "know" presupposes a personal involvement.

It wants to tell you that God's hand is on you personally, that He created you, that He chose you to be His special child long ago.

And because you belong to Him, He also accepted the ownership of your life. You belong to God. He created you and delivered you from sin. Nothing can come between you and Him any more. And for this reason you need not fear, because if you belong to God, you also have the assurance that one day you will have eternal life.

*Heavenly Father, how wonderful that You know my name! Thank You that I belong to You, and can know with certainty that I will one day have eternal life. Amen.*

# You are precious

> Since you are precious and honored in my sight, and because I love you, I will give men in exchange for you, and people in exchange for your life.
>
> ISAIAH 43:4

Even though the Israelites caused the Lord much sorrow, He continued to love them. They were so precious to Him that He was willing to give men in exchange for them, and nations in exchange for their lives. Every single time He was willing to forgive them and to accept them as His people again.

And this message is directed at you too. The Lord not only knows your name, He also regards you as extremely valuable: you are precious to Him. He will forgive your sins time and time again, if only you confess them.

There are many different things that people value highly: things such as wealth, security, power and status. And yet you cannot take any of these things with you when you die. A shroud has no pockets, as the proverb goes.

Death removes the value of all the things that we value so much. Ultimately, on your deathbed, your value depends only on how God sees you. And if you belong to Him, you can be sure that you are preciosus to Him.

Perhaps someone very precious to you recently passed away. If this is the case, you can also be assured that death is not the end for a Christian. Because you belong to Jesus, you can look beyond the grave to a life that will continue forever. Jesus died on the cross so that you – and the people you love – will one day have eternal life if you believe in Him.

*Lord Jesus, thank You that I am precious to You, and thank You for loving me. Amen.*

# Don't be afraid

"Have I not commanded you? Be strong and courageous. Do not be terrified; do not be discouraged, for the Lord your God will be with you wherever you go."

JOSHUA 1:9

Joshua must definitely have been very apprehensive about taking over from Moses to lead Israel into the Promised Land.

Not only was Moses a legendary figure who lived close to God every day, but the people over whom Joshua had to rule were a troublesome bunch. Fortunately the Lord Himself had a comforting message for Joshua: "You need not be terrified or discouraged, Joshua," He said, "I will be with you wherever you go."

Adults don't like admitting that they are afraid, and yet there are so many things that we fear. None of us likes to feel threatened or restricted. Most of us are also scared of death. But God's children can and must live fearlessly in this world. God's love provides us with temporal as well as eternal security.

This love drives all fear away, "There is no fear in love. But perfect love drives out fear, because fear has to do with punishment. The one who fears is not made perfect in love" (1 Jn. 4:18).

Love also takes the threat out of death since because you love God, you no longer need to be afraid of dying. On the cross Jesus conquered death so that you can have eternal life with Him.

Lord Jesus, thank You for the assurance that there is nothing that I need to fear, because Your presence in my life causes fear to vanish. Amen.

# God goes ahead of you

Then Deborah said to Barak, "Go! This is the day the Lord has given Sisera into your hands. Has not the LORD gone ahead of you?"

JUDGES 4:14

In Deborah's time things were not going well for God's people. They were defenseless against the superior numbers of the pagan nations, and were at the mercy of Sisera, the cruel general of King Jabin of Canaan. But Deborah refused to give up, even though Barak did. She prophesied that the Lord would give Sisera into their hands.

Deborah's secret was her absolute trust in God. She knew that you will always be victorious if God goes ahead of you. For this reason she inspired the fearful Israelites with courage. She knew that the Lord would give victory to His people, regardless of how much they were outnumbered by the pagan nations. Sisera was eventually killed by a woman and the Israelites defeated the Canaanites, just as Deborah predicted.

God wants to use you in His master plan as He used Deborah, as long as you are willing to follow Him and to trust in Him. If you are willing to allow the Lord to go ahead of you, He will level all the uneven paths for you and solve all your problems for you. In times of pain and suffering He will enfold you with His love.

Are you willing to be an inspiration and support to the people around you, as Deborah was?

If you are, you can make these words from Deborah's song of praise your own: "May they who love you be like the sun when it rises in its strength" (Judg. 5:31).

*Heavenly Father, please go ahead of me every day, so that I will be able to encourage and strengthen the people I meet along the way. Amen.*

# *S*uffering

Lord Jesus,
I know that I am not immune to hurting and suffering even
though I belong to You,
but I also know that You will be with me
when things are bad,
that You will hold my hand
and that Your arms will be around me.
Thank You for knowing me so well
that You see every one of my tears,
that You also know of each one of my problems,
that You understand me so well because You Yourself
were a human being who knew suffering.
Lord, I have even discovered that this suffering
is good for me
because it draws me ever nearer to You
and teaches me to comfort others in turn.
Please help me when the suffering becomes too much:
give me Your strength so that I can persevere and endure.
Make me willing to take up my cross and follow You.
Thank You for the certain knowledge
that the suffering in my life can never have the last word.
I cling to Your promise that my suffering
will one day in heaven be something of the past.

*A*men.

# God sees your tears

---

O people of Zion, who live in Jerusalem, you will weep no more. How gracious he will be when you cry for help! As soon as he hears, he will answer you.

ISAIAH 30:19

---

God need not have shown mercy to the people in Jerusalem. He told them that they need not weep any longer because He would answer them if they called on Him.

When our family once experienced a great trauma this verse gained special meaning for me. When I read it, I heard the Lord Himself speaking to me. "Don't worry, My child," I clearly heard Him say, "you don't have to cry any more, I will have mercy on you and hear your prayers."

When a small child falls and gets hurt, he cries profusely. A hurt child knows only one way: straight to his mother. He knows well that mommy will pick him up and comfort him and wipe away his tears.

In the same way, when you are sad, you can go straight to your heavenly Father with your pain; with Him there is always comfort. He can use even your tears positively in your life.

If things are very difficult for you at present, God wants to say to you personally today to dry those tears. He has seen every one of them and although He doesn't undertake to always remove all difficulties, He does undertake to comfort you and be with you always.

*Heavenly Father, thank You very much that You know of every one of my tears and that You are always there for me when I need comfort. Amen.*

# God wipes away all your tears

"God himself will be with them and be their God. He will wipe every tear from their eyes. There will be no more death or mourning or crying or pain, for the old order of things has passed away."

REVELATION 21:3-4

Only when it is dark enough can we see the stars, writes Emerson. Tears are sometimes necessary so that you can see God's love and grace in your life in a new way. Just as physical tears are good for you because they wash the eyes, hurting is also good for you because it makes your relationship with God more intimate again.

Nevertheless, tears are not pleasant for anybody. Christians can be sure of one thing: their tears will not keep flowing forever. Although tears are part of your life on earth, someday these tears will come to an end.

The Lord can and wants to wipe away your tears. It is part of the great song that tells of Jesus' Second Coming. In Revelation 21 John writes about the new Jerusalem, the city that is going to be the home of God and His children. There the Lord will be with His children every day and there will be no more tears, because God Himself will wipe them away.

Although life on this earth is full of hurt and hardship you can hold fast to the promise that heaven, where there is no more hardship or death, mourning, sorrow or pain, is waiting for you after all this suffering.

Lord Jesus, You know that my life at present is full of hurt and sorrow. Thank You for Your promise that one day in Heaven there will be no more tears. Amen.

# God keeps His promises

So she said to Abram, "The LORD has kept me from having children. Go, sleep with my maidservant; perhaps I can build a family through her."

SENESIS 16:2

Sarai was tired of waiting. In contrast to her husband she definitely did not believe that God's promise of many descendants would ever come true, and therefore she made her own little plans. She persuaded Abram to take her maidservant, Hagar, as his concubine so that she could produce a son for him. And surprisingly, Abram agreed!

Sarai's plan caused great misery for millions of people after her: the offspring of Hagar and that of Sarai are still at war with each other. It often happens that when we question God's promises and then make our own plans, the outcome of our plans is to our own detriment.

God's promises are certainly steadfast and true, but we can never attach our own timetables to them and then deduce from them that He does not fulfill His promises. We must be willing to wait for the fulfillment of God's promises.

God will answer your prayers too, although it will be in His own time and His own way. Sometimes God also answers differently from what you imagined He would.

However, of one thing you may be certain: God always does what He promises, "Every word of God is flawless" (Prov. 30:5). Remember this when you are tempted to doubt God's promises.

*Heavenly Father, make me patient to wait for the fulfillment of Your promises for me. Thank You that I may know that You will fulfill every one of them. Amen.*

# A God who sees and hears

She gave this name to the LORD who spoke to her: "You are the God who sees me," for she said, "I have now seen the One who sees me."

GENESIS 16:13

God heard the boy crying, and the angel of God called to Hagar from heaven and said to her, "What is the matter, Hagar? Do not be afraid; God has heard the boy crying as he lies there."

GENESIS 21:17

Abraham's slave, Hagar, did not belong to the people of God, but nevertheless, the Lord saw her when she needed help. Hagar fled twice from her master: the first time when she was pregnant and the second time when Sarah drove her away. Both times she landed in difficulties in the desert and both times God came to save her.

In the desert Hagar got to know God as a God who loved her and truly cared for her. She called the fountain where God met her Beer Lahai Roi, which means "a God who sees me."

If you belong to the Lord you can also be sure that God is still seeing you today. He knows when things are difficult, He hears you every time you call upon Him and He stands ready to help you.

Perhaps you need God's help and assistance very much right now. Follow Hagar's example. If you are in a tight corner you can call on God. He is always there for you, He can always help you as He helped Hagar in the desert.

*Heavenly Father, I praise You for being a God who sees me and hears me every time when I call on You for help. Amen.*

# Can God forget you?

"Don't call me Naomi," she told them. "Call me Mara, because the Almighty has made my life very bitter ... The LORD has afflicted me; the Almighty has brought misfortune upon me."

RUTH 1:20-21

When Naomi had lost her husband and her two sons in the heathen country of Moab, she and her daughter-in-law, Ruth, returned to Bethlehem. Naomi was bitter and sorrowful. She was of the opinion that all her suffering was the fault of the Lord, that she was suffering because the Lord had forgotten her. Nevertheless, she clung to the Lord in her suffering and she again experienced the joy in her life that comes from the Lord.

Sometimes you suffer so much that you, like Naomi, think that the Lord has forgotten you. How else could He allow so much adversity in your life? But the Lord can never forget His children. "Can a mother forget the baby at her breast? Though she may forget, I will not forget you!" the Lord promises His people in Isaiah 49:15.

The Lord gave Ruth a new husband. When Ruth and Boaz had a son, life once again became worthwhile for Naomi and she acknowledged that the glory for all this belonged to the Lord.

God can give a new future to people who seem to have arrived at a dead end .

He can turn your current negative circumstances around so that they will work out positively for you in the end. But forget you? Never!

*Heavenly Father, thank You for the assurance that You will never forget me, but that You will always save me if I trust You. Amen.*

# When your strength fails you

Remove your scourge from me; I am overcome by the blow of your hand.

PSALM 39:10

In Old Testament times people attributed everything that happened to them to God, including the negative things. The poet of Psalm 39 did likewise, but nevertheless he did not stop waiting for God. Today we, who live after the crucifixion, know that God does allow negative things in our lives, but that they are not necessarily His will. He does not bring them upon us.

He tests our faith by means of these things. The problems in our lives are, as it were, God's "examination" for us, determining how our faith is doing when life becomes difficult.

What do you do with the crises in your life? Do you blame God as David, Job and Jeremiah did at times, or have you learned to cling to God in the midst of your crisis?

"My hope is in You ... For I dwell with You as an alien" the poet confesses (Ps. 39:7, 12). This confession is still valid today for each of God's children.

When your own strength fails you, God's power to work miracles is still available to you. Take note of Isaiah 40:31 in your Bible when your own burden becomes so heavy that your strength fails you, "Those who hope in the Lord will renew their strength. They will soar on wings like eagles; they will run and not grow weary, they will walk and not be faint."

*Heavenly Father, thank You that Your power is always available to me when my own strength fails me. Please give it to me even today. Amen.*

# "Why" questions

If only I knew where to find him; if only I could go to his dwelling! I would state my case before him and fill my mouth with arguments. I would find out what he would answer me, and consider what he would say.

JOB 23:3-5

Joni Eareckson Tada, a popular American author, was paralyzed in a diving accident when she was a teenager. She started bombarding God with questions soon after this accident. "Why me, Lord?" she wanted to know from Him. "I am still so young, my whole life is stretched out before me." However, she received no answers.

Like Joni, Job also asked God "why" questions. He was of the opinion that he was guiltless and could not understand why God had punished him so severely. His three friends were shocked because he dared question God. However, God was not shocked. Moreover, He did not condemn His child, Job, for his bitterness and confusion.

What He did do was take him for a walk. "Look Job," He said to him, "look closely at all the things I have made." The more Job looked at the wonders of nature, the smaller he felt himself. Then at last he had to admit that God is elevated above questions, that God owed him nothing.

Joni professed that she eventually did receive an answer from God to all her "why" questions. This answer is recorded in Romans 8:38-39: "Nothing can ever separate us from God's love." That is answer enough to all of the "why" questions with which you are struggling today.

*Heavenly Father, thank You for the knowledge that I can leave all my questions with You today because I know that nothing can ever separate me from Your love. Amen.*

# In emergencies

The needy will rejoice in the Holy One of Israel.

ISAIAH 29:19

In Isaiah 29 God proclaims a judgment on Jerusalem because they lived so far removed from Him. Nevertheless, this judgment was again balanced with a message of redemption: the suffering people will again rejoice in the Lord.

The newspapers of August 26 1998 featured lengthy reports on the bomb that had exploded in a restaurant at the Waterfront in Cape Town the previous day. Several people died in this explosion and a family from England – father, mother, two children and grandparents – were all seriously injured. The six-year-old girl lost a foot.

When I paged through that paper I couldn't help wondering why the Lord allowed such things to happen. He is powerful enough to stop bad things.

Perhaps things had gone too well for us in the past, so that we acted as if we didn't need the Lord any more ... I also wondered whether we as a nation would ever rejoice in the Lord in crises, like Israel did. I received my answer in Isaiah 30:18 where the prophet Isaiah declares that the Lord longs to be gracious to us.

The Lord will also be gracious to you if you call on Him for help. He wants to be your strength every day, your rescuer in emergencies.

*Heavenly Father, thank You that I can place my hope in You in the midst of unrest and violence, in the steadfast knowledge that You will always be there for me when I call on You for help. Amen.*

# Stumbling-blocks and thorns

To keep me from becoming conceited because of these surpassingly great revelations, there was given me a thorn in my flesh, a messenger of Satan, to torment me.

2 CORINTHIANS 12:7

Paul struggled with a stumbling-block, a thorn in his flesh he really wanted to get rid of. He often prayed to God to remove this thorn, but God had a better plan: He did not remove the thorn. He did, however, tell Paul that His grace was sufficient for him, and that His power was made perfect in weakness.

No person is without a specific, personal thorn in his life. Perhaps your thorn is an illness, a sin of which you cannot rid yourself, an issue that keeps on hampering you and prevents you from becoming the person God wants you to be. Perhaps, like Paul, you have also prayed to the Lord many times to remove your thorn.

If He has not yet done so, listen closely to His message to Paul. Although the Lord has not yet removed your thorn, He wants to equip you, like Paul, to endure the thorn.

He wants to show you how you can be a better, more obedient child with the thorn rather than without it, precisely because it not only keeps you humble, but also teaches you to depend on His strength completely.

*Heavenly Father, I am also not at peace with my personal thorn, and I have often wondered why You do not want to remove it from my life. Now I know that You strengthen me through suffering. Please be glorified through me. Amen.*

# The advantage of thorns

That is why, for Christ's sake, I delight in weaknesses, in insults, in hardships, in persecutions, in difficulties. For when I am weak, then I am strong.

2 CORINTHIANS 12:10

The same thorn with which Paul had wrestled so much ultimately became a positive power in his life. It taught him that his own strength was not sufficient for the thorns and stumbling-blocks in his life, but God's was.

Without the stumbling-blocks and thorns in your life you risk the danger thinking that you can help yourself, that you do not really need God. By allowing thorns in your life, God shows you that you cannot manage without Him, that you need Him every day of your life. He makes His power available to you when you are willing to admit your dependence on Him.

In the end Paul was thankful for his thorn: "I quit focusing on the handicap and began appreciating the gift. It was a case of Christ's strength moving in on my weakness" (*The Message*, p. 457).

Why don't you take a page from Paul's book today? Look at the stumbling-blocks in your life from a different angle. The Lord has a purpose for every one of them. He wants to use them to teach you to trust Him more. Like Paul you might discover that your weakness has taught you to depend wholly on God.

*Heavenly Father, today I want to thank You for the thorns in my life, because they teach me to live in total dependence on You. Amen.*

# You may complain

"Look, O LORD, and consider, for I am despised."

LAMENTATIONS 1:11

The Book of Lamentations consists of five songs composed by the prophet Jeremiah while the people of Israel were exiled in Babylon and were suffering hardship. In this book Jeremiah expresses his confusion and hurt about the difficulties his people faced. He pleads with the Lord to see the suffering of the people and to deliver them from it.

It always helps children of the Lord to speak about things that bother them. In crisis situations you, like Jeremiah, can also ask, "Help me, Lord." The children of the Lord are not spared suffering: each one of us gets his fair share.

Believers handle this suffering in a totally different way from unbelievers. They have an unbreakable bond with God because He chose them to be His children and because He saved them from the power of sin.

They know that crises cannot tear them away from God. On the contrary, sometimes crises bring about a deeper and more intimate relationship with God. Sometimes the Lord uses hurt and suffering in your own life to draw you nearer to Him.

This fact can help you to experience your own crises differently. Although you know that the suffering in your life is not going to be erased, you also know that you have a God who will assist you in crisis situations. This knowledge will make it easier to bear your own personal suffering.

*Heavenly Father, thank You that I can know for certain that Your arms will be around me in every crisis. Help me never to panic, but to bring my problems to You. Amen.*

# Take off the mask

I am the man who has seen affliction by the rod of his wrath. He ... made me walk in darkness rather than light.

LAMENTATIONS 3:1-2

Jeremiah was a prophet who did not hide his sorrow in adverse circumstances. He lamented about every one of his afflictions before the Lord.

In the end Jeremiah discovered that he could keep on trusting the Lord, no matter how dark his circumstances were. "Because of the LORD's great love we are not consumed, for His compassions never fail. They are new every morning; great is Your faithfulness," he declares in verses 22-23.

What do you say when people want to know how you are? "Fine, thank you," although things are perhaps not going so well for you? Christians do not have to wear a mask. We may admit that at times things are not as good as they could be. Faith does not mean that you must always say that things are fine. On the contrary, an open, honest relationship with God means that you may speak about your crises. Only then will you be healed, as a doctor must first lance a boil before it can heal.

In conclusion, you, like Jeremiah, can know that crises and hardship never have the last word in a Christian's life. The love of the God in whom you believe is unchangeable. His compassion for you is new every morning.

Therefore, in the midst of your problems, you can keep on hoping in God today. He will deliver you once more.

Heavenly Father, thank You that I can keep on hoping and that I can cling to Your promises, even though it feels as if I, like Jeremiah, am also walking on a dark road. Amen.

# A lifeline for you

Yet this I call to mind and therefore I have hope: Because of the LORD's great love we are not consumed, for his compassions never fail. They are new every morning; great is your faithfulness.

LAMENTATIONS 3:21-23

When the prophet Jeremiah wrote the Book of Lamentations things were going very badly for him. He was despondent because it felt as if the Lord had refused to answer his prayers, "Even when I call out or cry for help, He shuts out my prayer (Lam. 3:8).

Just a little further on he complains: "My splendor is gone and all that I had hoped from the LORD" (Lam. 3:18).

Nevertheless, this suffering did not estrange Jeremiah from God. In the midst of his suffering his hope in God still burned like a bright flame, and he depended on the mercy of God.

Joni Eareckson Tada calls this chapter in Lamentations her "lifeline verses." When she was totally discouraged, these verses helped her to keep a strong heart, to cling to God and keep hoping in Him.

Perhaps you too feel that your hope in the Lord is gone. Prolonged suffering sometimes makes us doubt God's love for us. When a crisis crops up in your life again, you should underline the beautiful promise in Lamentations 3:31-32, "For men are not cast off by the LORD forever. Though He brings grief, He will show compassion, so great is His unfailing love."

*Heavenly Father, today I want to praise You in the midst of my suffering because Your love for me is so great and unchanging. Thank You for the promise that You will show compassion. Amen.*

# Don't lose heart

Therefore we do not lose heart. Though outwardly we are wasting away, yet inwardly we are being renewed day by day.

2 CORINTHIANS 4:16

Paul suffered much. He was persecuted and imprisoned, beaten and tortured. Nevertheless, he never really lost heart.

He learned to look away from his physical circumstances and to keep his eyes fixed upon Jesus. So we fix our eyes not on what is seen, but on what is unseen, he wrote to the church in Corinth (2 Cor. 4:18).

Don't allow the many problems in your life to discourage you. There is always a purpose in the crises that come your way. Often the Lord is testing your faith with them. He wants to see whether you keep on trusting Him in spite of these things.

Problems have several advantages:

❋ They help us to remember that Jesus suffered on our behalf.
❁ They prevent us from becoming proud and help us to stay totally dependent on God.
❀ They ensure that we look further than only this short life.
❁ They are proof to other people of our perseverance in faith.
❁ They make it possible for God to reveal His great power in and through us.

Try to see problems as opportunities rather than becoming rebellious about them.

*Heavenly Father, please make it possible for me to use my problems to demonstrate to other people my perseverance in clinging to You and trusting You. Amen.*

# Job as demonstration model

"Does Job fear God for nothing?" Satan replied. "Have you not put a hedge around him and his household and everything he has? ... But stretch out your hand and strike everything he has, and he will surely curse you to your face."

JOB 1:9-11

Satan very quickly saw that Job was a model believer. He told God that it was because everything was going well for him.

Then God used Job as a model for demonstration: He first took away all his possessions, then his children and then his health. Job could not understand why these disasters came his way, because he knew that he had not sinned against God.

God wants to treat us with the story of Job: He gives us a peek behind the curtain. Job's testimony had much more value when things turned against him than in the days when everything was still well with him. God tested Job to see whether he would pass the examination of faith and prove the devil wrong.

It is interesting that it is difficult to date the Book of Job historically, and similarly the locality of the city where Job lived is unknown.

Perhaps the reason for this is so that each of us can write our own name in here. By means of the suffering in your life God is testing and demonstrating your faith.

Through this suffering He wants to make you a better witness for Him than in the times when everything is going your way.

*Heavenly Father, please forgive me for being a bad demonstration model for You most of the time. Help me to be a good witness for You, especially through times of suffering. Amen.*

# Is suffering punishment?

Suppose a man says to God ... teach me what I cannot see; if I have done wrong, I will not do so again. Should God then reward you on your terms, when you refuse to repent?"

JOB 34:31-33

Job's friends believed that his suffering was really caused by his sin and that it would disappear as soon as he repented.

However, Job refused to accept this because he knew that his punishment was unjustifiable. It is ironic that Job was far from being as guiltless as he imagined, because before God everyone is sinful and deserves His punishment.

In the Old Testament people were punished severely for their sins. However, unlike Job, we live on this side of the cross and we know that our suffering in this world has little connection to our sin. Jesus bore the punishment for your sins and mine on the cross once and for all. Although God does discipline His children from time to time to show them that they are on the wrong path, He no longer punishes us because we are sinners.

In his own eyes Job was a "righteous" man, but God nevertheless punished him, not so much because he was sinful, but because He wanted to demonstrate His omnipotence to and through Job. In the last chapter Job eventually got the message and he immediately stopped proclaiming that he was guiltless.

Fortunately God does not punish you because of your sins, but He does teach you through them. When problems come your way again, ask yourself what God wants to teach you through them.

*Lord Jesus, thank You very much that You bore God's punishment for my sins on the cross, so that I will never again be punished for my sins. Amen.*

# Suffering is a magnifying glass

My ears had heard of you but now my eyes have seen you. Therefore I despise myself and repent in dust and ashes.

JOB 42:5-6

Instead of answering all Job's many "why" questions, God gave him a practical, visible demonstration of His omnipotence.

He showed him the world He had created. Job was speechless before the Creator of light and darkness; the Maker of snow, hail and ice; the God who created the lion, the hippopotamus and the crocodile.

When Job discovered God's absolute power, he discovered also that God owed him nothing. Ultimately his suffering was the magnifying glass that showed Job what God is like. When Job acknowledged God's omnipotence in chapter 42, he testified of his own free will: "My ears had heard of You but now my eyes have seen You. Therefore I despise myself and repent in dust and ashes" (Job 42:5-6).

Often the same is true of you. When everything is going well, there are so many things occupying your attention that there is very little time left for God. When you suffer, however, it is only you and God.

God wants you to see Him in a new way in the pain He allows in your life so that eventually you will know, love and serve Him in a new way. Thus your suffering becomes the magnifying glass through which you can see God.

*Heavenly Father, forgive me for sparing You so little time when everything is going my way. Thank You for hurt and suffering that show me again how wonderful You are. Amen.*

# God is glorified by your suffering

"Neither this man nor his parents sinned," said Jesus, "but this happened so that the work of God might be displayed in his life."

JOHN 9:3

Jesus and His disciples saw a man who had been born blind. The disciples in accordance with the opinion of that time wanted to know from Jesus whether this blindness was the result of the man's own sin or that of his parents. Neither, Jesus answered them. The man was blind so that the glory of God might be displayed in his life.

When Jesus then put clay on the eyes of the man born blind and told him to wash himself in the Pool of Siloam, he was able to see. Then all the people who knew him realized that Jesus had done a miracle.

Sometimes negative things happen in the lives of the children of God so that He can reveal Himself more clearly through their lives. Have you ever thought that perhaps your suffering was because God wants to demonstrate His omnipotence in your life so that people may glorify Him?

What do you do in times of suffering? Through them you may discover that you are totally dependent on God. Through your hurt you can know for certain that God is walking with you; indeed, your pain will eventually serve to glorify Him.

*Heavenly Father, this is a new insight: that You use pain in my life so that You can be glorified through it. Help me to handle my suffering in such a way that Your works may be seen in my life. Amen.*

# When you do not understand

Surely in vain have I kept my heart pure; in vain have I washed my hands in innocence. All day long I have been plagued; I have been punished every morning.

PSALM 73:13-14

"Lord, I do not understand," is the cry of the psalmist. "Why are the unbelievers prospering, but I, who have always done my utmost for You, am suffering? Each new day brings new problems, every new morning new punishment."

Perhaps you too have had the same thought as the poet of Psalm 73: Everything is so difficult for you while unbelievers around you prosper.

However, the Lord's reckoning differs from ours. We can never understand Him by our human logic. It is wonderful that Psalm 73 does not end with verse 14. When the psalmist meets God face to face in verse 17, he sees everything differently. The final destiny of the "prosperous" wicked will be terrible, whereas God fills the life of the psalmist with wonderful meaning.

If there are things in your life that you cannot understand, perhaps it is time to come into God's presence and realize that nothing is more important than Him.

In the end it doesn't matter *what* is in God's hand for you, but *that* you are in His hand. In reality God owes you absolutely nothing. Everything that you receive from His hand is pure grace. Remember to thank Him for it.

*Lord, please forgive me for trying to understand You with my puny human brain. Thank You for the insight that everything that I have is a gift of grace from Your hand. Amen.*

# Suffering as a plus

Surely it was for my benefit that I suffered such anguish. In your love you kept me from the pit of destruction ... But what can I say? He has spoken to me.

ISAIAH 38:17, 15

Hezekiah's illness taught him a few valuable lessons. Eventually he saw his suffering as an advantage. Not only did it bring him closer to God, but it also made him conscious of God's love for him once again.

In his illness he heard God speaking to him. He experienced the joy of forgiveness of sin, which can happen only when you have been on your knees before God. Then he discovered that it was his destiny as man to praise God and profess His grace.

Although nobody enjoys suffering, it does make us conscious of our human frailty. It makes us realize again how dependent we are on God, and through our suffering we discover once again just how close to God we ought to live.

After my husband had a heart attack, he realized that the Lord had given him another chance. His priorities and outlook on life changed drastically. Other things are important to him now. He has discovered again what a wonderful gift health is and how good it is to be alive.

When you are ill, remember that inner healing is often more important than physical healing. Suffering and illness can also guide you to the awareness that you can praise God more than before and can profess His grace with greater certainty.

*Heavenly Father, thank You that illness and suffering are plusses for me, because they teach me to love You more and bring me closer to You. Amen.*

# Trial by fire

Dear friends, do not be surprised at the painful trial you are suffering, as though something strange were happening to you. But rejoice that you participate in the sufferings of Christ, so that you may be overjoyed when his glory is revealed.

1 PETER 4:12-13

Believers must learn not to be surprised by suffering, Peter writes. We must rather expect it and even welcome it, because it is the proof that we will partake in the glory of Jesus when He comes again.

Your own trial by fire should not be something strange to you. We are often overcome by suffering, and we can adapt to it more easily when we expect it and realize that we are not the only ones who are staggering under it. Every person experiences suffering. We feel the vibration of the anger of God for sin when we suffer, but in the end it changes into a symphony of joy because God is so merciful to us.

You too may expect to suffer, because you are living in a broken world. Your suffering is not the will of God. It is the result of the Fall, but God can control that suffering so that it ultimately works for your good (see Rom. 8:28).

Sometimes your pain reveals something about your relationship with God. Perhaps you need an intensification of your faith, brought about by pain.

Sometimes it is good for you when God makes you face reality again. It causes you to get perspective on yourself, on your neighbor and on God again.

*Heavenly Father, make it possible for me to thank You for pain and suffering, because I can partake in Your glory through it. Amen.*

# When God feels remote

But when you hid your face, I was dismayed. To you, O LORD, I called; to the LORD I cried for mercy.

PSALM 30:7-8

Here the poet looks back upon his life. In this psalm we see very clearly that nothing makes one as conceited as prosperity, but also that nothing makes one as humble as dependency. When I felt secure, I said, "I will never be shaken," the psalmist writes in verse 6. However, when some problems cropped up in his life it was a totally different matter, "But when You hid Your face, I was dismayed" (Ps. 30:7).

When we are in a tight corner, we often call upon the Lord, only to discover that He feels far removed and strange. Whenever this happens to you, ask yourself whether it is God who withdrew Himself from you or whether it is you who wandered away from Him.

God promised that He would never forsake you. He sent His Holy Spirit to live in you. When the shadows fall upon your life, it is often because you are standing with your back to the Sun, writes Johan Smit.

When next you are in a tight corner you should turn around so that you can see God. He will bring light into your life again so that you will be able to praise Him as the psalmist did.

*Heavenly Father, I now see that it is I who wandered away from You when You felt far removed from me. Thank You that You can never be far from me because You are living in me. Amen.*

# God changes mourning into a feast

You turned my wailing into dancing; you removed my sackcloth and clothed me with joy.

PSALM 30:11

God's children have the assurance that He will eventually change their mourning into a celebration, that He will exchange their sackcloth for festive clothes.

The Dutch theologian van Ruler writes that man must dance and sing and enjoy God's favor. However, he must also be careful never to forget the Lord: "He must not keep on dancing by and for himself; there is something foolish in that. And ultimately also something arrogant. In the end man starts to think that he is his own creator and also the creator of his life. That is ultimate foolishness."

God understands your grief and loss of joy in life. He wants you to learn to dance and celebrate again, but He also wants you never to lose sight of Him. Therefore He wants to clothe you with joy. "We must not mourn away our precious time for living," Johan Smit said in one of his Bible study classes. "Life must be a celebration for us. In the portal of heaven one must sing and dance!"

Are you despondent at the moment? God wants you to exchange your sackcloth for festive clothes right now. He wants to clothe you Himself. He can deliver you from the unnecessary fear and sadness that are the bane of your life. Remember to praise Him for His goodness to you.

*Heavenly Father, thank You that You always give me the opportunity to dance for joy in the midst of grief because I know that I belong to You. Amen.*

# God wants to use you

[God] comforts us in all our troubles, so that we can comfort those in any trouble with the comfort we ourselves have received from God.

2 Corinthians 1:4

Paul had a wonderfully comforting message for the Christians in Corinth. In this passage he writes that when problems occur in your life, God will comfort you. But even more, God uses these adversities to equip you for comforting others as God has comforted you in your crisis.

Suffering in your own life becomes the way in which God is able to use you so that you can reach out appropriately to others who are also suffering.

One of my friends, who lost her daughter in a car accident, wrote a book about her experience. It meant a lot to many other people who had also lost a child, "Then I realized that as a spiritual being it is easy to accept these things, but I am also a physical being who lives in this world. God does not keep me from anything just because I am His child. On the contrary, if He wants to use me because of this experience, I have to experience it deeply and realistically. How else will I be able to identify with others' pain?".

The next time something happens in your life that makes you reach out for God's comfort, remember that God wants to use you as a result of this experience. Pass this comfort on to somebody else who may need it.

Heavenly Father, Thank You for Your comfort and encouragement that are always available when I am in anguish. Help me to comfort others as You comfort me. Amen.

# In crisis situations

> David was greatly distressed because the men were talking of stoning him; each one was bitter in spirit because of his sons and daughters. But David found strength in the LORD his God.
>
> 1 SAMUEL 30:6

A crisis situation developed when David and his men reached Ziklag and saw that the Amalekites had totally destroyed the city in a raid. All the women and children had been carried away and the city was razed by fire. David's men had lost everything. Now they were angry at David and they wanted to stone him. In reality they were acting totally illogically. It was not David's fault. He had also lost both his wives in the raid.

In contrast to his men David kept his composure and sought help from God, "But David found strength in the Lord his God." God helped immediately and David and his men succeeded in slaying the enemy and getting back their families and possessions.

When serious problems in your life make you lose your composure, remember what David did, and calm down and focus on God. Ask help and advice from Him. Although you often cannot handle your crises yourself, the Holy Spirit is there to help you with them.

God's purpose with suffering is always to draw you nearer to Him. Thus, confess the things that are still standing between God and you. Finally, look at your own situation through God's eyes. He is completely able to help you and assist you as He did David.

*Heavenly Father, forgive me for so often losing my composure in crises. Help me to focus on You and from now on to ask Your help immediately. Amen.*

# God is good!

Good and upright is the LORD; therefore He instructs sinners in his ways. All the ways of the LORD are loving and faithful for those who keep the demands of his covenant.

PSALM 25:8, 10

The Lord is loving and faithful to those people who obey Him, writes the psalmist. In your own life you will experience the Lord's goodness and love first-hand every day if you are willing to trust Him unconditionally.

Gary Thomas writes that there are three things that help God's children through times of hardship: we know that God is good, that God is in control and that God knows best.

God wants only the best for you because He loves you. During those times when unpleasant things happen to you, remember that these things are also part of His plan for your life. Hardship is also good for you.

Nowhere do we read that it is pleasant or comfortable, but God uses this hardship as a sculptor uses his chisel, to make you more and more like His Son.

Even in the midst of problems you can experience God's goodness. Amy Carmichael, a missionary among Indian children, declared that she trusted in God and in God's character. She believed firstly that God is a loving Father and she always trusted Him as a small child trusts her father.

From now on be willing to relate whatever happens to you to the goodness of God.

*Heavenly Father, I want to experience Your goodness every day in my life, including in my times of hardship. Thank You that I need never doubt it. Amen.*

# God is in control

And we know that in all things God works for the good of those who love him, who have been called according to his purpose.

ROMANS 8:28

In all things God works for your good. That doesn't mean that He keeps all adversity (measured according to our standards) from you, but that He uses everything, even the foolish things that you do and your sins, for your good. This knowledge means that no bad thing happening to you can ever unbalance you permanently. You know that it fits in with God's good plan for your life.

God can use even negative things positively in your life. He causes everything to work according to His plan. "God ... is the blessed controller of all things" reads the Phillips translation of 1 Timothy 6:15.

He is totally in control, even of those things that are out of your control and of which you can change nothing at the moment. With Him there are no accidents or mistakes: what He does, is always good and right and in accordance with His plan for your life.

Therefore, you can trust Him with your smallest doubt and with your biggest problem, even though you cannot understand Him. He uses everything in your life, good or bad, to achieve His purpose for you. However, there is a condition: God wants you to love Him more than anything else.

*Heavenly Father, thank You for being in control of my life and for using everything – including the negative things – to fulfill Your perfect will in my life. Help me to love You above all. Amen.*

# God knows best

"For my thoughts are not your thoughts, neither are your ways my ways," declares the LORD. "As the heavens are higher than the earth, so are my ways higher than your ways and my thoughts than your thoughts."

ISAIAH 55:8-9

God cannot be compared to human beings. His thoughts and actions differ widely from ours. That is why we struggle to understand God. If we could understand God, He would not be God. He is eternal and omnipotent. What He does is good and right. He can do anything, except make mistakes!

Job's friend Zophar had already discovered this secret when Job was still struggling to understand God's ways. "Can you fathom the mysteries of God?" he asked Job. "Can you probe the limits of the Almighty? They are higher than the heavens – what can you do?" (Job 11:7-8).

Sometimes it seems to us as if God does the wrong thing, so that we want to say, "Not like this, Lord!" Sometimes the Lord works too slowly for us and we want to help Him along as Abraham's wife, Sarah did. However, the Lord always knows best.

When there are times in your life when you cannot understand God, do not even try. Rather try to see things from God's perspective. Then you will discover that He always knows best, even when initially you do not agree with Him.

*Heavenly Father, forgive me for trying so hard to understand You. Thank You for the insight that it is impossible, however hard I try. Help me to believe that You always know best. Amen.*

# Cast your anxiety on Him

> Humble yourselves, therefore, under God's mighty hand ... Cast all
> your anxiety on him because he cares for you.
>
> 1 Peter 5:6-7

*The Message* translates this verse as follows, "So be content with who you are, and don't put on airs. God's strong hand is on you; He'll promote you at the right time. Live carefree before God, He is most careful with you," (p. 583). "You can throw the whole weight of your anxieties upon Him, for you are his personal concern," reads the Phillips translation. God cares for you personally. You may safely cast each one of your problems on Him – He will take care of them for you.

Never let circumstances control you; rather surrender yourself to God; He indeed has full control of your circumstances. To surrender to God means that you are willing to trust Him totally, to yield your whole life, will, plans and being to His will.

It also means that you will once and for all give up the tendency to want to help Him, and be willing to wait on Him patiently. In His own time and in His own way He will solve your problems.

When you try to bear your daily worries yourself it means only one thing: that you do not yet trust the Lord completely. Make a list of all the things that cause you to lie awake at night and tell the Lord about every one of them. He will look after you.

*Heavenly Father, I now bring each one of my many worries to You. Please take care of them and care for me. Amen.*

# Trust God

He will be the sure foundation for your times, a rich store of salvation and wisdom and knowledge; the fear of the LORD is the key to this treasure.

ISAIAH 33:6

Today's Scripture verse is a testimony of God's people who trust Him totally and who find their treasure in serving Him.

All through the Bible it is stressed that we can trust God unconditionally, that He is worthy of our trust at all times.

One reason why we can trust God unconditionally is that nobody who has trusted Him has ever been disappointed.

"Commit your way to the LORD; trust in Him and He will do this" the psalmist writes in Psalm 37:5. "Trust in the LORD with all your heart and lean not on your own understanding," is the advice of the writer of Proverbs (Prov. 3:5). "Those who hope in the LORD will renew their strength" writes the prophet Isaiah (Is. 40:31).

You can safely trust the God whom you worship. Trust Him for great things, but also for the ordinary everyday things.

When you trust God in this your whole life will change. If you truly believe that God is in control, you won't be so concerned if your plane is not on time, or if your washing machine broke at an inconvenient moment or even if you lost your job. Switch off and be calm. God is in control. Trust Him when crises occur. If you can do this, you will experience perpetual peace in your life.

*Heavenly Father, teach me to trust You completely for every crisis that may cross my path. Thank You that You are worthy of my trust and will never disappoint me. Amen.*

# Be a disciple

Dietrich Bonhoeffer wrote a book called *The Cost of Discipleship*. When Jesus calls someone, Bonhoeffer writes, He calls that person to die.

To be a disciple of Jesus is going to cost you something. Disciples are people who are willing to sacrifice other things to be able to follow Jesus. Discipleship demands absolute obedience, the willingness to take up your cross and follow Jesus, the willingness to put others first, to relinquish your attachment to material things, and to take up the mission to serve other people. It will require of you to be obedient to God's will, to renew your mind, to love unconditionally and to bear fruit for God.

You will have to be willing to put your hand deep into your pocket, and to set a good example. To be a disciple of Jesus means that you will have to walk in His footsteps.

How to do this is the theme of this month's devotions.

# What does a disciple look like?

To the Jews who had believed him, Jesus said, "If you hold to my teaching, you are really my disciples. Then you will know the truth, and the truth will set you free."

JOHN 8:31-32

A disciple is someone who is a pupil or follower of Jesus: someone who unconditionally believes in what He says, who clings to His teachings and lives according to them. Every disciple is indeed a Christian, but every Christian is not necessarily a disciple.

A Christian is someone who has accepted Jesus as his Redeemer, someone who is on his way to heaven with the key of the cross in his hand, while a disciple is someone who is reporting for service.

To the disciple the cross is more than a key: it is a way of life. This is not to say that disciples are better than other Christians; the issue is not one of value. Rather, it centers on love and the willingness to serve.

A disciple is someone who is willing to affirm his love for the Lord in his life; someone who lives his faith in everything that he says and does. Actually the word "disciple" simply determines your commitment as a Christian.

When Jesus called Peter and John to be His disciples, they immediately left their nets and boats. They were immediately willing to follow Him. Would you do the same thing today? Are you willing to relinquish all other things so that you can follow Jesus with all your heart? Think carefully about which one of the two you are: a Christian or a disciple?

*Lord Jesus, I see now that I am really just a Christian. Make me a disciple who is willing to follow You to the end, to hold to Your teachings and to do Your will. Amen.*

# The characteristics of a disciple

And anyone who does not carry his cross and follow me cannot be my disciple.

LUKE 14:27

The demands of discipleship are so taxing that many people cannot live up to them. "If anyone comes to Me and does not hate his father and mother, his wife and children, his brothers and sisters – yes, even his own life – he cannot be My disciple," Jesus says very clearly in Luke 14:26.

There are three characteristics that every disciple should possess:

※ A disciple is willing to relinquish his own interests.
🦐 A disciple is willing to take up his cross and to follow Jesus.
🐚 A disciple does not mind relinquishing his possessions.

Being a disciple firstly requires that you will be prepared to put your own interests in second place, and surrender your will to God's.

Secondly, discipleship means that you will be willing to take up your cross and follow Jesus – and a cross always indicates humiliation and sacrifice.

Disciples are not materialistic. They are willing to give up all their possessions for the sake of the Lord. If your possessions are more important to you than the Lord, you are not yet His disciple. You invest in God's kingdom by giving things away.

To which things in your life do you still cling? To be a disciple you will need to sacrifice these things and to let the Lord use your life as He wills.

*Lord Jesus, I very much want to be Your disciple. Help me to take up my cross and follow You. Amen.*

# Disciples renew their minds

Do not conform any longer to the pattern of this world, but be transformed by the renewing of your mind.

ROMANS 12:2

Disciples are people who not only live differently, but also think differently. Your thoughts have a tremendously powerful influence on your life. Whether you think positive or negative thoughts makes a profound difference to your way of life. The things you think ultimately also determine the things that you are going to say and do.

Therefore discipleship is much more than an attitude: it means that you must choose to live according to an entirely new way. Start with your thoughts and decide whether you are prepared to risk making the change. Hone your thoughts to maturity as Paul advises the church in Corinth (see 1 Cor. 14:20). Ask the Lord Himself to give you the necessary experience and discernment to accomplish this.

Have you learned to think like a disciple yet? "Finally, brothers, whatever is true, whatever is noble, whatever is right, whatever is pure, whatever is lovely, whatever is admirable – if anything is excellent or praiseworthy – think about such things," Paul writes in Philippians 4:8.

Do you still sometimes struggle with improper thoughts? Ask God to help you to filter the information that you allow into your mind carefully. Learn to think like a true disciple. Then you will also find it much easier to live like one.

Heavenly Father, I pray that You will teach me not only to live like Your disciple, but also to think as Your disciple. Grant that the things I think will be in accordance with Your will. Amen.

# Disciples obey God's will

> Then you will be able to test and approve what God's will is – his good, pleasing and perfect will.
>
> ROMANS 12:2

When you allow God to renew your mind, you will simultaneously become more sensitive to the will of God. Furthermore, you will have to be willing to obey God's will by making your will subservient to His.

In order to know God's will, it is essential for you to have a good relationship with Him. People who live close to God know what His will for their lives is.

God also reveals His will to you when you are studying His Word. If you are serious about understanding God's will, you must be willing to do intensive Bible study, because in your Bible you will find very clear guidelines concerning the will of God. God also reveals His will to His children when they ask Him in prayer to do so. Pray that the Lord will truly show you what His will is.

Lastly, the Holy Spirit who lives in you also discloses God's will to you. The Spirit intercedes for us in accordance with God's will, as Paul writes to the church in Rome (see Rom. 8:27).

Do you still occasionally have doubts about God's will for your life? If so, commit yourself to become truly willing to do what He asks of you in His Word.

*Heavenly Father, I pray that You will teach me what Your will for my life is. Make me sensitive to the voice of Your Holy Spirit, so that I will truly know what You want me to do. Make me willing to obey Your will. Amen.*

# Disciples are not paid

Heal the sick, raise the dead, cleanse those who have leprosy, drive out demons. Freely you have received, freely give.

MATTHEW 10:8

In this passage Jesus gives a rather odd instruction to His disciples – an instruction that seems very strange to our modern mentality. In essence, Jesus is telling His disciples to go out and help people without expecting or asking for payment. Because they received freely, they should also be willing to give freely.

Everything that we receive from God's hand is pure grace. All the blessings that we receive from the Lord are completely free. And how abundantly He blesses us! We don't work for it and we cannot earn it. But there is one thing that we can do: we can generously share the love, time and possessions that we have received from God with other people.

You can do so by joining a Bible study group, by sharing particular truths from the Scriptures that have meant a lot to you with your friends, by making time for other people – but primarily by sharing your material assets with those who have less than you.

This is one of the most obvious ways in which other people will see that you are a disciple. "If anyone has material possessions and sees his brother in need but has no pity on him, how can the love of God be in him?" asks John (1 Jn. 3:17).

Allow the Holy Spirit to use your services to encourage and comfort other Christians, and to use your possessions to help people who really need them.

Heavenly Father, please teach me today that everything I have comes from You, and make me willing to share freely what I have freely received from You. Amen.

# Disciples do not stand still

So come on, let's leave the preschool fingerpainting exercises on Christ and get on with the grand work of art. Grow up in Christ. The basic foundational truths are in place ... But there's so much more. Let's get on with it!

HEBREWS 6:1, THE MESSAGE, P. 547

The writer of Hebrews is making an urgent appeal to Christians not to keep relying on baby's milk for sustenance, but to move on to solid food, so that they can grow spiritually. Here the milk refers to the basic foundational truths of the gospel, while the solid food refers to the Bible's call to live life according to God's will.

When you are pedaling on a bicycle, it is impossible to stand still or to go backwards. There is only one way to go when you are on a bicycle, and that is forward. In the same way disciples always have to move forward by growing spiritually. They should never stagnate by fixating only on the basic foundational truths of the gospel.

A disciple is someone who doesn't stay in the same place, someone who is constantly on the move. He grows in faith and does not get bogged down in the basic things that he learned about Christ when he was first born again.

He is willing to prove his love for God in practice. As John writes, "Dear children, let us not love with words or tongue but with actions and in truth" (1 Jn. 3:18).

Is this true of you?

Lord, I am sorry that I still try to sustain myself with baby's milk. Help me to grow spiritually and to be willing to prove my love for You in the things I do. Amen.

# Disciples remain in Jesus

Remain in me, and I will remain in you ... If you remain in me and my words remain in you, ask whatever you wish, and it will be given you.

JOHN 15:4, 7

In the Old Testament the Israelites were often compared to a vine if they lived close to God. Jesus is the true vine. Only when His children live so close to Him that they form part of Him as the branch is part of the vine, will they truly be able to bear fruit for Him.

To live in Jesus means, among other things, to believe in Him; to profess that He is the Son of God; to know Him as Redeemer and Lord; to be obedient to God's commands; to persevere in faith and to share in the fellowship of the faithful.

Disciples are people who live close to Jesus, people who are inextricably bound to Jesus in their faith, people who remain in Jesus. Only by living this close to Him will you be able to bear fruit for Him. When a disciple bears fruit he fulfills his divine task. Prayer, joy and love are all fruit.

And when you, as a disciple, remain in Jesus, a wonderful thing happens: Jesus also remains in you through His Holy Spirit.

You are assured of His guidance every day of your life. No one can ever separate you from His presence. For this reason He will also give you everything that you ask of Him, as long as it is in accordance with His will.

Lord Jesus, I want to remain in You as the branch remains in the vine. Help me to bear fruit for You every day. Amen.

# Disciples bear fruit

This is to my Father's glory, that you bear much fruit, showing yourselves to be my disciples.

JOHN 15:8

Yesterday we discovered that if we remain in Jesus as the branch remains in the vine, we will bear fruit for Him. And it is to His Father's glory, as Jesus Himself says, if we bear much fruit and show ourselves to be His disciples. God equips people to be His disciples and to bear fruit for Him. If you love God and bear fruit for Him, other people will be able to see by these two things that you are truly His disciple.

Bearing fruit finds its expression in a life of sacrificial love. If you are truly serious about your discipleship, you will strive to live in such an atmosphere of love.

In John 15:12 Jesus says: "My command is this: Love each other as I have loved you." And this is by no means an easy task, because the love that Jesus has for us is an unconditional, sacrificial love; a love that does not ask what it can gain, but rather what it can give. Such a love is impossible for human beings, but God Himself comes and places His love in our hearts.

Love is the very first part of the fruit that Paul describes in Galatians 5:22-23, but there are also other characteristics that need to be evident in your life, "But the fruit of the Spirit is love, joy, peace, patience, kindness, goodness, faithfulness, gentleness and self-control."

Prayerfully consider those qualities that are still lacking in your life.

*Lord Jesus, I want to bear fruit for You. Help me to love other people in the same way that You love me. Amen.*

# Disciples are people who love

"A new command I give you: Love one another. As I have loved you, so you must love one another. By this all men will know that you are my disciples, if you love one another."

JOHN 13:34-35

Of all the characteristics of a disciple, love is the most important. Sincerely loving God and our neighbor is the distinctive mark by which other people can see that we are truly disciples. Just as the pupils of a particular school can be recognized by their school uniforms, disciples can be recognized by the love that emanates from them.

Jesus was the living example of God's love, and disciples should in turn be a living example of His love. This love demands everything of us, but this love also gives everything to us, as Jesus proved.

A disciple is someone who obeys God's command that His children should love Him with heart and soul and with all their strength. A disciple is someone who has discovered that love is willing to make sacrifices and hold nothing back; someone in whose life there is no longer a battle between obedience and love. To love is to be obedient.

John knew this secret, "Dear friends, let us love one another, for love comes from God. Everyone who loves has been born of God and knows God" (1 Jn. 4:7).

The world around you is hungry for the love of Jesus. Are you willing to be a channel for His love to others, so that people will be able to see that you are truly a disciple by the way you love?

*Lord Jesus, I pray that You will put Your love in my heart, so that other people will be able to see that I am Your disciple by the love that radiates from me. Amen.*

# Disciples estimate the cost

"Suppose one of you wants to build a tower. Will he not first sit down and estimate the cost to see if he has enough money to complete it?"

LUKE 14:28

It is simply foolish to buy thousands of dollars worth of clothes on credit at the start of a new season if you know very well that you will not be able to pay your account. Before you buy something, you should first make sure whether you can afford it. The same applies to being a disciple.

The requirements of discipleship that Jesus points out in this passage are demanding. To be a disciple means that you will have to be willing to relinquish all other things. Discipleship demands devotion. It is essential for you to estimate the cost before you decide to follow Jesus.

You must know precisely what you are letting yourself in for, so that you won't later succumb to the temptation of turning back when the demands start becoming too burdensome. Your discipleship is probably going to cost you dearly. If you truly want to be a disciple, you will have to follow Jesus with complete commitment.

Being a disciple by no means implies that your life is going to be problem-free from now on. Being a follower of Jesus may require you to be willing to suffer for Him – even to die for Him. If this sounds too burdensome to you, perhaps now would be a good time to sit down and decide whether you are really willing to be His disciple.

*Lord Jesus, sometimes I become afraid because of the burdensome demands that discipleship places upon me. Help me to be willing to continue on my path, even after I have estimated the cost. Amen.*

# Disciples follow Jesus

Then Jesus said to his disciples, "If anyone would come after me, he must deny himself and take up his cross and follow me."

MATTHEW 16:24

Disciples are cross-bearers. There is an entire list of requirements that people who wish to follow Jesus have to meet.

The Jews understood Jesus' comparison of "taking up one's cross" very well, because people who were condemned to death often had to carry their own cross to the place of their execution – as Jesus Himself also did. To follow Jesus in this way demands the complete surrender, devotion and commitment of His disciples.

Furthermore, disciples are people who are willing to deny themselves. This means that you need to be willing to relinquish your sense of your own importance and to follow Jesus unconditionally, every day of your life. It also means that you will follow His example by becoming more and more like Him.

A disciple is someone who has discovered that God demands everything of him, but also that God is willing to sacrifice everything for his sake, even the life of His Son. All the relationships in which a disciple is involved are determined by his relationship with God: his relationships with his marriage partner, children, family, himself and his possession are all subservient to his relationship with the Lord.

Are you willing to devote your entire life to the Lord, to earnestly try to live up to God's expectations of you, to make God the number one priority in your life, and to be obedient to His Word?

*Lord Jesus, You know that I am not yet willing to follow You in this way. Help me so that I will be able to devote my entire life to You. Amen.*

# Disciples choose the right friends

Perfume and incense bring joy to the heart, and the pleasantness of one's friend springs from his earnest counsel. As iron shapes iron, so one man sharpens another.

PROVERBS 27:9, 17

Your friends can make or break you. This is especially true in the case of young people: the wrong friends can cause even the best children to go off the rails, while the right kind of friends can keep them on track.

Disciples need the right kind of friends: Christian friends who have also made a choice for God, friends who are also willing to follow Jesus with complete commitment and to obey the commands of the Bible.

Therefore, choose the right friends for yourself. Keep away from those friends whose do things that go against what you believe. However, be willing to cherish your friendships with other Christians. Make time for your friends; time to pray together, to study the Bible together, to share your faith with one another.

What does your circle of friends look like? Do they help you or hinder you in your service to the Lord? And do you help to strengthen their faith?

Disciples also know the best Friend of them all. They know that Jesus is always there to support and help them, and that He will never abandon them, but will always protect and enfold them with His love. Jesus Himself said: "You are my friends if you do what I command" (Jn. 15:14).

*Lord Jesus, help me to choose the right friends, friends who know You. Thank You that I can also be Your friend if I am obedient to Your commands. Amen.*

# Disciples are not lazy

A little sleep, a little slumber, a little folding of the hands to rest – and poverty will come on you like a bandit and scarcity like an armed man.

PROVERBS 24:33-34

In this passage the writer of Proverbs sketches an accurate picture of a foolish man: his life is characterized by slovenliness, laziness, and ultimately poverty and lack. But before you judge this man too quickly, take a minute to consider whether there aren't any similarities to your own life in this description. Are you perhaps also sometimes too lazy to get up early, too lazy to be self-disciplined about your Bible study and prayer?

Laziness leads to poverty on the material as well as the spiritual levels. Lazy people are never wealthy, because success always requires hard work and dedication. The same is true of discipleship.

If you want to grow spiritually, you will have to be willing to be spiritually disciplined. This means that you will have to set aside enough time in your busy schedule for focused Bible study and diligent prayer. It also means that you will have to be faithful in your attendance of church services and prayer meetings.

If these words leave you with a sense of guilt, answer the following questions for yourself:

※ Are you a lazy disciple? How much time do you give to the Lord?
❀ Do you utilize all the opportunities for spiritual growth offered in your congregation, or are you simply too lazy?

*Lord Jesus, I stand before You with a guilty conscience. I confess that I am lazy. Please forgive me and make me diligent in Your service. Amen.*

# Disciples are willing to learn

He wakens me morning by morning, wakens my ear to listen like one being taught. The Sovereign Lord has opened my ears ...

ISAIAH 50:4-5

Disciples are people who are willing to listen and learn in order to make spiritual progress. People are shaped by the experience and insight of their teachers.

No one really likes being taught or criticized; it usually causes us to become angry and defensive. But teachers' legacy of faith is tremendously important to disciples: disciples should be willing to be taught by the Bible, to be guided by their pastors, and to draw inspiration from books written by other people who have lived close to the Lord.

What does your spiritual library look like? Do you regularly buy Christian books for yourself? Do you study the Bible with the help of a concordance, a Study Bible or Bible study course? Make time for reading spiritual reading matter. You can be assured that it will assist you in your spiritual growth.

You also learn by what you hear during the Sunday church service. Take a notebook to church and write down the things that you find striking in the sermon. When you are at home, you can read it again and apply it to your own life. Johan Smit likes to say, "The best sermons are never the ones that confirm your own views." When was the last time that you were admonished by God's Word? And did you accept the admonition?

Learn to listen to God – as well as to those sensible and wise people He sends across your path.

*Heavenly Father, thank You for teaching me to listen to Your Word, to other Christians and to books that help me to grow spiritually. Help me to never stop learning. Amen.*

# Disciples are living sacrifices

Therefore, I urge you, brothers, in view of God's mercy, to offer your bodies as living sacrifices, holy and pleasing to God – this is your spiritual act of worship.

ROMANS 12:1

The sacrifices of the Old Testament were symbols of the worshiper's confession of his sins and his surrender to the Lord. Jesus was willing to sacrifice Himself on the cross for us. His perfect sacrifice replaced the sacrifices of the Old Testament, because it never has to be repeated.

If you want to practice your Christianity in your everyday life, you need to be willing to follow His example and to offer yourself as a sacrifice to God. Disciples are people who are willing to offer themselves as living, holy sacrifices, to put themselves at His disposal. This means that they are in His service fulltime, twenty-four hours a day.

To be a living sacrifice requires you to put yourself fully at God's disposal. It is much easier to give of your money or your possessions than to give of yourself. But God wants you to be willing to lay yourself down on the altar, to relinquish your old, sinful nature and to allow your life to be controlled by His Spirit. It means that you will always be available for His work, that you will use your time, your strength and your gifts in such a way in His service that it will cost you something.

You also have to be a holy sacrifice. This requires you to be devoted to God, to be pleasing to Him. Your entire life should be worthy of God's approval.

Heavenly Father, I find it hard to put myself completely at Your disposal. Help me to accomplish this goal, because Jesus did the same for me. Amen.

# Disciples are willing to give

"Give, and it will be given to you. A good measure, pressed down, shaken together and running over, will be poured into your lap."

LUKE 6:38

The central idea of Jesus' Sermon on the Mount is that we should be merciful and compassionate, as His Father is merciful and compassionate. If we read carefully, we will find that we should give to everyone who asks something of us (see Mt. 5:42). If we think of the number of beggars we encounter every day, it seems impossible to follow this command. Surely we can't give to everyone who asks – surely we have to draw a line somewhere? Reading these words causes us to wonder whether Jesus would still say the same thing today, or whether His words were meant only for the people of His time.

Jesus' message of compassion is still directed at every Christian. Disciples are people with hearts devoted to others, people who are willing to give more than they can afford. Often this requirement of discipleship is the one that causes us to turn back, because all of us tend to grow attached to our possessions.

Jesus was even willing to sacrifice His life for you. If you are His disciple, your life should have the same quality of compassion and caring. You should be willing to provide for the needs of others. What people do with the things that you give to them or do for them is not important. What is important is that they will see Christ's attitude and love in your behavior toward them; that God will practically touch their lives through you.

Are you willing to be a disciple who gives?

*Lord Jesus, thank You for giving Your life for me. Make me willing to give to everyone who asks something of me. Amen.*

# Disciples set a good example

But set an example for the believers in speech, in life, in love, in faith and in purity.

I TIMOTHY 4:12

It is essential that disciples will live in such a way that others will look at their lifestyle and behavior and see Christ in them.

Paul leaves the young Timothy with a difficult duty. He expects Timothy to set an example for the other believers in five different areas: in speech, in life, in love, in faith and in purity.

Setting an example in speech encompasses everything that you say, not only when you are trying to impress others with your Christianity, but also when you are alone, when you become angry, or when you are disparaged by others. Disciples should learn to speak carefully. Your mouth says only what is going on in your heart. Setting an example in life means that the things you do and the way in which you choose to live will show others that you believe in Christ.

The love of which Paul speaks is the unconditional love of the Bible, a love that demands sacrifice and self-denial, a love that will cause you to reach out to others.

Faith is the way in which you walk with God: your personal relationship with Him should be evident in your way of life.

Purity relates to the relationships in your life, and it is usually also associated with sexual matters, but it ultimately relates to the entire law of God: live in such a way that you obey God's commandments.

Unfortunately your testimony has no value if your way of life does not agree with your words. Does your life correspond with your testimony as a Christian?

*Heavenly Father, make me an example for others in speech and in life, in love, faith and purity. Amen.*

# Disciples can be imitated

Whatever you have learned or received or heard from me, or seen
in me – put it into practice. And the God of peace will be with you.
PHILIPPIANS 4:9

In this passage Paul is discussing what the lives of Christians
should look like. We should always be joyful as well as gentle,
we should present our requests to God in prayer, we should
renew our thoughts, and then he says, "What you have heard
from me or seen in me, is what you should do. Do as I have
done."

There are very few people who can say what Paul says in this
passage. Most of us tend to say: Do as I tell you! We know all
too well that there is a vast difference between what we preach
and what we practice.

But isn't Paul a little conceited? We almost get the impres-
sion that Paul thinks too highly of himself. But he is actually
absolutely sincere when he writes these words. Just as Jesus
did, Paul also practiced what he preached.

It was of the utmost importance to him to set a pure example
to other believers; to live in such a way that he could tell them
to follow his example with a clear conscience. This is also why
Paul can testify in Galatians 2:20, "I no longer live, but Christ
lives in me."

Disciples are people who can be imitated. And you? Are you
living as an example to other Christians? If not, why not try to
do so from now on?

*Lord Jesus, forgive me for keeping my own ego alive. Help me
to live in such a way that I will also be able to tell other people
to follow my example. Amen.*

# Disciples are Christ-like

Follow my example, as I follow the example of Christ.

1 Corinthians 11:1

Jesus was obedient to the will and bidding of His Father in word as well as in deed. And His disciples are called to live as Christ did. We should follow the example of Christ at all times, as Paul did.

In Matthew 23:3 Jesus speaks about the teachers of the law and the Pharisees, the most distinguished religious people of His time, but people who did not practice what they preached. They were quick to point out the way that others should follow, but did not follow this way themselves. The words and example of such people are false. They have no real value as testimony. Their actions speak so loudly that their words have no effect.

This picture of the teachers of the law and the Pharisees that Jesus sketches, points out our own shortcomings. We try so hard, but we can't manage to live like Jesus.

There are areas in all our lives where we fail to walk in Jesus' footsteps. However, we have the consolation that Paul also occasionally became discouraged and exasperated with himself. The same Paul who asked others to follow his example complains in Romans 7:21, "When I want to do good, evil is right there with me."

You need not be discouraged: Jesus will provide you with the strength to follow His example. He will free you from the burden of sin and help you to become more like Him every day.

*Lord Jesus, I try so hard to live as You did, but I seldom succeed. Help me to follow Your example in word and in deed. Amen.*

# Disciples are never in want

The LORD is my shepherd, I shall not be in want.

PSALM 23:1

David declares that the Lord is his shepherd and that he will never be in want. This state of affairs seems quite impossible to us when we try to apply it to our own lives. After all, there are so many people who lack something in their lives. Some have lost their life partner or a child through death, others are seriously ill or have had to go through a divorce, still others have lost their job and their security.

When we consider David's life, we see that he too suffered a great deal. He often had to flee for his life, his own son wanted to kill him, and he lost more than one of his children. Therefore today's Scripture cannot be interpreted without certain qualifications. There are many things that we lack, because life is never only moonshine and roses, even if you are a Christian.

And yet the first line of Psalm 23 says it all: The LORD is my shepherd ... If you follow this Shepherd, you know the reason why you want for nothing. The exclusive guarantee of Psalm 23 is only applicable to certain people: Jesus' disciples, those people who are followers of the Shepherd.

In Jesus' time there was no fencing. The shepherd carried the sole responsibility for the safety of his flock. And the flock knew their shepherd's voice and followed him. If you follow Jesus in this way, you will discover that you will not lack anything, after all. However, then you will have to be willing to follow in the footsteps of your Shepherd day after day, and to obey Him unconditionally.

Lord Jesus, I praise You as the Shepherd who was willing to sacrifice Your life for me, so that I may want for nothing in my life. Amen.

# Peace and contentment

He makes me lie down in green pastures, he leads me beside quiet waters.

PSALM 23:2

We can know true contentment and peace only if we allow God, our Shepherd, to lead us. He knows exactly where to find the green pastures and the quiet waters that will restore and strengthen us.

The shepherd not only protects his flock, he also provides for their needs: their needs for rest and food to sustain them. Our Shepherd still wants to do this: He wants to give us all those things that make life beautiful and meaningful. For this reason we can live in peace; we know that our Shepherd will provide for us.

However, there is a condition: disciples must not stray from their Shepherd. They must be willing to depend on the Lord as sheep depend on their shepherd, and to trust God completely for the fulfillment of all their needs.

In Psalm 23 mention is also made of dark valleys: times of danger. Whenever his flock is in trouble, the shepherd is there to lead them out of the dangerous situation, to protect and keep them. Our Shepherd also carries us through our dark times. Regardless of how terrible things seem, you can be sure that your Shepherd will lead you, walking ahead of you every step of the way.

David experienced the Shepherd's caring love and protection. Have you claimed your share of God's protection yet?

*Heavenly Father, thank You for being the Shepherd who cares for me, who provides for all my needs and who carries me through valleys of darkness. Amen.*

# *Looking forward to God's feast*

You prepare a table before me in the presence of my enemies. You anoint my head with oil; my cup overflows. Surely goodness and love will follow me all the days of my life, and I will dwell in the house of the LORD forever.

PSALM 23:5-6

The first part of this psalm tells of the Lord who is like a Shep-herd caring for his flock, while the second part describes the marvelous feast that the Lord prepares for His children. It is indeed a lavish table that is prepared here: an abundance of love and goodwill is poured out on the guests.

God always gives in abundance: our Father not only gives us what is necessary, He spoils His children with luxury. He is the perfect Host who promises to lead and protect us throughout our lives, and finally to receive us into His house with a marvelous feast. Disciples are people who look forward to and yearn for this feast that awaits them in the house of the Lord.

Remember that everything you have comes from God. It is important for you to notice all the things that the Lord spoils you with.

If you have God on your side, there is one thing that you can be sure of: the things that you lack will be in the minority, and the things that the Lord wants to give to you will be much more than anything you could ever lose.

As His disciple, as one of His sheep, you can be assured that you will one day dwell in the house of the Lord forever, and that not even the grave can keep you from eternal fellowship with Him.

*Heavenly Father, I look forward to the abundant feast that You are preparing for me. Help me to live in such a way that I will one day be fit to dwell in Your house forever. Amen.*

# Disciples are people with courage

A man's spirit sustains him in sickness, but a crushed spirit who can bear?

PROVERBS 18:14

When you are faced with a major crisis, it is all too easy to become panicky and to lose your courage in the process.

People who depend on God for the strength to bear their suffering courageously, are exceptional witnesses for the Lord, and their courage astonishes the people around them time and time again.

There is a vast difference in the ways in which unbelievers and Christians cope with suffering. Unbelievers are easily discouraged. A disciple, on the other hand, is always someone with extraordinary courage, someone who can radiate joy despite suffering and pain.

I met someone like this in a town where I was asked to deliver a speech. During back surgery the surgeon had accidentally cut her spinal cord, so that her spinal fluid continually drains away through the incision. She can no longer get up and walk around; she is in continual pain, and yet she is a beautiful, radiant woman. Everyone who goes to visit her with the intention of comforting and encouraging her discovers that the opposite happens. After a visit with Heléne you go home with wonder in your heart and a faith that is restored and fortified. And this courage of spirit that enables her to bear her suffering with so much grace can only come from God Himself.

The next time you experience a time of suffering in your life, trust the Lord to give you the same kind of courage and fortitude of spirit.

*Heavenly Father, You know that my courage quickly falters. Help me to remain courageous in the midst of suffering, so that I may also comfort others because I believe in You. Amen.*

# Disciples rely on God

I do not concern myself with great matters or things too wonderful for me. But I have stilled and quieted my soul; like a weaned child with its mother, like a weaned child is my soul within me.

PSALM 131:1-2

In this Scripture passage the psalmist sketches a picture of absolute trust. When incomprehensible events occur in our lives, we are often like naughty children who insist that God should provide us with the answers to our many "why" questions.

But this is not what disciples do. They are willing simply to become still in the presence of God, as a child is still at its mother's breast. They do not insist on explanations; they do not tire themselves out over things that they cannot change in any case. They trust God unconditionally and believe that He will help them when the time is right, and therefore they are willing to wait for God's answer.

Unless we become like little children we will not enter the kingdom of heaven, as Jesus said to His disciples. What do you do when things in your own life start spiraling out of control? Have you learned the secret of surrendering everything to God yet? Have you learned how to stop worrying about things that you cannot change, and how to become peaceful and quiet in the presence of God and trust in Him?

If you can do this, He will give you the grace to wait for Him until He decides that the time is right to deliver you from your difficulties.

*Heavenly Father, forgive me for still sometimes being rebellious when things don't go my way. Make me peaceful in Your presence and willing to wait for You. Amen.*

# Disciples report for duty

When he had finished washing their feet, he put on his clothes and returned to his place. "Do you understand what I have done for you?" he asked them. "Now that I, your Lord and Teacher, have washed your feet, you also should wash one another's feet."

JOHN 13:12, 14

To wash the feet of the people at a dinner feast was the work of a slave. And because there was no slave present at the celebration of the Passover feast, Jesus' disciples hesitated. None of them was prepared to do this slave's duty. Then Jesus stood up, took off His outer clothing and wrapped a towel around His waist. Then He poured water into a basin and started washing His disciples' feet.

Despite the fact that none of them wanted to do it, the disciples weren't really comfortable with the idea of their Teacher, the most important One among them, washing their feet. Peter, in particular, objected vehemently, but Jesus stated unequivocally that He wanted His disciples to follow His example and to be willing to wash one another's feet.

The most important reason why Jesus washed His disciples' feet was so that they would continue His example of service on earth after He had left them. Disciples are people who are willing to roll up their sleeves and serve others. They are willing to serve God, to serve one another and to serve those to whom they bring the message of redemption.

Are you prepared to love others so much that you will be willing to set your pride aside and to serve them?

*Lord Jesus, teach me what I should do to be of service to other people. Make me willing to follow Your example. Amen.*

# Disciples are joyful people

You have filled my heart with greater joy than when their grain and new wine abound.

PSALM 4:7

$A$ woman who was a complete stranger to me stopped me in a parking lot and asked me whether I was a Christian. I was quite taken aback, but nevertheless answered affirmatively. She replied, "I knew it; I could see it on your face!"

No one is able to walk around with a beaming smile every day – we all have days when we feel "down" – but nevertheless people should be able to see who you belong to by simply looking at your face.

When you have the joy of Christ in your heart, you cannot hide it. And the source of this inner joy is God Himself. It is He who gives joy to His children, regardless of their circumstances.

The psalmists were people who knew this secret. "You will fill me with joy in Your presence" the writer of Psalm 16:11 testifies. "Let the hearts of those who seek the LORD rejoice," as is written in Psalm 105:3. This is the reason for our joy: the God who gives us joy is always with us.

We can even be joyful in times of hardship, as the people of Macedonia were. Paul writes, "Out of the most severe trial, their overflowing joy ... welled up in rich generosity," (2 Corinthians 8:2).

Disciples are joyful people. They radiate joy even in times of suffering – the joy that comes from God.

Can you do this yet?

*Heavenly Father, thank You for the overflowing joy in my heart because I know that I belong to You and that You are always with me. Help me to radiate this joy so that others can see it. Amen.*

# Disciples live gratefully

Sing and make music in your heart to the Lord, always giving thanks to God the Father for everything, in the name of our Lord Jesus Christ.

EPHESIANS 5:19-20

It is an unfortunate fact of life that we usually have to lose something before we really appreciate it. When you are struck by illness, you discover how precious your health is. When you lose your husband, you realize how much you loved him. When your sight and hearing start deteriorating, you discover just how wonderful it is to be able to see and hear.

Disciples should be grateful people, people who are attuned to all the wonderful things that God gives and does for them in His grace. We should thank God for each of His blessings, Paul writes to the church in Ephesus.

The word "everything" indicates that we should also give thanks for those things that we aren't really grateful for, things that are disagreeable to us, but nevertheless things that the Lord wants to use positively in our lives. He can make all things, even suffering and hardship, work for our good.

When last did you thank the Lord not only for all the great and wonderful gifts that He gives you, but also for all the small, insignificant things that you so often take for granted? Always remember that you don't deserve anything that you receive from Him. Everything you have comes only from the grace of God. Notice God's blessings in your life and make a point of thanking Him for them every day.

Heavenly Father, I am sorry for being so ungrateful. Grant that I will notice every blessing in my life and thank You for each one. Amen.

# Disciples are people with hope

I say to myself, "The LORD is my portion; therefore I will wait for him." The LORD is good to those whose hope is in him, to the one who seeks him.

LAMENTATIONS 3:24-25

When Jeremiah wrote the Book of Lamentations things were going very badly for him and his people. And yet he clung to his hope in the Lord. He gives us the reason for this tenacious hope, "Yet this I call to mind and therefore I have hope: Because of the Lord's great love we are not consumed, for His compassions never fail. They are new every morning; great is Your faithfulness" (Lam. 3:21-23).

According to the dictionary hope is the knowledge that your expectations will not be disappointed. And it is precisely because they see their expectations disappointed every day that so many people lose hope. Fortunately no one who has hoped in the Lord has ever been disappointed.

Not even suffering and hardship can cause people who place their hope in God to be discouraged. They can even be joyful in their suffering, because they know, "We also rejoice in our sufferings, because we know that suffering produces perseverance; perseverance, character; and character, hope. And hope does not disappoint us, because God has poured out His love in our hearts by the Holy Spirit, whom He has given us" (Rom. 5:3-5).

Are you feeling discouraged at the moment? Focus on God for a change. Continue hoping in Him and you will discover that all the things you hope for will come true.

*Heavenly Father, thank You that I am free to hope in You, because You never disappoint those who place their hope in You. Amen.*

# Disciples care for others

But love your enemies, do good to them, and lend to them without expecting to get anything back. Then your reward will be great, and you will be sons of the Most High, because he is kind to the ungrateful and wicked. Be merciful, just as your Father is merciful.

LUKE 6:35-36

In this passage Jesus provides us with an overview of exactly how disciples should act. They should do good to others without expecting anything in return. And this is by no means easy! It is much easier to do good to others if you know that they are going to reward you for your hospitality or generosity.

But Jesus wants you to be willing to lend without expecting to get anything back, to help those who are trying to harm you, and to reach out to others and provide for their needs without first trying to determine whether they deserve it. In short, you should do to others as you would have them do to you (see Lk. 6:31).

The reason is to be found in verse 36: "Be merciful, just as your Father is merciful." Just think of how good God is to you, even though you don't deserve His grace at all.

In the same way you have to be willing to do good to others who might not deserve it; to notice the distress of people around you and to do something about it. If you can do this, you are obeying God's commands, and then you will truly be His disciple.

*Heavenly Father, I struggle to do good to people who try to harm me. Help me to notice the distress of other people and to help them, as You help me every day. Amen.*

# Disciples do not squander time

Be careful, then, how you live – not as unwise but as wise, making the most of every opportunity, because the days are evil.

EPHESIANS 5:15-16

Time is extremely valuable and time squandered is time lost. Every person has exactly the same 24 hours at his disposal every day. People's time is chock-full of things that need to be done and there have never been so many things taking up our time as there are now: computers, courses, sport, work pressures and family.

We spend much of our time trying to finish the work that we are obliged to do so that there will still be some time left for the things that we would like to do. But good things can also be detrimental. Going walking at five o'clock in the morning is very beneficial for your health, but it is detrimental to you if you do it in the time that ought to be set aside for fellowship with God.

Disciples are people who make the best use of every opportunity that comes their way. Decide today which things are the most important to you, and in future spend the most time on these things.

Be sure to utilize your time optimally: give preference to the important things, the things with eternal value, the things of God. Try to find out what it is that God wants you to do. Always put His kingdom first. Then you will be able to use your time in the best possible way.

*Heavenly Father, I must confess that I still waste my time on unnecessary things. Help me to use my time well, and to give enough of my time to You. Amen.*

# Disciples make disciples

Then Jesus came to them and said, "All authority in heaven and on earth has been given to me. Therefore go and make disciples of all nations, baptizing them in the name of the Father and of the Son and of the Holy Spirit, and teaching them to obey everything I have commanded you."

MATTHEW 28:18-20

Jesus not only wants us to be disciples, he also wants us to make disciples. He not only wants people to be converted to the Christian faith, he wants them to be guided towards discipleship.

And the field has never been as ready for harvesting as it is now. There are currently about 5.7 billion people in the world, and every day 75 000 of them die never having heard of Jesus.

No one has an excuse for not being a maker of disciples. "Even if you are too young or too old to go yourselves, you can do your missionary work on your knees!" said someone in a recent missionary sermon.

It is God's ideal for His church that everyone who professes to being a disciple will also be a maker of disciples, so that the harvest of the kingdom of God may be brought in.

If you are willing to be a maker of disciples you may take the promise in verses 18 to 20 as your own: to Jesus belongs all the power and authority in heaven and on earth. He Himself will help you with your great commission. He also promises to be with you until the very end of the age.

Heavenly Father, help me to make disciples of others, so that even people who have never heard of You will have the opportunity to become Your children. Amen.

# Seeking God

God created us to seek Him. He is not far from each one of us, for in Him we live and move and have our being, Paul tells the people of Athens (see Acts 17:27-28). Augustine agreed with Paul's sermon: You are not completely whole until you have found God.

According to Paul it is not difficult to find God. He is close to us, because it is only by His grace that we actually exist. Fortunately nobody seeks God in vain. "Seek and you will find" Jesus promises in the Sermon on the Mount (Mt. 7:7). Unfortunately many people are seeking God in the wrong places.

This month we are going to reflect on how we can seek God in such a way that we will truly find Him.

# Communion with God

> O God, you are my God, earnestly I seek you; my soul thirsts for you, my body longs for you, in a dry and weary land where there is no water. I have seen you in the sanctuary and beheld your power and your glory.
>
> PSALM 63:1-2

As a deer thirsts for water, even so the psalmist thirsts for God's presence in his life. The psalmist's relationship with God is inextricably part of his life. He longs passionately to meet God in the sanctuary, the temple in Jerusalem where the Jews worshiped God.

If you seek God with a true heart, you must truly thirst for God. The verbs used here stress the intensity of this longing, namely "seek," "thirst" and "long." To feel like this about God, to long for His presence in your life in this way, supposes that you will have a living, intimate relationship with Him.

How is your relationship with the Lord? Is it a personal relationship, like that of the psalmist, or has your relationship become simply a matter of convention? You still go to church on Sundays, you read the Bible and pray regularly, but the bubbling enthusiasm is totally absent.

Won't you truly seek God again and renew your communion with Him? Fortunately you no longer need a temple to reach God. You yourself are now a temple in which God is living through His Holy Spirit. He is available for you every day and He wants to bestow His grace on you.

*Heavenly Father, forgive me that my seeking for You has become so powerless. I do want to renew my relationship with You, Lord, so that I can experience true communion with You again. Amen.*

# Experiencing God's grace

Because your love is better than life, my lips will glorify you. I will praise you as long as I live, and in your name I will lift up my hands.

PSALM 63:3-4

In these verses the psalmist describes exactly how he experiences God's grace and love: God's love is better than life and therefore he will always glorify Him. The psalmist wants to sing about God's love for him, he wants to praise Him as long as he lives. Even at night (when he is suffering) he will keep on praising God for His grace.

In this confession of faith he expresses the quality of his communion with God. Most modern people have not learned to be so completely dependent on God.

There are so many other matters that draw our attention, matters that are important and necessary to us, and so we forget to focus fully on God. The result is that He is no longer more important than life to us.

The Christian's life should be a service of worship to the glory of God, not only on Sundays, but every day. To praise God in all circumstances should be a way of life to God's children.

How do you respond to God's love for you? Does the way you do things give evidence that you are living in close communion with the Lord? Then your life will also be a song of praise to the honor of God even when your circumstances are negative. Then you will succeed, as the psalmist did, in making praising God a way of life.

Heavenly Father, I praise You for Your all-encompassing love for me. Make it possible for me to answer Your love with my life. Amen.

# Evidence of communion

Because you are my help, I sing in the shadow of your wings. My soul clings to you; your right hand upholds me.

PSALM 63:7-8

The strength of the poet's relationship with God is manifested in the fact that he addresses Him in verse 1 as "my God."

God has always helped and protected him and therefore he wants to rejoice in that protection. Verse 8 is the key to the psalmist's life of intimate communion with God: "My soul clings to you; your right hand upholds me." Nothing can ever separate him from God.

However, God never forces Himself on people. Whether you, like the psalmist, will decide of your own free will to remain near the Lord, to allow Him to support you in everything you undertake, rests completely with you.

Whether you are going to continue trusting Him, even in the night and also when you are suffering, is your choice. Through His Holy Spirit God is already dwelling in you. He promised that He would help, lead and support you.

Make a decision now to claim God's love and protection for yourself. Remember, you may not keep quiet about this. Like the psalmist, sing a song of praise to God, give testimony to other people of God's love and faithfulness in your life. Then you will experience it firsthand: nobody can ever wrench you from His hand, or can ever separate you from His love.

*Lord Jesus, I choose to trust You now, to accept Your direction for my life and to praise You for it. Thank You for being with me always. Amen.*

# Come near to God

Submit yourselves, then, to God. Resist the devil, and he will flee
from you. Come near to God and he will come near to you.

JAMES 4:7-8

The initiative to bring people to God always comes from God
first. He not only invites you to be His child, but also places the
desire to accept the invitation in your heart. However, there is
a condition attached to it: Before you can reach God, you first
have to be willing to submit yourself to Him and to resist the
devil.

You need to end your flirtation with the world and the things
of the world. You will have to face your sins, confess them and
leave them behind.

If you are willing to do this there is a wonderful promise in
today's verse: If you come near to God He will also come near
to you. "Say a quiet yes to God and He'll be there in no time"
(*The Message*, p. 571).

To come near to God will demand work; it never comes by
itself. It will mean that you must be willing to work on your
relationship with God every day. It will also mean that you must
deliberately try to let go of your sins and live close to God. It
may not be easy, but it is always totally worth it.

*Heavenly Father, I want to come near to You. Thank You for
assuring me that You will also come near to me and will hold
my hand fast. Amen.*

# Remain in Jesus

"I am the vine; you are the branches. If a man remains in me and I in him, he will bear much fruit; apart from me you can do nothing."

JOHN 15:5

Water and food can reach the branches only through the vine. The branch is inextricably part of the vine. Branches are pruned so that they can be even more fruitful, but when a branch is cut from the vine it is useless and withers.

If we are not willing to live in a relationship of faith as close to God as the branch is to the vine, we are also useless to Him. When we remain in Him, He gives us life as the vine gives life to the branch. He makes it possible for us to execute His divine command: to bear fruit for Him. However, if we move away from Him, if we place our faith in other things, we shall bear no fruit, because apart from Him we can do nothing.

If you want to remain in God it is necessary for you to realize your total dependency on Him every day. "Blessed are the poor in spirit, for theirs is the kingdom of heaven," Jesus says in the Sermon on the Mount (Mt. 5:3).

Although you know well that you will be able to do nothing on your own, you also know that when you remain in God His immeasurable power is available to you. Then you will not only be able to bear fruit for Him, but you will be able to accomplish everything through Him who gives you the strength.

*Lord Jesus, I want to remain in You like the branch in the vine – very close to You – so that I can bear much fruit. Amen.*

# Do God's will

"Not everyone who says to me, 'Lord, Lord,' will enter the kingdom of heaven, but only he who does the will of my Father who is in heaven."

MATTHEW 7:21

Jesus is speaking here about the day of His Second Coming when He will judge everybody. He says that those people who make pious confessions of faith or do the right things for their own gain, but do not have a personal relationship with Him, will not enter heaven. Only those people who obey will eventually enter the kingdom of heaven.

Jesus is always more concerned about how you live than about what you say. If your life does not correspond with your faith it is not a worthy testimony. Jesus places a very high premium on obedience. If you want to live close to God, you will obviously have to be willing to relegate your own will to the background and to focus on God's will for your life, even if it differs widely from your own. A good testimony is of no use if it is not underscored by your deeds: for Matthew deeds are the mold in which faith is molded.

It is true that you can only be saved by grace, but because you are saved, you now obey God's will out of gratitude. "Obedience is an answer to mercy, as a song of thanks for mercy. This is precisely what God demands of you. If you are willing to do this, you will remain in Him.

*Heavenly Father, help me to obey Your will out of gratitude for Your great mercy toward me. Amen.*

# Lose to gain

"If anyone would come after me, he must deny himself and take up his cross and follow me. For whoever wants to save his life will lose it, but whoever loses his life for me and for the gospel will save it."

MARK 8:34-35

Many Christians are of the opinion that they will enter heaven "on a bed of roses" as somebody aptly described it. Unfortunately, however, it is not as simple as that. Seeking God, remaining in Him, will not free your life from problems and crises. It will actually increase your problems and crises, because, as Jesus Himself said, people who follow Him must be willing to sign their own death warrant.

People who live only for themselves will eventually lose their lives forever, whereas people who are willing to lose their lives for Jesus and for the gospel will continue to live forever.

If you want to seek God and remain in Him you will have to be willing to lose your life in order to gain life. The love God wants from you is a demanding love. It demands of you to deny yourself, which means to give of yourself unconditionally.

It demands that you sacrifice your pride, reputation and self, to take second place so that God's kingdom can take first place.

It also demands that you will give up the things that you want to do for the things that God asks of you.

Are you willing to try?

*Lord Jesus, it is not always easy to follow You if it demands of me to first lose so that I can gain. Please make me willing to give of myself unconditionally. Amen.*

# Treasure in heaven

---

Jesus looked at him and loved him. "One thing you lack," he said. "Go, sell everything you have and give to the poor, and you will have treasure in heaven. Then come, follow me."

MARK 10:21

---

When the rich young man asked Jesus what he had to do to inherit eternal life, Jesus simply answered that he had to sell everything he had so that he could have treasure in heaven. Unfortunately the rich young man was not willing to go that far because his earthly wealth was very great.

The rich Jews of Jesus' time believed that they could enter heaven more easily than poor people because they had more money to use for doing good. In this way they could virtually "buy" their salvation. However, this is not the way it works in God's kingdom.

Eternal life cannot be bought with money. God gives free grace to everybody who believes in Him. Only a spiritual "treasure" can guarantee eternal life for you. This is what Jesus advised in the Sermon on the Mount: "But store up for yourselves treasure in heaven, where moth and rust do not destroy, and where thieves do not break in and steal" (Mt. 6:20).

People who seek God cannot find Him while they are still bound to their earthly treasures. Only when you are willing to make God the most important priority in your life, when you store up for yourself a treasure in heaven, will you know what it means to find God.

Lord Jesus, I pray that You will make me willing to deny my earthly treasure so that I may have a treasure in heaven. Amen.

# You must be born again

In reply Jesus declared, "I tell you the truth, no one can see the kingdom of God unless he is born again."

JOHN 3:3

Nicodemus was an important Jewish leader. He came to Jesus in the night because he did not want to people see him with Jesus. However, he did realize that Jesus was special because of the miracles He performed. Just like the rich young man, Nicodemus wanted to find a recipe to reach God. Jesus told him that he would have to be born again to succeed in this, but this simply increased his confusion.

Nicodemus understood the words of Jesus literally and answered that he could not enter into his mother's womb a second time and be born again. However, what Jesus was saying in effect is that he had to be born into the spiritual world.

You do not need to understand this spiritual rebirth, even as you do not have to understand the origin of the wind to be able to feel it blowing.

The Holy Spirit works like the wind in your life: it is not necessary to understand the working of the Holy Spirit. The only thing you have to do is to make yourself available to the Spirit and submit your whole life to His control.

To know God you must be spiritually sensitive, and this can only happen if you are born again in the Spirit. God wants to intervene in your life and make you His child. The only thing you have to do is to accept His gift of grace.

*Heavenly Father, thank You that I do not need to understand You with my human brain, that I need only accept Your offer of grace with open hands. Amen.*

# Salt and light

"You are the salt of the earth ... You are the light of the world. A city on a hill cannot be hidden."

MATTHEW 5:13-14

In Jesus' time salt was used to prevent food from spoiling and to make it tasty. However, when salt loses its saltiness it is worthless. Light is necessary so that people can see in the dark. One does not light a lamp and hide it under a bowl. It must shine so that everybody in the house can have light.

Believers should be the salt of the earth and the light of the world. If we have no influence on the world we are worthless. Like salt we must make food tasty and stop the decay. As light cannot be hidden, we also must not hide our light; everybody must be able to see it so that they can glorify God.

If you know God then His love must be visible in your life.

As a Christian you need to make a difference in the world in which you live: you must stop decay and be a bearer of light. When you look around you it is obvious that sin is becoming ever more acceptable.

Always remember that you are the salt and light of Jesus in this world. By your actions you must make life more beautiful for other people and show them the road to the true Light of the world.

*Lord Jesus, You are the light of the world. Make me a light too that will show Your love to other people, and salt that will make a positive difference to the people around me. Amen.*

# Totally dependent

> "Blessed are the poor in spirit, for theirs is the kingdom of heaven."
>
> MATTHEW 5:3

Blessed is the person who knows that he is dependent on God for everything, Jesus said in the Sermon on the Mount. Many adults find it quite difficult to admit that they are dependent. All of us prefer to play off our own bat, to do things ourselves, to be independent.

On the other hand, children live in complete dependence. Listen to the children's conversations: they always boast about their parents, never about themselves. Children ask their parents when they want something because they cannot provide for themselves. They know that they need their parents. No wonder Jesus said that if we do not become like children, we cannot enter the kingdom of heaven.

People living close to God are those who have discovered their own bankruptcy. They are people who know for certain that they can do nothing without God. As one author puts it: "A man who knows that he is dependent upon God is a wealthy beggar. He is a beggar because he acknowledges his dependency on God. He is wealthy because the Lord has promised him the kingdom of God."

Sometimes, especially when things are going well for you, you might think that you do not need God so much. However, that is a big mistake! Discover today exactly how dependent you are on God. Then you can live without worry in God's bounty and know too that heaven will be yours one day.

*Lord Jesus, forgive me that I so badly want to be independent. Make me willing to trust only You so that I may inherit Your kingdom one day. Amen.*

# First the kingdom!

> But seek first his kingdom and his righteousness, and all these things will be given to you as well.
>
> MATTHEW 6:33

It is only human to worry when you see social conditions deteriorating around you daily. Many People are discouraged by the low value of the rand, problems in our schools, conditions in our hospitals and the daily occurrence of crime. Even Christians cannot help wondering what tomorrow and the day after will bring.

People living in the time of Jesus were also worried. They wondered (like us) what they would eat and what they would wear. It is definitely not necessary to be so worried, Jesus said. Our Father in heaven knows exactly what we need. The secret is that we should know what the right order of things is: if we first seek the kingdom of God and His will He will give us all the other things about which we are so worried.

Are you still worried about many things? Listen to the advice of Jesus: Stop worrying. Follow your King every day, work for the expansion of His kingdom here on earth, do the things that are in accordance with His will for your life. Then you will discover that your worries will diminish because you are safe in His hands and He will look after you every day.

*Lord Jesus, from now on I want to follow You unconditionally and put Your kingdom first. Thank You for Your promise that You will give me all other things as well. Amen.*

# God will comfort you

"Blessed are those who mourn, for they will be comforted."

MATTHEW 5:4

Another group of people Jesus called blessed are those who mourn. The blessedness in sadness lies in the comfort you can get. People mourning without God are inconsolable. They have no prospect of being comforted by God Himself.

The people about whom Jesus is talking here are those who go to God with their grief. These people know that their grief is limited. It will not continue forever because there is a heaven waiting for them where there will be no more grief or tears. These mourners know the comfort of the arms of God around them when they are grieving.

They also know that God can use their grief to their benefit. If you have suffered yourself, it becomes a school in which God teaches you to comfort other people who are dejected. You pass the comfort that you received from God on to other people, "God comforts us in all our troubles, so that we can comfort those in any trouble with the comfort we ourselves have received from God" (2 Cor. 1:4).

Are you sad at present? Share your grief with God, He wants to comfort you. When He has done it, look for somebody else who is sad and comfort him.

*Heavenly Father, I do not always know what to do with my own grief. Thank You very much for the assurance that You Yourself will comfort me and will also teach me how to comfort others. Amen.*

# Pure in heart

"Blessed are the pure in heart, for they will see God."

MATTHEW 5:8

For Jesus true happiness is never connected to outward conditions. He thinks differently from us. He promises His peace and joy to those people who live near God, serve Him and obey Him.

"Blessed are the pure in heart, for they will see God," Jesus says. "You're blessed when you get your inside world – your mind and heart – put right. Then you can see God in the outside world," is how this verse is translated in *The Message* (p. 20). We are not pure in heart. All of us are sinful by nature. We blame Adam and Eve for that, because they brought sin into the world. Since then not even one of us has been free from sin.

To be pure in heart means that you will live a pure, impeccable, faultless life, that your heart, which is the center of your life, will be pure and righteous. A pure heart is a heart that is dedicated completely to God.

When you measure yourself according to these standards you are most probably going to fall far short of the requirements. However, it is possible to live a pure life, although you will never succeed on your own.

Ask the Holy Spirit to take full control of your life and to forgive your sins. He will give you the wisdom so that you will be able to discern between right and wrong. He will show you when you sin and help you also to let go of that sin.

Lord Jesus, I pray that You will give me a pure heart, that You will make me sensitive to sin so that I will see You one day. Amen.

# God chooses you to be holy

For he chose us in him before the creation of the world to be holy and blameless in his sight.

EPHESIANS 1:4

Every person is sinful by nature. We can never approach God by ourselves. However, through His act of redemption on the cross Jesus made it possible for sinners to be children of God.

If you believe in Jesus, He chose you long ago (before the creation of the world) to be His child. It is an unbelievable miracle that a holy God especially chose insignificant, sinful people to belong to Him. You have no part in this predestination; it is the pure grace of God. God chose you purely because He wants to and therefore not one of us can boast that we are redeemed. However, once He has saved us, He asks of us to be holy and blameless before Him.

God now looks at you through the cross of His Son. Jesus has already paid for every one of your sins; now you need to live like somebody whose sins have been eradicated.

To be holy means that from now on you will be set apart for God, that you will be willing to walk the road of sanctification with God so that you can become more like Jesus every day.

"God loves you just as you are, but He refuses to leave you like that. He wants you to become like Jesus," says Max Lucado. Are you willing to obey Him?

*Heavenly Father, I praise You because You love me, and because You chose me long ago to be Your child. Help me now to live a holy life. Amen.*

# Be holy!

The Lord said to Moses, "Speak to the entire assembly of Israel and say to them: 'Be holy because I, the Lord your God, am holy.'"

LEVITICUS 19:1-2

God's people differed from all the heathen peoples. They were set apart for God and served Him alone. For that reason they had to obey dozens of purity laws, health laws and sexual laws. God did not allow them to eat anything that was impure or to marry Gentiles.

They had to be different, set apart for Him, so that the heathen peoples could see clearly that they were God's people. They also had to closely obey the law of God set out in the Ten Commandments.

As He expected from Israel, God is still expecting His children to act differently from the rest of the world, to speak differently, to live differently. He wants His children to live holy lives because they worship a holy God.

Paul explains how to do this in Ephesians 4:23-24, "You are to be made new in the attitude of your minds; and to put on the new self, created to be like God in true righteousness and holiness."

Can your friends see in the things that you do and say (and *don't* do and say) that you are different because you belong to God? If not, it is time for you to look carefully at yourself and to ask God to show you those things that keep you from living a holy life.

*Heavenly Father, there are still so many wrong things in my life. Please show them to me so that I may live only for You from now on. Amen.*

# Holy temples

If anyone destroys God's temple, God will destroy him; for God's temple is sacred, and you are that temple.

1 Corinthians 3:17

Every Christian is a temple of God because the Holy Spirit is living in all of us. Thus we no longer belong to ourselves, but to God. He must be glorified in our bodies. For this reason Christians are not to live sexually promiscuous lives.

God created man in His image. When Adam and Eve turned against God that image was destroyed for ever. Only Jesus could restore it again, so that now we can be temples of God, holy homes where God Himself comes to live.

Sanctification is always a long process; it is not completed in a short while. Sanctification demands that God's children think, live, act and speak differently. It demands that we die to sin, that we bear fruit for God and declare war on our sinful natures every day. It demands of us to live so that the characteristics of Jesus can be seen in our lives.

Holiness is always a gift of God, never your own achievement. Only the Holy Spirit living in you, whose temple you are, can help you to become more holy every day so that you will ultimately be as complete and holy as Jesus.

However, then you will have to decide to obey the voice of the Holy Spirit from now on, to renounce those little habitual sins that you like so much.

Are you ready?

*Holy Spirit, I try so hard to be a holy temple for You, but I fail every time. Please help me to become more like Jesus every day. Amen.*

# Living like Jesus

Whoever claims to live in him must walk as Jesus did.

1 JOHN 2:6

Jesus Himself asks that we remain in Him so that we can bear fruit. However, it is a command that few of us succeed in obeying. We try hard, but do not succeed in living like Jesus lived.

God wants us to reflect the glory of Jesus. Paul said, "And we who with unveiled faces all reflect the Lord's glory, are being transformed in His likeness with ever-increasing glory which comes from the Lord, who is the Spirit" (2 Cor. 3:18).

The further you proceed on the road of sanctification, the more you will resemble Jesus so that His glory will be reflected in your life.

Look at the face of somebody who truly loves the Lord. Most probably the eyes of that person will shine and there will be a smile on his lips. God's peace and joy cannot be hidden. It is impossible to keep that joy to yourself; it shines forth so that everybody who comes into contact with you will be able to see it.

When you next walk past a shop window, peep at your own reflection. Is your face shining, or is it impossible for you to get rid of the frown? Remember that the glory that shines forth from you must be ever-increasing. Fortunately you don't have to do it yourself, God will do it for you.

Lord Jesus, I so dearly want to live like You did. Please make it possible for me, so that Your glory may shine forth from me. Amen.

# Perfecting holiness

Since we have these promises, dear friends, let us purify ourselves from everything that contaminates body and spirit, perfecting holiness out of reverence for God.

2 CORINTHIANS 7:1

The Lord hates half-heartedness. He is a jealous God and wants all of our lives. He seeks total dedication from us. That is not very easy! Most of us avoid total commitment. We reckon that it is right if we give over about 50% of our lives to God, while we ourselves keep control of the rest.

In this passage of Scripture Paul warns the believers in Corinth against the negative influence that sinners could have on them, and urges them to live in complete dedication to God.

You are also living in the world like the people of Corinth, and therefore you also find yourself up against worldly standards every day.

Perhaps you are of the opinion that you may lower your own standards a little for that reason; that it is not necessary for you to be quite so honest, work exactly so hard and give precisely so much. Unfortunately that is not true of the life of a Christian. God demands everything or nothing. He expects complete dedication from you. To tell the truth, He prefers you to be cold rather than lukewarm.

Are you willing to live a hundred percent for God, to turn your back on the world, to give your everything for Him, to be completely dedicated to Him? Then He will make every promise in His Word true for you.

Heavenly Father, please forgive me for my half-heartedness. Make me willing to give You my everything, to live completely dedicated to You. Amen.

# Sexual sin

It is God's will that you should be sanctified: that you should avoid sexual immorality. For God did not call us to be impure, but to live a holy life.

1 THESSALONIANS 4:3, 7

The moral standards of Paul's time were often very low. For that reason he continuously warned the children of God to avoid sexual sin. They needed to submit to the commands of Jesus in the sphere of sexuality too.

Sexual transgressions have become so common that in the eyes of most people they are not even sinful any more. It is nearly impossible to switch on your television set or to open a book without being confronted by extramarital sex or by the all but naked bodies. This is the case even in the Sunday newspapers.

A popular women's magazine recently published an article about a well-known (unmarried) author who is pregnant. The whole story was told in such a way that it was clear that the editors have no problem with premarital sex. Literary awards are given indiscriminately to pornographic stories. If you dare to question these things you are regarded as if you come from Mars!

Your children are growing up in this immoral world. It will depend on you whether they will one day uphold the right standards or whether they will also go with the stream. God demands of you to be sanctified in the sexual sphere. Are you ready not only to live a holy life yourself, but also to express your opinion, or are you still doing what the world does?

*Heavenly Father, You know I do not like always being the one who protests. Make me willing to stand by my convictions. Amen.*

# Be careful what you say!

We all stumble in many ways. If anyone is never at fault in what he says, he is a perfect man, able to keep his whole body in check.

JAMES 3:2

One of the things about which James has very strong feelings is that believers must watch their tongues. The tongue is certainly the one part of the body that keeps the holiness that God demands out of our reach. The tongue is a fire, says James. It corrupts the whole person, sets the whole course of his life on fire, and is itself set on fire by hell.

If you use your tongue correctly it can be an instrument in God's hand. However, if you use it incorrectly, it can influence your whole life negatively. It is not for nothing that the proverb says that the tongue is mightier than the sword.

Most of us speak easily; we say things about other people without considering that they may hurt or harm them. Just think: Can everything you said today be published? Do you slander and abuse even your best friends? If you (like me) have to hang your head in shame, you can take heart. Christ can control your tongue: the Lord, by letting His Holy Spirit live in us, gives us a bit for our mouths, so to speak.

Pray with the psalmist today that the Lord will set a guard over your mouth and keep watch over the door of your lips (see Ps. 141:3).

*Lord, You know precisely in what great trouble my tongue has landed me already. I pray that You will set a guard over my mouth and keep watch over the door of my lips. Amen.*

# Think right!

Finally, brothers, whatever is true, whatever is noble, whatever is right, whatever is pure, whatever is lovely, whatever is admirable – if anything is excellent or praiseworthy – think about such things.

PHILIPPIANS 4:8

In vain you are going to try to grow spiritually and be holy if you do not sift your thoughts carefully and summarily get rid of the sinful and wrong ones. That which you allow into your thoughts determines what kind of words and deeds will flow from you. As water reflects a face, so a man's heart reflects the man (Prov. 27:19).

Do you time and again catch yourself thinking about wrong things? Your thoughts have a very strong influence on your life. If you think negative thoughts all day long, you can be sure that all the negative things that you fear will happen to you. If, however, you can succeed in thinking joyful, positive thoughts, in filling your thoughts with whatever is true, whatever is noble, whatever is right, whatever is pure, whatever is lovely, whatever is admirable, excellent or praiseworthy (see Phil. 4:8), you will most probably find that your life will reflect these things.

From now on, focus deliberately on thinking right. Ask God to renew your thoughts so that you can approve what God's will is for your life (see Rom. 12:2).

Heavenly Father, I pray that You will renew my thoughts; that You will help me to think positively so that my life can reflect my thoughts. Amen.

# Out of the overflow of the heart ...

The good man brings good things out of the good stored up in his heart, and the evil man brings evil things out of the evil stored up in his heart. For out of the overflow of his heart his mouth speaks.

Luke 6:45

Not only your thoughts, but also your heart must be right if you want to live a holy life dedicated to God. The inclination of your heart always comes out in the things that you say and do. Small wonder that the last part of today's verse has become a proverb!

Sin always begins with your thoughts: "For from within, out of men's hearts, come evil thoughts, sexual immorality, theft, murder, adultery, greed, malice, deceit, lewdness, envy, slander, arrogance and folly," says Jesus in Mark 7:21-22. The list is very long and decadent.

Perhaps you think that you are not nearly as bad as the people described in this verse. Unfortunately you are wrong. Read the verse again carefully. All the things mentioned form part of your sinful nature; they are present in your heart if it has not yet been cleansed by the blood of Jesus.

Out of the overflow of your heart your mouth will speak. Why not accept the invitation in Isaiah 1:18 today? "Come now, let us reason together ... Though your sins are like scarlet, they shall be as white as snow."

*Lord Jesus, thank You very much that You have made it possible for me to exchange my dirty heart for a pure heart because Your blood has cleansed me for ever. Amen.*

# Dead to sin

In the same way count yourselves dead to sin, but alive to God in Christ Jesus.

ROMANS 6:11

People who seek God are holy: set apart for the Lord. They should not keep on sinning, because they are dead to sin. They are people who are living for God, because they are one with Jesus, as Paul writes to the believers in Rome.

Alas, not one of us can really testify that we are truly dead to sin. We commit sin every day. Even Paul confessed that he did the things that he did not want to do. However, there is a difference to be seen in the lives of people who have been set apart for God. Sin is no longer their master. They are no longer its slaves.

Do you succeed in resisting sin in your life, or is sin still your master? You need not allow sin to control your life and give in to the desires of your sinful nature.

Ask the Holy Spirit to help you live a holy life. Then dedicate yourself to the service of God so that every part of your life is useful to Him. If you do that, you can accept the promise in Romans 6:22 as your own: "But now that you have been set free from sin and have become slaves to God, the benefit you reap leads to holiness and the result is eternal life."

*Heavenly Father, please help me to resist the sins in my life, and to dedicate myself to Your service. Amen.*

# God is merciful

For their sake he remembered his covenant and out of his great love he relented.

PSALM 106:45

When we read Psalm 106 we get a review of the whole history of Israel. It takes our breath away when we realize the extent of God's mercy for His obstinate people. Time and again they turned from Him to worship idols, they ignored His grace. Nevertheless, God remained true to His covenant. Although He sometimes punished them for their sin, He was always willing to forgive the sinners and to renew His covenant with them again.

Before you judge Israel too harshly, think about what you are doing with God's mercy. Do you not repeatedly do wrong things even though you often decide turn from sin? Do you not often take God's love and grace lightly? There is not one of us who can succeed in being without sin.

Although we dare not cheapen God's grace, it is wonderful to know that God will also forgive us again and again as He did the Israelites.

You are in an even better situation than Israel. God does not punish you for your sins, because Jesus has already paid the full penalty for those sins on the cross. The only thing you have to do to earn God's forgiveness is to confess your sins and to remind Him of His compassion for you.

*Heavenly Father, please forgive me when I am unfaithful to You time and again just like Israel of yore. Thank You very much for Your mercy by which You forgive me again and again. Amen.*

# The peace of Jesus

Peace I leave with you; my peace I give you. I do not give to you as the world gives. Do not let your hearts be troubled and do not be afraid.

JOHN 14:27

Jesus promises His followers a peace that differs from the peace that the world gives. H. B. McCartney recounts that he once visited Hudson Taylor, who was doing missionary work in China. It struck him that Taylor was always calm and peaceful although his work often was mortally dangerous and – because of the great number of people – virtually impossible.

"How do you succeed in being so calm and peaceful? You are working with millions of people. I, who am only working with hundreds, am so nervous and tense!" McCartney wanted to know from Hudson.

"I would never have succeeded in doing my work without God's peace which transcends all understanding," Taylor answered him. "Hudson Taylor was for me the personification of John 14," wrote McCartney after his visit to China. "I could clearly perceive how he lived in Christ and Christ lived in him."

Can you bear witness, like Hudson Taylor, that you can handle your daily portion of stress calmly because you have the peace of Jesus in your life?

If not, try surrendering all your problems to Him and trusting Him for the solutions. Then His peace will also flood your life, so that you will be able to exchange your present stress and worries for God's peace and calm.

Lord Jesus, You know exactly how stressed and worried I am. I now want to bring each one of my problems to You and exchange them for Your peace in my life. Amen.

# Fear is unnecessary

The men were amazed and asked, "What kind of man is this? Even the winds and the waves obey him!"

MATTHEW 8:27

When a violent storm broke on the sea of Galilee and Jesus continued sleeping in the back of the boat, His terrified disciples woke Him. "You of little faith, why are you so afraid?" Jesus wanted to know. He got up, rebuked the wind and the waves, and immediately it was completely calm.

A charming story is told about a passenger liner that was caught in a violent storm on its way from London to New York. Everybody was terribly afraid, including the captain's eight-year-old daughter. She wanted to know, "Is Daddy on the bridge?" When her mother affirmed it, she turned around and fell asleep immediately. She had complete faith that her father would steer the ship safely through the storm.

The faith of Christians does not safeguard them against the storms of life. Nobody can escape hurt and hardship; they form an inextricable part of life. When you belong to God, however, you can face these storms of life without fear, because you know that your Captain is on the bridge and that He will steer your life safely through every storm.

God does not calm every storm in your life, but He is with you in the storm. Like the ship captain's little daughter, you need not fear the storms; your Father will guide you safely through them.

*Heavenly Father, I praise You for the knowledge that You do not safeguard me against all storms, but that You do promise to guide me safely through them. Amen.*

# The advantages of hardship

Our fathers disciplined us for a little while as they thought best; but God disciplines us for our good, that we may share in his holiness.

HEBREWS 12:10

It is necessary for children to get a hiding occasionally; it is the only thing that will drive folly far from them, the author of Proverbs wrote (Prov. 22:15). The rod of discipline makes a child obedient; it causes him to let go of the wrong things, because he does not want to feel the burn on his backside again.

In the same way and for the same reason God allows hardship in your life. Then you can draw closer to Him, trust Him more fully, hold faster to Him and eventually emerge as a more holy person. We know that only God can help when crises that we cannot handle ourselves come into our lives. They urge us to live closer to Him.

When you feel as if you can no longer handle the crises in your life, bring them to God. He promised that He will not let you be tempted beyond what you can bear, but that when you are tempted, He will also provide a way out so that you can stand up under it (1 Cor. 10:13).

Eventually you will experience firsthand that God can also use the hardship – His way of disciplining you – for your good; that you will be a more holy, more obedient and more dedicated child for Him as a result of it.

*Heavenly Father, just like my own children I do not enjoy it when You sometimes discipline me. Thank You for the assurance that You do it only to draw me to You. Amen.*

# Grief is sometimes good for you

Godly sorrow brings repentance that leads to salvation and leaves no regret.

2 CORINTHIANS 7:10

Grief is hard to bear. It hurts to lose somebody you love, or to be left in the lurch by people you trust, or to be scolded by somebody. When Paul made the people of Corinth grieve by sending them a letter called the "tears letter" (it was later lost), it was only for their good.

In writing this letter Paul wanted to bring the Corinthians to understanding and repentance. According to Bible authors this "letter of tears" indeed had the desired result: the Corinthians started to change for the better and the letter brought them back to God.

The right kind of grief always produces positive results. In 2 Corinthians 7:11 Paul speaks about the change that he observed in the Corinthians, "See what this godly sorrow has produced in you, what earnestness, what eagerness to clear yourselves, what indignation, what alarm, what longing, what concern, what readiness to see justice done." Because they were grieved about the admonishment, they repented and changed their way of life.

Sorrow in your life always draws you to God because nobody can comfort you like He can. When on occasion you cause sorrow to people whom you love because you scold them in love, it can only do them good. Well-meant confrontation can also bear fruit.

Heavenly Father, thank You for the comfort that sorrow can be good for me because it draws me to You and because it can change people for the better. Amen.

# At the baptismal font

Peter replied, "Repent and be baptized, every one of you, in the name of Jesus Christ for the forgiveness of your sins. And you will receive the gift of the Holy Spirit."

ACTS 2:38

In the New Testament baptism replaced circumcision, which was the visible sign of God's covenant with His people. When a baby of believing parents is baptized God invites the little person to be His child, although the baby does not understand anything of the ceremony. One day when that baby is grown up, he has to respond personally to God's invitation. At the baptismal font the parents undertake to teach their child about the Lord.

On the first Sunday of every month babies are baptized. We have become so used to the baptismal ceremony that we tend to forget that every such ceremony is not just about the parents and their babies who are baptized, but also concerns every church member who is present in church. The whole congregation takes part in the sacrament of baptism.

Recently I read a moving story about an unmarried mother who brought her baby to be baptized. There was nobody to stand next to her before the pulpit. The whole congregation rose to their feet and made the baptismal promise with her.

When you next attend a baptismal ceremony, remember that you too have an obligation that must be kept.

Pray every month for the babies who are baptized in your congregation and ask that their parents will keep the baptismal promise.

Heavenly Father, thank You that You invite little human children to be Your children. Help me to be personally involved in every baptismal ceremony in my congregation. Amen.

# At the holy communion table

While they were eating, Jesus took bread, gave thanks and broke it, and gave it to his disciples, saying, "Take and eat; this is my body." Then he took the cup, gave thanks and offered it to them, saying, "Drink from it, all of you. This is my blood of the covenant, which is poured out for many for the forgiveness of sins."

MATTHEW 26:26-28

When Jesus passed the bread to His disciples during the celebration of Passover He told them to eat it, because it was His body. He did the same with the wine, but this time He said, "This is my blood."

Most probably the disciples did not understand that this first holy communion pointed to the imminent crucifixion of Jesus. There His body was broken and His blood flowed so that sinners could approach God.

As the blood of the Passover lamb had to be put on the doorframes before the exodus from Egypt so that the angel of death would pass over the Israelites, so Jesus' blood was shed on the cross, so that you, if you believe in Him, can have eternal life. Jesus is also the bread that gives life. If you believe in Him, you will live forever, even after your death.

God gives His sacraments to strengthen the faith of His children by means of an object-lesson. Holy communion should be a very special feast for every Christian. When you take part in holy communion, you can taste and see how the body of Jesus was broken for you and His blood was shed for you so that your sins could be forgiven.

*Lord Jesus, I praise You because Your body was broken for me and Your blood was shed for me. You died so that I can live eternally. Amen.*

# Walk with God

The ministers of my congregation drew up a congregational policy. The first point of this policy reads that our vision for our congregation is that we will "walk with God in profound dependence, care for each of our members, and reach out to all people in distress."

To walk with God means that you, like Enoch of old, will walk with God every day of your journey through life. Someone who walks with God always has God with him. God promises, "I will instruct you and teach you in the way you should go; I will counsel you and watch over you" (Ps. 32:8).

God is there for you at all times. He is by your side when your journey leads you along steep paths or through dark valleys. There is nothing that you need fear, because He will never abandon or forsake you. And at the end of the road heaven awaits those who walk with God.

This month we are going to take some time to contemplate exactly what it means to walk with God on your journey through life.

# On God's path

I will instruct you and teach you in the way you should go; I will counsel you and watch over you.

PSALM 32:8

When a child has to walk to school for the very first time, his mother will almost certainly walk with him, or watch him very carefully to make sure that he takes the right route. And this, says Psalm 32, is precisely what the Lord does with us.

He wants to make sure that you don't lose your way. He wants to keep His eye on you so that He can immediately give you advice when you take a wrong turn. He wants to lead you lovingly through each day, and He also promises to guide you along the very best path for you.

Sometimes you fall out of step with God because you want to make your own decision about which way to go, or you want to set the pace yourself.

This usually happens when you are so involved in your own agenda that you have no time left for God. Sometimes you reject His advice because you want to follow your own head. Sometimes you are impatient and run ahead without waiting for God to lead you. Perhaps you need a few walking lessons today:

- ❃ Learn to hold on to God with trust and confidence in those times when you cannot see the way ahead.
- ❃ Trust in Him when the road becomes steep.
- ❀ Take His hand when you are walking on the precipice.
- ❀ Live every day in complete dependence on Him.

*Heavenly Father, thank You for the assurance that You keep watch over me, that You want to show me the path I should take. Make me willing to walk with You on Your path. Amen.*

# A light for your path

Your word is a lamp to my feet and a light for my path.

PSALM 119:105

I am a hopeless driver and an even worse navigator, and since I have to venture upon unfamiliar roads on a weekly basis, because of my commitments as speaker in various places, I cannot manage without a road map. To be honest, my husband actually also has to show me exactly how the road map works beforehand! And despite all my forward planning I still manage to get lost. At night it's even worse. At night even familiar roads seem completely strange to me.

Every traveler needs a road map that indicates the right road to take to arrive at his destination, otherwise he will probably get seriously lost. It is also very dangerous to set out on an unfamiliar path in the dark. None of us knows what the paths of our lives are going to look like in the future. To travel this unknown road, we need a guide, a road map. And the Lord gives us His Word to be the light for our path.

If, at times, you don't know where to go next; when you lose your way in the dark, all you need to do is open His Word. In the Bible God teaches you step by step how to walk the path of your life, "I gain understanding from Your precepts; therefore I hate every wrong path" (Ps. 119:104).

The Lord's Word will also help you to recognize wrong paths and to avoid them. With the Word as the light for your path you will be able to set out on your life's journey with joy – even in darkness.

Lord, thank You for my Bible that is the light for my path every day. Help me to obey the commandments that You give me in Your Word. Amen.

# Keep away from side roads

My feet have closely followed his steps; I have kept to his way without turning aside.

JOB 23:11

When we traveled through Europe with a tour group for the first time, I was horribly frustrated. There were dozens of the most fascinating little side roads turning off from the main road, leading to centuries old little villages, but our tour bus drove right past all of them.

When we eventually managed, with great effort, to convince our bus driver to turn off on one of these little roads, we ended up on a narrow dead-end street next to a river. To get us out of there and back on the main road he was forced to reverse the big bus all the way down the narrow and winding little road.

Side roads may look very interesting, but they are usually a bad choice, especially if you end up on a side road that causes you to stray from God's path. Job testifies that God knows the path of his life (see Job 23:10) and that he follows God and does not deviate from his way. Can you say the same?

We all struggle to keep in step with God on God's way. There are so many interesting little side roads that entice us, and in addition God's way isn't always the easy or enjoyable way. And yet it is the only right way for you, and also the only path to heaven.

Perhaps you would now like to pray with the psalmist, "Teach me Your way, O LORD, and I will walk in Your truth; give me an undivided heart, that I may fear Your name" (Ps. 86:11).

*Heavenly Father, please keep me from all the many side roads that entice me, and help me to follow Your road and not to deviate from Your ways, as Job did. Amen.*

# *When the road becomes dangerous*

I lift my eyes to the hills – where does my help come from? My help comes from the LORD, the Maker of heaven and earth. The Lord will watch over your coming and going both now and forevermore.

PSALM 121:1-2, 8

In the psalmist's time traveling was extremely dangerous, especially in mountainous areas. Robbers hid among the rocks and attacked and robbed unsuspecting travelers. In this passage the psalmist is all too aware of the danger in which he finds himself and asks for the Lord's help and protection. The Lord undertakes to protect him from all danger, to watch over him wherever he may go – both now and forevermore – as verse 8 so beautifully puts it.

Today it is just as dangerous to go on a journey. You never know when your car will be hijacked or when it will break down in a dark and lonely place.

Fortunately you can hold onto the promise of God's protection on your journey through life. God is always available; He neither slumbers nor sleeps. He is fully capable of protecting you – wherever you may go – and keeping you from all danger.

Unfortunately this does not necessarily mean that you won't be involved in an accident or that you will never find yourself in a dangerous situation. But when these things do cross your path, you can be assured that the Lord is with you and that He has the power to protect you, yes, even after death.

*Heavenly Father, I know that I may look up to You in times of danger. Thank You for the assurance that You will protect me and keep me from all the dangers that come my way. Amen.*

# Time to turn around

See if there is any offensive way in me, and lead me in the way everlasting.

PSALM 139:24

In this psalm the poet asks the Lord to watch over him and to make sure that he does not end up on a wrong path, and to lead him in the right way.

Sometimes we accidentally end up on the wrong road. Shortly after my husband and I were married we took a short-cut through the Karoo on our way from Bloemfontein to Cape Town. We got so lost that we ended up driving about twice the distance of the main road. And this just because we refused to turn around. We thought that we would find our way back to the main road at any moment.

The best thing to do when you discover that you are on a wrong road is to turn around immediately. In doing so you will save yourself a great deal of time and effort in the long run. The same is true of your path through life. You often end up on side roads which seem like short cuts to you, but which can turn out to be a costly mistake.

When this happens, the Lord often warns you through His Holy Spirit. You have probably heard a little voice warning you that you are busy with the wrong things.

When you don't pay enough attention to your quiet time with God, when you don't set aside enough time for God or spend enough time reading the Bible and praying, you can be sure that you are on the wrong path. Turn back, because the only place where you will be truly happy is on God's right path.

*Heavenly Father, I pray that You will clearly show me when I take a wrong turn and make me willing to turn back immediately. Amen.*

# With feet like a deer

It is God who arms me with strength and makes my way perfect. He makes my feet like the feet of a deer; he enables me to stand on the heights.

PSALM 18:32-33

The psalmist writes that God makes his feet like the feet of a deer. God makes his way perfect and enables him to stand steadfastly on the heights. God arms him with strength.

Have you ever seen mountain deer jumping nimbly from cliff to cliff? They move with great assurance on the steepest cliffs. They are not afraid of slipping or falling. And they also always reach the mountaintops safely.

There are times on your journey that you too wish for feet like the feet of a deer, because it feels as if the road is becoming too steep, as if you can't manage the uphill climbs in your own limited strength.

In times like these you can be assured that the Lord will give you new strength when your journey through life tires you. He will put His miraculous strength at your disposal, so that you will be able to soar on the wings of an eagle, will run and not grow weary, will walk and not grow faint (Is. 40:31).

The Lord will keep His children safe on their journeys through life, even if they travel through dangerous places. God wants to offer you His strength today, so that you will have the feet of a deer to help you travel safely and so that your journey through life may be successful.

*Heavenly Father, I praise You for Your promise that You will give me feet like the feet of a deer when my path through life becomes too steep for me. Thank You for Your strength which is at my disposal every day. Amen.*

# The valley of the shadow of death

> He guides me in paths of righteousness for his name's sake. Even though I walk through the valley of the shadow of death, I will fear no evil, for you are with me; your rod and your staff, they comfort me.
>
> PSALM 23:3-4

All our paths sometimes take us through dark places and dangerous valleys; places where we can't see God or hear His voice. In all our lives there are times of crisis when it seems as if God is far away and a stranger, as if He is no longer acting like the loving God we are used to. The psalmist also experienced times like these. In Psalm 10:1 he asks, "Why, O LORD, do You stand far off? Why do You hide Yourself in times of trouble?"

Children of God are by no means exempted from hardship and suffering, but we know that God is with us throughout these times; that He walks with us through the valley of the shadow of death; that He is able to protect us against all dangers; that He never lets go of our hands, even though we sometimes pull our hands from His. And in God's hands His children are always safe.

You may take this promise with you on your journey through life. God is there for you in times of crisis, in times of suffering, in times of sorrow.

Even if you are lost in the valley of the shadow of death, you can still be assured that He will lead you safely through every danger, and that you will one day have eternal life with God.

*Heavenly Father, it is so wonderful to know that You are with me when I have to travel through the valley of the shadow of death; that Your hand guides me even there, and that You will ultimately lead me safely home. Amen.*

# Live close to God

Enoch walked with God; then he was no more, because God took him away.

GENESIS 5:24

Enoch walked with God, always living close to Him. And then one day God came and took this faithful child of His to be with Him. One moment Enoch was on earth, and the next he was in heaven. This remarkable tale of Enoch has always captured my imagination. When I was still in school I thought up dozens of ways in which the Lord could have taken Enoch away.

Enoch was a man who walked every day of his journey through life with God. And the Lord noticed this and rewarded him for it. Enoch did not die, God one day simply took him to heaven.

Do you walk with God every day of your life, as Enoch did? Do you live a life that is tuned in to Him? Is there an intimate relationship between you and God? If your answer is yes, it means that you will have to be willing to make some time in the midst of your busy schedule to focus on God. It means that you will have to put all other things, even important things, aside to make sure that you spend enough time with God.

Enoch's life was such that the people of his time could see that he walked with God. Can people say the same of you?

*Heavenly Father, show me how to walk with You through every day of my life, as Enoch did. Help me to stay close to You so that nothing in my life will become more important than You. Amen.*

# Conversations along the way

The LORD spoke with Moses. The LORD would speak to Moses face to face, as a man speaks with his friend.

EXODUS 33:9, 11

Moses was a great thinker, leader and organizer in the history of Israel. Even though he sometimes came up with many excuses for not being able to follow God's instructions, there was one thing that he was adamantly sure about: he flatly refused to go where God had not promised to walk with him.

On one occasion, when God refused to continue traveling with His people, Moses said unequivocally, "If Your Presence does not go with us, do not send us up from here" (Ex. 33:15). Without God, Moses was not prepared to continue the journey.

On Moses' journey with God communication with God was very important: God spoke to him as a man speaks to his friend. God also gave Moses his law to lay before the people.

Moses teaches us what true communion with God means. In the tent of meeting he spoke to God and listened to His instructions, while God spoke to him as a man speaks with his friend.

Have you learned to refuse to continue on your journey if God is not with you? Have you learned to listen to God at the beginning of each day and to speak to Him before you set out on your day's journey? If you do this, God will also speak to you personally through His Word and walk with you every day of your life's journey, as He did with Moses.

*Heavenly Father, I cannot attempt my life's journey without You. Please walk with me every day and speak to me through Your Spirit and Your Word. Amen.*

# Traveling with a song in your heart

Sing to the LORD, you saints of his; praise his holy name. You turned my wailing into dancing, you removed my sackcloth and clothed me with joy.

PSALM 30:4, 11

It is clear that David's journey with God was a continual joy to him. There is one thing that sets David apart from all the other characters of the Bible: his journey with God was a tremendous joy to him. You only have to read the Psalms to realize how enthusiastically he praised God and how he sang and danced before God to express his joy.

But David also knew the art of complaining to God when things didn't go well. In verse eight of this psalm he writes, "When You hid Your face, I was dismayed." All David's emotions were involved in his walk with God

Your journey with God can sometimes be joyful and sometimes quite dismal and discouraging. Know that you can take your joys as well as your problems to God.

To embark on a journey with God is a way of life in which you and God are intensely aware of each other, in which He is an inextricable part of your entire life.

Someone who walks with God does not keep Him only for use on Sunday, but is involved in a relationship with Him every day of his life. Someone who journeys with God knows that His anger lasts only a moment, but His favor a lifetime.

*Heavenly Father, I praise You for making my life beautiful and enjoyable, so that I can walk Your path with a song in my heart. Thank You for also being with me in times of crisis. Amen.*

# On a painful path

As the two of them went on together, Isaac spoke up and said to his father Abraham, "Father?" "Yes my son?" Abraham replied. "The fire and wood are here," Isaac said, "but where is the lamb for the burnt offering?"

GENESIS 22:6-7

When God asked Abraham to sacrifice his son to Him, Abraham immediately declared himself willing to follow the Lord's command. Abraham had to walk for three days with this incomprehensible command of God in his heart. We don't read of Abraham offering all kinds of excuses, as Moses did. He simply did exactly what God asked of him, despite the fact that it meant the end of all his dreams for the future.

While Abraham traveled for three days on this painful path thousands of questions must have filled his thoughts: How could God possibly expect this kind of sacrifice from him? What plan could God possibly have with bringing this kind of suffering into his life? How could it possibly be for his own good to kill his son? But Abraham never voiced any of these questions.

He also did not travel the road to Moriah by himself; Isaac was with him. And he also had to answer Isaac's innocent questions, "Father, where is the lamb for the offering?" Abraham's answer shows us his trust in God, "The Lord will provide, my son." And God never disappoints those who trust in Him. He indeed provided a ram to be sacrificed in Isaac's place.

God also wants to provide for you when you have to travel on paths of suffering. Trust in Him to fulfill His promise.

Heavenly Father, I praise You for never failing those who trust in You. Thank You for also providing for me in times of hardship. Amen.

# Traveling with the Spirit

Since we live by the Spirit, let us keep in step with the Spirit.

GALATIANS 5:25

On our journey through life the Holy Spirit accompanies us all along the way, but we must be willing to listen to Him, to follow His guidance, and to keep in step with Him.

The Holy Spirit not only lives in you, He also wants to walk with you every step of your journey through life. He wants to grant you sufficient grace for every new day. He doesn't walk with you mile by mile, but step by step.

We are often so obsessed with things that lie in the faraway future; we dream and plan so intensely for the years ahead, that we completely forget about today. And today is actually the only time that really belongs to us, the only time in which we can really make a difference.

Therefore you should stop worrying about the future. Embark on today's brief stretch of the journey with the help of the Holy Spirit. He wants to accompany you every step of the way. When Jesus told His disciples about the Holy Spirit, He promised them that this Comforter would always remain with them, and that He would verify everything that Jesus taught them.

He wants to do this for you too. Walk with Him from this day onwards, and He will be your Comforter and Companion in the days and years that lie ahead.

*Holy Spirit, thank You for living in me and for accompanying me on every step of my journey through life. Thank You for being there to guide and teach me every day. Amen.*

# Sanctified to God

May God himself, the God of peace, sanctify you through and through.
May your whole spirit, soul and body be kept blameless at the coming
of our Lord Jesus Christ.

1 THESSALONIANS 5:23

Paul prays that God will set aside the people of Thessalonica completely for His service so that they will live lives that are completely sanctified and dedicated to Him. When this prayer becomes a reality in your life, it changes you completely. You become a bearer of God's good news and embark on your journey through life with dedication.

In my husband's study there is a picture of the broad and the narrow way. The broad and easy way is filled with pleasurable things, and there are many people traveling it.

On the other hand there is the narrow way, a tortuous and steep path with no pleasures on it. Very few people choose to travel this path. And yet the destination of the broad way is hell while the narrow and difficult path leads to heaven.

In this world it is very difficult to remain on the narrow path, to remain dedicated to God. If you are willing to do this, you will have to set yourself aside for God. If you want to be holy, set apart for God, you must allow Him to detach you from the world and to draw you to Himself. You will also have to be prepared to exchange the pleasant broad path of the world for God's narrow path.

Are you up for the challenge?

*Heavenly Father, I struggle to remain on Your narrow path and to live truly dedicated to You. Please enable me to accomplish these ideals. Amen.*

# God gives peace

May God himself, the God of peace, sanctify you through and through.
May your whole spirit, soul and body be kept blameless at the coming
of our Lord Jesus Christ.

I THESSALONIANS 5:23

It is interesting that the Hebrew word that is translated as
"through and through" only occurs once in the Bible. Its meaning is "completely, totally, without exception." Therefore, when
Paul prays that God will sanctify the church in Thessalonica
through and through, he literally means that every last piece
of their lives should be dedicated to the Lord's service and put
at His disposal.

Complete dedication to God is something that never starts
with yourself. The initiative comes from God. The Lord has to
do something with you before you can be completely sanctified. Sanctification and dedication center on the work of the
Holy Spirit in your life. Without Him it is vanity to even try to
be dedicated and sanctified.

The One who sanctifies you is the God in whom there is
peace. Peace is always related to your relationships with God
and with your fellow human beings. You cannot be completely
dedicated to the Lord unless His peace has become part of
your life.

There is only one true peace and that is the peace given by
Jesus. Through His death on the cross He made peace between
the holy God and sinful people once and for all. His crucifixion
also implies a lasting peace among people. Do you experience
His peace in your life because you are sanctified and dedicated
to Him?

*Heavenly Father, I fall so far short of Your ideals. I pray that
You will sanctify me through and through and grant me Your
peace. Amen.*

# Keep your spiritual fervor

Never be lacking in zeal, but keep your spiritual fervor, serving the LORD.

ROMANS 12:11

We become enthusiastic about many things. Men tend to be very passionate about sport. They can spend hours in front of the TV watching game after game. Women, on the other hand, tend to be enthusiastic about the latest fashions and about shopping.

Sometimes we are enthusiastic about something at first, but later, when we start getting tired, our initial enthusiasm starts to wane. This is often the case in our journey with God. At the beginning of the journey we are fresh, rested and zealous, but the longer and steeper the road, the less enthusiastic we become.

Unfortunately there is precious little enthusiasm to be seen among the members of many congregations. The vast majority of congregations struggle to find people who are willing to help. Evening services and prayer meetings are poorly attended. We complain about more or less everything that we have to give to or do for the Lord: from our offerings of thanks to our service in the church.

You must be enthusiastically committed to the Lord. Where do you stand? Do you still have that same enthusiasm as when you became a Christian? If not, now is the time to pray that He will once again rekindle your first love.

*Heavenly Father, I confess that I am so often tired, discouraged and without enthusiasm. Please grant me an enthusiasm for You that will never waver. Amen.*

# Protection for your journey

---

But the Lord is faithful, and he will strengthen and protect you from the evil one.

2 THESSALONIANS 3:3

---

The Lord promises to protect His children every day of their journey through life; not only from wicked desires and evil men, but also from the evil one.

We often use the verb "protect" when we pray: when we entrust our children to the Lord, when we pray for people who are on a journey, and also when we pray that the Lord will protect us from the evil one. Indeed, we won't get far on our journey through life without God's protection.

However, this verb has another meaning as well: to preserve something. In biblical times salt was used to keep food from spoiling. In the same way, Paul asks the Lord to preserve His children from the decay of sin; to protect us from the influence of the evil one. We are so willing to give in to the temptations that the devil sends our way. And this is precisely the reason why we are sometimes so lacking in enthusiasm for God's kingdom. Only if God protects us from the evil one in this way, will we be able to be immaculately pure when He returns.

The Lord wants to protect you from the evil one for the entire duration of your journey. He promises to strengthen you so that you will be able to resist the attacks of the evil one with the help of His divine armor. In addition you will also possess a new passion for and dedication to Him. Will you allow Him to do this by opening your heart to the work of His Spirit?

---

*Heavenly Father, I pray that You will protect me on my journey through life, that You will also protect me from the evil one, so that I will be able to serve You with ever increasing dedication. Amen.*

# God knows you

O LORD, you have searched me and you know me. You know when I
sit and when I rise; you perceive my thoughts from afar.

PSALM 139:1-2

The psalmist is astonished by the fact that God knows him
so completely. God knows about all the wrongs in his life, He
knows what he is about to say before a single word is on his
tongue, He even knows his thoughts before they enter his mind.
The psalmist concludes with a prayer that God should search
him and test him, and lead him in the way everlasting.

God knows you through and through. There is nothing that
you can hide from Him. He saw you even before you were born;
He Himself wrote each of the days of your life in His book (see
Ps. 139:16).

Actually we dislike being known so completely. In our relationships with others we are used to wearing a mask or playing
a role by pretending to be something we are not. We sometimes
don't even want to admit to ourselves exactly how sinful and
wicked we truly are.

But God knows of every sin that you hide – even the ones
that you hide from yourself. He knows every single ungodly
thought that you secretly think. He knows very well whether
you are traveling the wrong paths on your journey through life.

Confess your sins before God right now. He already knows
about each one of them anyway, and He is willing to forgive
you for all of them.

*Heavenly Father, I don't always like the fact that You know me
so completely, that You know everything that I would prefer to
hide. Please forgive me my sins. Amen.*

# God is everywhere

Where can I go from your Spirit? Where can I flee from your presence? If I go up to the heavens, you are there ... If I rise on the wings of the dawn, if I settle on the far side of the sea, even there your hand will guide me.

PSALM 139:7-10

When the psalmist contemplates the extent of God's knowledge of him, he is filled with fear. His initial astonishment is replaced with fear. He now wants to flee from this God who can see right through him.

He tries to flee to various places – to the heavens, to the depths, to the east or the west – until he finally comes to the conclusion that God is everywhere and it is impossible to hide from Him. No one can flee from God.

Perhaps you have also wanted to flee from God. Unfortunately it is simply impossible. For you it is even more difficult than for the psalmist, because he lived before the crucifixion. When Jesus sent His Holy Spirit to the world, He came to live in each of His children. Through His Spirit God also lives in you; He is an inextricable part of you. You cannot go anywhere without His being with you.

Fortunately you don't need to flee from God. Even though He knows each of your sins, He still loves you. He wants to change you so that you can become more and more like Jesus.

Are you willing to allow Him to do so?

Lord, I know now that I cannot run away from You, because You are everywhere, because You live in me. Transform me and make me holy, so that I can become more and more like Jesus. Amen.

# You are wonderfully made

For you created my inmost being; you knit me together in my mother's womb. I praise you because I am fearfully and wonderfully made; your works are wonderful, I know that full well.

PSALM 139:13-14

The psalmist experiences a third emotion besides wonder and fear. He is consoled by the knowledge that the God who knows him and from whom he is trying to flee, loves him. This God created him wonderfully. He accepted him completely, with all his shortcomings. Even though God knows of every one of the psalmist's sins, He still loves him, and so he has no reason to try to flee from God.

Now he asks God to examine him more thoroughly; to search his thoughts and deeds; to test him and lead him in the way everlasting.

When our granddaughter was born I was once again overwhelmed by the wonder of God's creation of life. How incredible that He can weave together such a perfect little human being in her mother's womb! All the things that He does should fill us with wonder every day of our lives. God is great and wonderful and almighty!

And this wonderful God loves you. He knows you through and through. He is always with you. You can embark on your journey through life with the comfort that God knows you and cares for you. He proved His love for you by the death of His Son. If you ever again doubt God's care, all you need to do is look at Jesus' cross.

*Heavenly Father, how great and wonderful You are! All the things You do fill me with wonder every day of my life. I praise You for the extent of Your love for me. Amen.*

# Make the right choice!

"But if serving the LORD seems undesirable to you, then choose for yourselves this day whom you will serve ... But as for me and my household, we will serve the LORD."

JOSHUA 24:15

Joshua gives the people a choice: they must decide whether they are prepared to serve God sincerely, faithfully and devoutly, and at the same time forsake the pagan idols once and for all. As far as Joshua is concerned, he and his household will serve the Lord.

Hereupon the people answer as one that they promise to serve the Lord, "Far be it from us to forsake the LORD to serve other gods!" (Josh. 24:16).

Unfortunately Joshua knows his people all too well. He knows from experience that they are not able to choose God and stick to their choice in their own strength. Therefore he warns in verse 20 that the Lord will bring disaster on them and make an end to them if they forsake Him.

We are sometimes just like the Israelites: we have already chosen God, but our lives do not bear testimony to this choice.

The Lord wants you to serve Him sincerely, faithfully and devoutly; to choose Him once and for all. Are you prepared to take on this challenge? Just remember that you cannot do it in your own strength, but through His Spirit who lives in you God will enable you to live up to His challenge.

Heavenly Father, I want to choose You as the King of my life and serve You faithfully from today on. Help me through your Spirit to live up to my calling. Amen.

# *All or nothing*

"If you forsake the LORD and serve foreign gods, he will turn and bring disaster on you and make an end of you, after he has been good to you."

JOSHUA 24:20

Joshua warns the people that if they forsake the Lord and serve idols, He will turn against them. This truth remains valid in your life too. Choosing God means that you will affirm your choice through your life. Your faith cannot just be idle words, but should be borne out by your life.

It is so easy to profess that you love the Lord sincerely and want to serve Him, but it is just as easy to become so enamored of the world and worldly matters that you completely forget about all your promises.

We may no longer worship idols of wood and stone, but there are still many things in our lives that we regard as equally or more important than God; things like financial security, our marriage partner, our children, our possessions.

God's people wanted to follow the Lord, but at the same time worship pagan idols. The Lord demands undivided faithfulness from His children. To Him it is all or nothing. He is willing to give you everything, and therefore He does not want His children to run with the hare and hunt with the hounds.

Where do you stand? Are you prepared to affirm your faith by your way of life from now on?

*Heavenly Father, I confess that the faith I profess and my life still sometimes differ radically from each other. Please forgive me and enable me to live in such a way that other people will be able to see that I choose You. Amen.*

# Be careful of wealth

Though your riches increase, do not set your heart on them.

PSALM 62:10

Of all the "idols" that can keep you away from the Lord, wealth is perhaps the most dangerous. Wealthy people are sometimes extremely miserly. I recently read that Paul Getty, one of the wealthiest people in the world, had a coin-operated phone installed in his guest house, to make sure that his guests wouldn't make phone calls on his account.

"Whoever loves money never has money enough; whoever loves wealth is never satisfied with his income" according to Ecclesiastes 5:10. People who believe that all they need to be happy is a little more money ought to be careful, they might never have enough.

In the Sermon on the Mount Jesus warns that we cannot serve God and Mammon. We will have to choose one or the other. When your money and possessions become too important to you, it is very possible that you might start neglecting the Lord.

In your personal financial planning you should distinguish between your needs and your wants. Despite the fact that God promises to care for you and to provide for you, He gives no guarantees that He will satisfy all your wants or desires.

"Better what the eye sees than the roving of the appetite" (Eccl. 6:9). Why not be content with what the Lord gives you, rather than perpetually harping after more? Make sure that your treasure is in heaven rather than here on earth.

*Heavenly Father, I confess that I so often still wish for more money. Forgive me and make me satisfied with what You have entrusted to me. Amen.*

# The Lord determines your steps

In his heart a man plans his course, but the LORD determines his steps.

PROVERBS 16:9

Man proposes but God disposes, is a true proverb. People may plan their journey through life to the last detail by deciding exactly where they are going and what they want to do. But the best of our human planning can go awry if we don't take God into consideration. The last word always belongs to Him.

There is nothing wrong with planning your future, but you must never forget that God has a plan for your life. When you make your own plans, when you dream about your future, when you carefully plot the path that you would like to take, you must never lose sight of the fact that things can turn out differently from what you expect, if God wills it so.

I know a young man who wanted to become a doctor, but because of a serious illness that he contracted in his final year at school it was impossible for him to pursue his chosen career. I also know a couple who were about to get married when the young man suddenly died in a car accident.

You can plan the path that you would like to take, as long as you always realize that the Lord is the one who ultimately decides what your journey through life is going to be like. Perhaps it will be very different from the way you would have wanted it to be.

If this is the case in your life, hold on to the knowledge that the Lord's way is the best way for you, even if it doesn't seem like it at the moment.

*Heavenly Father, I am sorry that I so often make big plans without consulting You. Help me to remember that You ultimately determine my path. Amen.*

# Traveling with hope

Let the morning bring me word of your unfailing love, for I have put my trust in you. Show me the way I should go, for to you I lift up my soul.

PSALM 143:8

When the psalmist wrote this psalm, he had reached a very steep incline on his path through life. His problems had become too much for him and therefore he implored the Lord to answer him quickly, because his spirit was failing (see Ps. 143:7). He didn't have strength for the road ahead.

Then he remembered how the Lord had always helped and supported him in the past, and his cry of distress became a beautiful testimony, "Let the morning bring me word of Your unfailing love, for I have put my trust in You. Show me the way I should go, for to You I lift up my soul."

He asked the Lord to lead him on level ground and to teach him to do His will. As God answered his prayer he became hopeful and strong again. He was no longer discouraged and weary.

On your journey through life there will be times when you are tired and completely discouraged. In times like these you would do well to follow the psalmist's example. Lift your hands to God in prayer. Focus on Him instead of the mountains ahead of you. Ask that He will once again give you hope and lead you on level ground. He wants to do this for you.

*Heavenly Father, You know that I am weary and discouraged and that I am not up to attempting the road that lies ahead of me. Thank You that I can still put my hope in You. Please provide me with strength for the journey. Amen.*

# God goes before you

"The LORD himself goes before you and will be with you; he will never leave you nor forsake you. Do not be afraid; do not be discouraged."

DEUTERONOMY 31:8

Joshua was rather apprehensive of following in the footsteps of the formidable Moses in leading the Israelites. When his courage started to fail him, Moses encouraged him with this beautiful promise of God's continual presence on this journey. Moses said that Joshua need not fear the road ahead, because God would not only go with him, but would actually go before him. He would never leave Joshua nor forsake him. "Be strong and courageous. Do not be afraid or terrified ... for the LORD your God goes with you" (Deut. 31:6).

The one thing that you can be absolutely sure of if you travel with God is that you will never have to walk alone. You have the assurance that God will go before you, as He went before His people in the desert.

Like Joshua you need not fear anything that awaits you on your journey, not even when your journey occasionally takes you through times of suffering. Even there in the darkness God is with you, even during times of hardship you can walk at His side.

It is precisely when your path becomes steep that you feel God's presence the clearest. He will lead you through the valley of the shadow of death so that you can one day arrive safely at the home of the Father.

*Heavenly Father, it is so wonderful that You go before me on my journey through life, and that I can lay claim to Your presence every day of my life. Thank You for never leaving me alone. Amen.*

# Safe in His hands

My soul clings to you; your right hand upholds me.

PSALM 63:8

You are with me; your rod and your staff, they comfort me.

PSALM 23:4

Here the psalmist testifies that his soul clings to the Lord in his distress because he can always count on the Lord's support. God's children are safe when His hands hold them up. We often read in the Bible of people calling on God in times of trouble, and we know that the Lord helped them every time.

Peter was very self-assured when he managed to walk on water, but when he realized that he was sinking, he called to Jesus, "Save me, Lord!" And Jesus immediately stretched out His hand and pulled Peter from the water.

In times of danger, God's hands are always there to save you when that becomes necessary. No danger is too great. God can save you from all dangers, but you have to promise to cling to Him.

If you remain close to Him, His hand will never let go of yours. Even when you let go of God's hand, He will still hold you, "I give them eternal life, and they shall never perish; no one can snatch them out of My hand," Jesus promises in John 10:28. And in James 4:8 He gives another promise, "Come near to God and He will come near to you."

*Lord Jesus, thank You for always grasping my hand tightly. Thank You that I am always safe in Your hand and that nothing will ever snatch me from You. Amen.*

# In God's presence

"Go up to the land flowing with milk and honey. But I will not go with you, because you are a stiff-necked people and I might destroy you on the way."

EXODUS 33:3

After the Israelites made the golden calf to replace the living God, the Lord finally became tired of their persistent disobedience. He told Moses and the people to continue the journey by themselves, because He was not prepared to travel any further with them. But Moses refused to take one step without the assurance of God's presence and assistance, "If Your Presence does not go with us, do not send us up from here," he said (Ex. 33:15).

Moses not only refused to continue the journey, but he also built a house for the Lord right there in the desert, the Tent of Meeting. The tent was erected outside the camp, not amid his stiff-necked people, and it remained a sign of God's presence among them.

When Moses went into the tent to speak to the Lord, the people could see the pillar of cloud in front of the entrance to the tent. And here, in the Tent of Meeting, the Lord spoke directly to Moses, as a man speaks to his friend.

If you want God to accompany you on your journey through life, you will also need to have a meeting place where you can commune with God, and where He can speak to you from His Word. Decide on a special time and place where you can meet with the Lord personally on a daily basis.

*Heavenly Father, I don't want to embark on my journey through life without You. Please speak to me every day and give me Your peace. Amen.*

# When you stumble

The LORD upholds all those who fall and lifts up all who are bowed down. He hears their cry and saves them. The LORD watches over all who love him.

PSALM 145:14, 19-20

The psalmist praises the Lord for lifting all those who have fallen and all who are bowed down; for hearing His children's cries of distress and saving them.

During your journey through life you will undoubtedly encounter steep uphills and loose treacherous rocks; places where you will easily stumble, lose your balance and fall and hurt yourself.

If you have ever had to console one of your children who had a bad fall, you will know how they feel. They don't want to walk any further. It is during times like these that you just want to sit down next to the road and stay there.

Fortunately you will never have to do this. The Lord is always there to help you up when you have fallen. He is always willing to uphold you, especially on those days when you feel discouraged and dejected.

With Him at your side you can embark on your journey with confidence, every day of your life. No uphill or incline will be too much for you with God's helping hand supporting you.

Dangers may be lurking on your journey through life. But here too you can call upon the Lord's protection. He will hear you when you call for help and He will protect you.

*Heavenly Father, it is wonderful that You are with me to help me when I fall, to uplift me when I am dejected, and to protect me when I am in danger. Amen.*

# The law as a road map

"This is the covenant I will make with them after that time, says the LORD. I will put my laws in their hearts, and I will write them on their minds."

HEBREWS 10:16

People who choose God are redeemed from sin for all eternity by Jesus' sacrifice of atonement. In the Old Testament God gave His people the Ten Commandments so that they could know how He wanted them to live. In the last days, the writer of Hebrews says, God institutes a new covenant, He writes His laws on the hearts and minds of His children.

God's law is a constant "dotted line" next to our path through life which shows us how the Lord wants us to walk. Contrary to what we believe, this law is not a bunch of "musts" and "must nots." Rather, it is a road map that shows us the dangerous areas to watch out for.

It is a tried and tested way to travel safely through life, so that we will reach the other side in one piece. But most important, the law also shows us what to do so that we can one day reach our desired destination.

God wants to write His law on your heart and mind, so that you can know how to walk in His way. However, before you can apply the law of God to your own life, you need to know exactly what it entails. Take some time to read Exodus 20 carefully and mark the commandments that you still need to work on in your own life.

*Heavenly Father, thank You for the road map of Your law that shows me how You want me to live. Make it possible for me to follow Your commandments conscientiously. Amen.*

# *Praise the Lord!*

> Praise God in his sanctuary ... Praise him for his acts of power ... praise him with the clash of cymbals ... Let everything that has breath praise the LORD. Praise the LORD.
>
> PSALM 150:1-2, 5-6

Music and song were inextricably part of worship in the Old Testament. And in this worship, praise played a crucial role. Psalm 150 is the conclusion and summary of the entire Book of Psalms, and the message of this psalm is that we should praise God with everything that is in us. What is more, we should call all other things – musical instruments and "everything that has breath" – to join us in praising the Lord.

In our contemporary setting the value of praise has diminished tremendously. A new brand of toothpaste or a new kind of car is presented to us with so much praise that we tend to take such excessive expressions of praise with a pinch of salt. This must definitely not be the case with the praise that we offer God.

Praising God should always come from deep inside us, and must never depend on external circumstances. We can and must also praise God in times of hardship and suffering.

Do you praise God daily with everything you have, because you love Him and have His joy in your heart? The more you praise the Lord, the greater your joy will become. Joy comes from seeing God in your circumstances and rejoicing over Him, even through difficult times.

*Lord, my Lord, I want to praise You with my whole heart, with everything that is within me. I want to praise You for all the good things that You bestow on me. Praise the Lord! Amen.*

# Getting to know Jesus

This month we are going to focus on the characteristics of Jesus so that we can be conformed to His likeness.

Jesus was a human being just like us, with one difference: He was without sin. However, Jesus is also God. He and the Father are one.

Jesus left heaven and died on the cross so that we can be saved. He is holy and without sin. He is our shepherd. He is willing to serve, although He is the King of the universe. He is omnipotent, merciful and full of love. He renews us, and without Him we can never enter heaven. He conquered death when He rose from the grave.

At present He is sitting at the right hand of God and one day He will come again, so that He can take us to the Father.

It is God's will for every child of His to become like Jesus. "For those God foreknew He also predestined to be conformed to the likeness of His Son" as Paul writes to the Christians in Rome (Rom. 8:29).

# Jesus is God

"I tell you the truth," Jesus answered, "before Abraham was born, I am!"

JOHN 8:58

When a group of Jews accused Jesus of being a servant of the devil, Jesus told them that He was in the service of His Father. He was greater than their forefather Abraham, because He existed long before Abraham.

When God introduced Himself to Moses at the burning bush He told Moses that His Name was "I AM WHO I AM" (Ex. 3:14). This Name was so holy for the Jews that they did not want to pronounce it. It was the same Name that Jesus used here when He told the group of Jews who He was. This declaration of Jesus is undeniable proof of His divinity.

His divinity is affirmed time and again in the Bible: He was with God in the beginning. "Through Him all things were made; without Him nothing was made that has been made," John witnesses (Jn. 1:2-3).

Therefore Jesus was already present at creation. "I and the Father are one," Jesus said in John 10:30.

The author of Hebrews writes as follows about the excellent greatness of the Son of God, "The Son is the radiance of God's glory and the exact representation of His being, sustaining all things by His powerful word." And God Himself says, "Let all God's angels worship Him" (Heb. 1:3, 6).

Jesus is great and glorious, eternal and omnipotent. He is God. If you believe in Him you must acknowledge and glorify Him as God.

*Lord Jesus, I now know that You are truly God; that the glory of God radiates from You and that You have existed for all eternity. I want to praise and worship You. Amen.*

# Who sees Him, sees the Father

Jesus answered: "Don't you know me, Philip? Even after I have been among you such a long time? Anyone who has seen me has seen the Father."

JOHN 14:9

When Philip asked Jesus to show them the Father, Jesus realized that His disciples did not yet understand that He was truly God. "Anyone who has seen Me has seen the Father" He told Philip.

In Old Testament times God was not visible to human eyes. He was too exceedingly holy. "You cannot see My face, for no one may see Me and live," God told Moses in Exodus 33:20. He did allow Moses to see His glory from behind. However, when Jesus came to earth, it became possible for humans to see God.

When Jesus came to earth as a human being it was possible for ordinary people to touch Him, see Him and talk to Him. John writes in 1 John 1:1, "That ... which we have heard, which we have seen with our eyes, which we have looked at and our hands have touched." For three years the disciples of Jesus could travel with Him and listen to what He taught.

In what He said and did on earth Jesus reflected His Father. In the body of His Son God Himself became accessible to the people. In Jesus God comes near to you. If you know and love Him, you also know and love the Father.

Lord Jesus, I praise You for making God accessible to me. Thank You that I can look at You and at the things You did and said and see God Himself in them. Amen.

# Jesus, our Redeemer

> But the angel said to them, "Do not be afraid. I bring you good news of great joy that will be for all the people. Today in the town of David a Savior has been born to you; he is Christ the Lord."
>
> LUKE 2:10-11

The first people who heard the message of the angels were a little group of fearful shepherds: the long expected Messiah whose coming they had been looking forward to for many years had at last been born.

The shepherds did not hesitate. Their initial fear soon changed into joy at the good news. They departed immediately for Bethlehem to see the Savior with their own eyes. After they had seen Him, they told everybody with whom they came into contact that the Messiah had been born.

Unfortunately the Jews had a wrong understanding of the coming of the Messiah. They believed that He would free them from Roman oppression. Because He did not comply with their expectations they crucified Him.

Jesus is still your Messiah. He is the only one who can save you from sin. He comes to everybody who believes in Him. He died on the cross so that you could be saved once and for all from your sins. Do you worship Him as the Redeemer? Do you meet Him daily by reading His Word? Do you follow the example that the shepherds set two thousand years ago: are you also willing to tell other people the good news about Jesus?

*Lord Jesus, I worship You as my Redeemer. Thank You that You make it possible for me to be saved from sin. Please help me to tell the joyful news to everybody. Amen.*

# The blood of Jesus purifies from sin

But if we walk in the light, as he is in the light, we have fellowship with one another, and the blood of Jesus, his Son, purifies us from all sin.

1 JOHN 1:7

Every time a baby is baptized and sprinkled with water, this sacrament becomes a lesson on God's love and mercy for His children. Just as water is necessary to cleanse us, so the blood of Jesus purifies us from sin.

In Old Testament times an animal was killed as a sacrifice for the sins of the people. Jesus died on the cross, His blood flowed so that we could be purified from sin. This purifying process is not completed at once. Just as we should wash our hands every time before we eat, the purification by the blood of Jesus is an ongoing process in our lives. The literal translation of today's Scripture is: We are being cleansed of every sin by the blood of Jesus.

If you believe in Jesus, His blood purifies you from sin. However, when you realize that you are once again sinning, you should ask Him immediately to wash away the sin. Jesus is willing to forgive your sins every time. However, be careful that you never make His grace cheap by continuing to sin because you are sure that He will keep on forgiving you.

Lord Jesus, thank You that You were willing to die so that I could be reconciled with God. Thank You for Your blood that flowed on the cross so that my sins could be purified. Amen.

# Jesus is the Prince of Peace

"The rising sun will come to us from heaven to shine on those living in darkness and in the shadow of death, to guide our feet into the path of peace."

LUKE 1:78-79

When Isaiah prophesied that God would change the destiny of His people by the birth of a child, he said that this child would be called Wonderful Counselor, Mighty God, Everlasting Father, and Prince of Peace. Jesus is the Prince of Peace. When He came to the earth He brought His peace into the prevailing strife. "For He Himself is our peace ... His purpose was to create in Himself one new man ... thus making peace," Paul writes to the church in Ephesus (Eph. 2:14-15).

The peace that Jesus brings is totally different from worldly peace, which usually only means a truce. Jesus' peace brings healing. It restores relationships, not only between God and man, but also between man and man and between man and nature.

A person with the peace of Jesus in his heart can live peacefully in the midst of violence and strife in the knowledge that God is in control. The peace that Jesus gives also demands of you to live in peace with other people. It makes you a peacemaker so that you will reconcile people with one another.

Jesus wants to place your feet on the path of peace because you serve and love the Prince of Peace. Are you ready to trust Him to do it for you?

*Lord Jesus, I pray for Your peace in my life. Make me a peacemaker so that people may be reconciled with one another, and place my feet on the path of peace. Amen.*

# Jesus is the bread of life

"I am the bread of life. He who comes to me will never go hungry, and he who believes in me will never be thirsty."

JOHN 6:35

The sixth chapter of John begins with the story of Jesus feeding the five thousand with five loaves and two fish. Jesus cared about hungry people and He supplied their needs. The crowd followed Him because they expected Him to supply their needs and not because they knew who He was.

Jesus knew it and therefore He said, "You are looking for Me, not because you saw miraculous signs but because you ate the loaves and had your fill" (Jn. 6:26). Then He added that He was the true bread of life who would give life to the world. People coming to Him would never again go hungry.

When we think about bread, we think about staple food, a necessity to survive. Therefore, Jesus Himself taught us to pray, "Give us this day our daily bread." When Jesus said that He is the bread who gives life, He wanted to stress that just as bread is a necessity for life, so we cannot live without Him.

"Jesus offers Himself as Savior of the world. He gives everyone a choice – the choice to live or die," Johan Smit writes. Have you already chosen Jesus as your bread of life? Then you have the assurance that you will never again go hungry.

Lord Jesus, thank You that You are the bread of life and that I can believe in You, so that I need never go hungry again. Amen.

# Jesus renews people

Therefore, if anyone is in Christ, he is a new creation; the old has gone, the new has come! All this is from God, who reconciled us to himself through Christ.

2 CORINTHIANS 5:17-18

When somebody believes in Jesus, God makes him a new creation. He shows him his sins and persuades him to let go of them. Such a person is less self-centered and more aware of other people's needs. Such a person becomes more and more like Jesus and His characteristics become visible in his life.

All this is from God, Paul writes. This change for the better is completely the work of God – you cannot do it yourself. The only thing that you have to do is to be willing to allow Him to change you.

This change must start in your mind, "Do not conform any longer to the pattern of this world, but be transformed by the renewing of your mind," Paul advises the church in Rome (Rom. 12:2).

"You were taught ... to be made new in the attitude of your minds; and to put on the new self, created to be like God in true righteousness and holiness," Paul writes to the Ephesians (Eph. 4: 22-24).

God wants to renew you so that you can become more and more like Jesus. He wants to teach you to live a new life and think new thoughts. Will you allow Him to do it for you?

Lord Jesus, I do want to become more and more like You, so that other people will be able to see You in my life. Change my life and my mind and help me to walk in Your footsteps from now on. Amen.

# The only way to heaven

Jesus answered, "I am the way and the truth and the life. No one comes to the Father except through me."

JOHN 14:6

In our era religion has become very people-friendly. People seem to do everything they can so that no one will be offended.

We try frantically to accommodate one another in such a way that everybody is right in the end. And ultimately people want to believe that every religion is the same: we are all on the way to the same place if we only live right.

It does not matter whether we worship Allah, Mohammed or Jesus. Most people do recognize Jesus as a great prophet, but they will not acknowledge that He is the only Savior, God's Son and God Himself.

There is only one way to get to heaven and that is through faith in Jesus. There is no other way in which we can go to heaven. Anyone who does not go by this way can reach the Father.

Jesus was speaking to His disciples about the future. He is not only the Way, but also the Truth and the Life. His words stand fast and only by believing in Him can one live eternally. He is not only the point of departure for heaven, but also the destination. Have you met God yet?

*Lord Jesus, thank You that I can know for sure that You are the Way and the Truth and the Life. Thank You that I will live eternally because I believe in You. Amen.*

# The good shepherd

> "I am the good shepherd. The good shepherd lays down his life for the sheep."
>
> JOHN 10:11

The people in Jesus' time understood the image of the shepherd very well. They all knew shepherds who tended their sheep. A shepherd in Jesus' time always stayed with his sheep. Such a shepherd knew every one of his sheep by name. He led his flock; the sheep knew his voice and followed him with great trust. He never left them alone.

He had to see to it that they had food and water and he had to protect his sheep from danger, sometimes putting himself in mortal danger. David killed a lion and a bear while he was tending his father's flock. The shepherd was even willing to die for the sheep if he had to.

In Psalm 23 the psalmist paints a beautiful picture of such a shepherd: He looks after his sheep, he takes them to a place where they can get grazing and water, he protects them from dangers.

In today's unsafe world we all need a shepherd: someone who knows us completely, someone who can look after us and protect us from danger. You do have such a shepherd. He has already laid down His life for you. He knows you, He wants to look after you, protect you and supply all your needs.

Jesus is not only the shepherd, but also the gate for the sheep. Only through Him can you enter heaven. Are you willing to follow Him unconditionally?

*Lord Jesus, I praise You for being my shepherd who looks after me every day, who leads me and who will protect me in dangerous places. Amen.*

# Jesus is our Comforter

He has sent me to bind up the brokenhearted ... to proclaim the year of the LORD's favor ... to comfort all who mourn, and provide for those who grieve in Zion – to bestow on them a crown of beauty instead of ashes, the oil of gladness instead of mourning, and a garment of praise instead of a spirit of despair.

ISAIAH 61:1-3

In this passage of Scripture the prophet Isaiah proclaims a message of comfort. God sent him to announce redemption for His people; to assure them that they no longer needed to be disheartened, because God Himself would bestow mercy on them. They received the promise that the Lord would comfort all who grieved.

Grief forms an inextricable part of our lives here on earth and not one of us can escape it. However, Christians have the guarantee that their grief will only last for a short while. At the end of their lives heaven is awaiting them. Their grief and hurt will come to an end forever.

When Jesus was born Isaiah's prophesy became true. (Mt. 11:2-9; Lk. 7:18-35). Jesus is the One who guarantees comfort for us and who will bind up the brokenhearted.

Jesus wants to be your comforter. He wants to know about your grief. Do tell Him about it. Through the grief you experience He wants to equip you to comfort others.

Lord Jesus, thank You that You are always there to comfort me in times of grief. Help me to see the hurt of other people and to comfort them as You do me. Amen.

# Jesus became poor for our sakes

For you know the grace of our Lord Jesus Christ, that though he was rich, yet for your sakes he became poor, so that you through his poverty might become rich.

2 CORINTHIANS 8:9

Paul is speaking here about Christian generosity. He tells the story of the poor congregation of Macedonia who were willing to give more than they could afford because they loved the Lord.

When you love somebody you enjoy sacrificing things for the sake of that person. We usually buy bigger presents than we can comfortably afford for those people whom we treasure. We are completely willing to make sacrifices so that they can benefit.

In the same way Jesus was willing to leave heaven and to give up His divine status and wealth for the sake of the people He loves.

In heaven He was rich and important – angels bowed down before Him. Nevertheless, He was willing to come to earth as an ordinary human. He was willing to be born in a dirty stable, to live a pauper's life on earth, to be humiliated on the cross and to die a cruel death so that we, who believe in Him, can one day share in heaven.

Jesus was willing to come to earth so that you can inherit heaven. He became poor so that you can share in God's wealth eternally. Have you accepted what Jesus did for you?

Lord Jesus, how can I thank You that You were willing to become poor so that I can be rich in God? Make me willing on my part to sacrifice things for Your sake. Amen.

# The light of the world

> The people walking in darkness have seen a great light; on those living in the land of the shadow of death a light has dawned.
>
> Isaiah 9:2

When the prophet Isaiah announced the coming of the Messiah, he said that the people walking in darkness had seen a great light, that on the people living in the land of the shadow of death a light had dawned.

At the birth of Jesus a bright light indeed shone on the dark fields of Bethlehem when an angel announced the coming of the Light of the world.

Jesus' birth put an end to the darkness of sin that had existed since the fall. All people who believe in Him are now children of light. They can live in light because they believe in the Light of the world. However, it is not enough only to live in the light of Jesus: He expects of us to be lights for Him as well.

"It is too small a thing for you to be My servant to restore the tribes of Jacob ... I will also make you a light for the Gentiles, that you may bring salvation to the ends of the earth," God told His people in Isaiah 49:6.

The Lord wants to make you a light like Israel of old, a light spreading His joyful message so that it will reach the ends of the earth and everybody will be able to become God's children.

Are you such a light?

*Lord Jesus, I adore You as the Light of the world that has driven away the darkness of sin. Make me a light for You so that other people can also believe in You. Amen.*

# Live in the light

> If you spend yourselves in behalf of the hungry and satisfy the needs
> of the oppressed, then your light will rise in the darkness.
>
> ISAIAH 58:10

God chose Israel to be His people out of all the peoples on earth. He made a covenant with them and promised to be their God if they would undertake to obey His commandments. Unfortunately the Israelites strayed from God and time and again exchanged the true God for heathen idols.

It is still possible for you to be religious without truly living close to the Lord. God's children proclaim their faith through the way they live. God told the prophet Isaiah what people should do to be living in His light, "If you spend yourself on behalf of the hungry, if you satisfy the needs of the oppressed, your light will rise in the darkness."

If you belong to the Lord, you are a child of the light. For you were once in darkness, but now you are light in the Lord. Live as children of light, Paul wrote to the Ephesians (Eph. 5:8).

To be a child of light requires that you will not only see the needs of other people, but that you will also be willing to do something about them. If you are willing, you can take the beautiful promise of Isaiah 58:11 for yourself, "The LORD will guide you always; He will satisfy your needs."

*Lord Jesus, I want to live in Your light. Open my eyes to the needs of others and make me willing to help those in need. Amen.*

# Forgiven through Jesus

When he had received the drink, Jesus said, "It is finished." With that, he bowed his head and gave up his spirit.

JOHN 19:30

When we pray, we like to ask God to forgive our sins "for Jesus' sake." God forgives us because Jesus earned forgiveness for us on the cross. Jesus Himself is the image of forgiveness. Even on the cross He prayed for the people who were killing Him, "Father, forgive them, for they do not know what they are doing" (Lk. 23:34).

All of us are sinners and therefore every one of us is guilty of the death of Jesus. Because Jesus paid the price for our sins on the cross, God is now willing to forgive our sins. By His death on the cross Jesus settled our sin account once and for all. On the cross He brought the supreme sacrifice.

Therefore we do not have to bring sacrifices again and again like the priests in the Old Testament. The single sacrifice of Jesus was enough.

Because Jesus died, there is forgiveness for everyone who believes in Him, everyone who accepts that He died in our place.

"It is finished," Jesus said before He died. These words mean that He had fulfilled God's will. As Jesus forgave the people who crucified Him, He asks that God will now forgive each one of your sins, because He has already paid for them in your place.

Lord Jesus, thank You for earning God's forgiveness for me on the cross. Make me willing to forgive others as You have forgiven me. Amen.

# Jesus is ready to forgive

Jesus ... asked her, "Has no one condemned you?" "No one, sir," she said. "Then neither do I condemn you," Jesus declared. "Go now and leave your life of sin."

JOHN 8:10-11

Adultery was a serious sin in Jesus' time. When a woman was caught in the act of adultery, the bystanders were immediately ready to stone her. Indeed, the law allowed it. However, in this instance they first wanted to know what Jesus had to say about it. He silenced the accusers by saying that the one without sin should throw the first stone. At this they all walked away quietly and left Jesus alone with the woman.

In contrast to all the others Jesus was immediately willing to forgive her sin. He did, however, add that she had to leave her life of sin.

Jesus is still willing to forgive each one of your sins. However, there is a condition: out of gratitude you must be willing to forgive other people who hurt you and damage you.

Bear with each other and forgive whatever grievances you may have against one another. "Forgive as the Lord forgave you," Paul wrote to the church in Colosse (Col. 3:13).

Therefore, stop asking whose fault it was. Be willing to forgive the other person even though you might have been totally blameless.

*Lord Jesus, how good You are for not holding my many sins against me, but forgiving each one of them. Help me to do the same with everybody who sins against me. Amen.*

# Jesus is willing to serve

"For even the Son of Man did not come to be served, but to serve, and to give his life as a ransom for many."

MARK 10:45

On a certain occasion when John and James asked Jesus whether they could one day sit at His right and left hand, Jesus told them that He did not come to this world to be served but to serve.

Jesus was ready to turn His willingness to serve into deeds. When not one of His disciples was willing to do the slave's work of washing feet, He did it.

In his book *Just Like Jesus* Max Lucado gives a beautiful description of Jesus kneeling to wash the disciples' feet. "In this case the One with the towel and bowl is the King of the universe. Hands that shaped the stars, now wash away filth. Fingers that formed mountains now massage toes. And the One before whom all the nations will one day kneel now kneels before His disciples. Hours before His own death, Jesus' concern is singular. More than removing dirt, Jesus is removing doubt. He wants His disciples to know how much He loves them." (p. 18).

Because Jesus was willing to wash His disciples' feet, you must also be willing to serve other people if you want to walk in His footsteps. "I have set you an example that you should do as I have done," Jesus says in John 13:15.

Are you willing to do this?

*Lord Jesus, it is difficult to serve other people. Thank You that You were willing to wash the disciples' feet; to be a servant. Help me do this too. Amen.*

# Jesus is omnipotent

He replied, "You of little faith, why are you so afraid?" Then he got up and rebuked the winds and the waves, and it was completely calm.

MATTHEW 8:26

When the disciples were caught in a storm at sea, they were indignant because Jesus was sleeping in the midst of the danger. They woke Him and begged Him to save them. Jesus did, but He first wanted to know why they were afraid and why they had so little faith.

Jesus is omnipotent. He can do anything. Even the elements of nature are subjected to His power. By His powerful word the waves and the wind abated. He has the power to make the blind see, to make the deaf hear, to heal the sick and even to restore the dead to life.

We all get scared in dangerous situations but we should remember that Jesus is omnipotent and that He can calm the storms in our lives. You too need not fear anything. If you believe in Him, His miracle-working power is available to you. The only thing you need to do is to trust Him.

When Jesus gave His disciples the great commission, He affirmed to them, "All authority in heaven and on earth has been given to Me" (Mt. 28:18). He is the Ruler over heaven and earth, He has the final word about everything. If you are willing to obey His commands, He will make it possible for you.

Lord Jesus, I praise You because all the power in heaven and on earth belongs to You, and You grant me that power when I need it. Amen.

# *Jesus is King*

"Say to the daughter of Zion, 'See, your king comes to you, gentle and riding on a donkey, on a colt, the foal of a donkey.'"

MATTHEW 21:5

When Jesus rode into Jerusalem, the crowd became delirious with excitement. They praised Him as the Messiah whose coming they had been awaiting for such a long time. When Jesus rode into Jerusalem, it was the only time when He acknowledged by His actions that He was King, and it was also the only time when the Jews acknowledged Him as King.

Their expectation of Jesus as King was, however, totally wrong. They believed that He was the king who would free them from the hated Roman oppression. When Jesus was not the kind of king they expected, they crucified Him, because, according to them, He acted in blasphemy by posing as a king.

When Pilate later pertinently asked Jesus, "Are you the king of the Jews?" ... He answered, "It is as you say" (Mt. 27:11). Before Jesus was crucified, the soldiers mocked Him. They clothed Him in the purple mantle of a king and put a crown of thorns on His head. When Jesus was crucified, Pilate let a written charge be put on the cross, THIS IS JESUS, THE KING OF THE JEWS (Mt. 27:37).

Jesus is King, the eternal King. His kingdom is no earthly kingdom, but a heavenly kingdom. This divine King wants to be the King of your life too and He wants you to be obedient to Him.

*Lord Jesus, I praise You as the King of my life. Help me to acknowledge and obey You as King in every sphere of my life. Amen.*

# Jesus became human

Who, being in very nature God ... made himself nothing, taking the very nature of a servant, being made in human likeness.

PHILIPPIANS 2:6-7

Jesus is God, but He was also completely human. When He was on earth, He experienced every human emotion: He suffered, was hurt and He loved. He cried when His friend Lazarus died, was afraid when He realized what the Way of the Cross entailed. On occasion He also suffered hunger and thirst. Satan even tried to tempt Him in His human capacity, but Jesus did not give in to temptation.

Although Jesus was fully human, there was one difference: Jesus was without sin. As a sinless human being Jesus was willing to bear the sin of all of humanity on the cross.

On the cross Jesus was lonely – His disciples all forsook Him and it seemed as if His Father abandoned Him. On the cross God's anger at the sins of all humanity was directed at Jesus alone. For this reason He called out, "My God, My God, why have you forsaken Me?" (Mt. 27:46). On the cross Jesus was forsaken by God so that we need never again be without God.

Because He was human Jesus understands you completely. He knows how people think and feel. Therefore, you can bring each of your problems freely to Him – He has compassion on human beings, because He Himself was one.

Lord Jesus, thank You that You were willing to become human so that my sins could be forgiven. Thank You that You understand me completely because You became human. Amen.

# *Water that gives life*

> "But whoever drinks the water I give him will never thirst. Indeed, the water I give him will become in him a spring of water welling up to eternal life."
>
> JOHN 4:14

Once when Jesus was on His way to Jerusalem, He stopped at a well and did something that in those days was unheard of. He asked a Samaritan woman for a drink of water.

He asked a Samaritan woman who came to the well to fetch water, to draw Him some water.

Immediately the woman wanted to know why Jesus, who was a Jew, would ask her for water. Jesus answered the woman by saying that if she knew who He was, she would ask Him for living water. Whoever drinks of the living water will never thirst again.

This offer sounded very attractive and immediately the woman asked, "Sir, give me this water" (Jn. 4:15). She didn't at all understand what Jesus meant. When He asked her to go and call her husband, she admitted that she had no husband. Jesus had already known this. Then He told her that He was the Messiah.

When the woman went back to her village, she told the people about Jesus and many Samaritans believed in Him.

Jesus knows everything about you too and He wants to offer His living water to you so that you will never again be thirsty. He wants to fulfill every one of your spiritual longings.

*Lord Jesus, thank You that I will never again be thirsty because I have learned to drink of Your living water. Help me to tell others about You. Amen.*

# Jesus made time for His Father

One of those days Jesus went out to a mountainside to pray, and spent the night praying to God.

Luke 6:12

Even though He was sometimes very tired and mostly very busy, Jesus always made time to communicate with His Father.

In this way He received strength for the things that His Father expected of Him, as well as the right guidance when He needed it.

The time that Jesus spent in prayer gave direction to His life. Before He selected His disciples, He prayed; before He had to die on the cross, He prayed again. For these times of prayer, Jesus isolated Himself. He made time to especially be alone with His Father.

You should also make time to be alone with God. It is very important to set aside enough time in your busy schedule so that you can actually meet with God in prayer and Bible study.

Perhaps the evening is not the best time if you are so tired that you fall asleep when you are praying. Set apart a special time and place where you can communicate with your heavenly Father in solitude.

Take the telephone off the hook and lock your door so that your children and husband know that you want to be alone to speak to your Father. Then you, like Jesus, will find the strength to face the tasks ahead of you.

*Lord Jesus, please make it possible for me to set apart enough time for You, time when I can be busy with Your Word and speak to You alone. Amen.*

# Jesus is the vine

"I am the vine; you are the branches. If a man remains in me and I in him, he will bear much fruit; apart from me you can do nothing."

JOHN 15:5

The vine and the branches form an inseparable unit. We cannot see where the vine ends and the branch begins. The branch is continually being fed by the vine. If the branch is cut from the vine, it will wither and die.

You must remain in Jesus like the branch in the vine. This implies that you will be willing to work on your relationship with Him, that you will grow and become stronger every day, so that you will be able to bear much fruit. It also means that you will get to know Him better, and love Him even more.

The comparison used here by Jesus reflects an intimate relationship. Jesus wants to be as near to you as the vine to the branch. Your body is the temple in which His Spirit lives. Without Him you can do nothing.

Fortunately the opposite is also true: you can do everything through Christ who gives you strength. The power of Jesus is at your command when you remain in Him. However, you first have to acknowledge that you cannot do anything without Him. If you are willing to remain in Him He guarantees that you will also bear fruit for Him, fruit that will last.

However, there is a warning: every branch that bears no fruit, He cuts off and throws in the fire. Thus, see to it that the lasting fruit of Jesus can be seen in your life.

Lord Jesus, I want to be as deeply attached to You as the branch is to the vine. Help me to bear much fruit. Amen.

# Jesus is the Lamb of God

The next day John saw Jesus coming toward him and said, "Look, the Lamb of God, who takes away the sin of the world!"

JOHN 1:29

When John the Baptist saw Jesus for the first time, he knew without a doubt that He was the Messiah "Look, the Lamb of God, who takes away the sin of the world!" he exclaimed. God hates sin and He has set the death penalty as punishment for sin. In the Old Testament a lamb was sacrificed to take the punishment for the sin of the people of Israel. Blood had to flow to take away God's anger over the sin before man's relationship to God could be restored.

Jesus is the Lamb of God, because God sent Him to be a sacrifice without blemish to die so that the sin of the world could be taken away. "God presented Him as a sacrifice of atonement, through faith in His blood," Paul writes to the church in Rome (Rom. 3:25).

When the blood of this sacrificial Lamb flowed on the cross, all your sin was washed away by His blood. God can now forgive you because His Son has already paid the price for your sin. God cannot leave sin unpunished, but He punished Jesus in your place.

Jesus took your debt of sin away and brought about reconciliation between you and God. Thus, you are not guilty any more; the only thing you have to do is confess your sins and let go of them. God gave His Son as a sacrificial Lamb so that you need never again doubt His love for you.

*Heavenly Father, thank You so much for sending Your Son to pay for my sins in my place. Lord Jesus, thank You that I may be reconciled to God through Your death on the cross. Amen.*

# Jesus really cares

Jesus reached out his hand and touched the man. "I am willing," he said. "Be clean!" Immediately he was cured of his leprosy.

MATTHEW 8:3

In Jesus' time people who suffered from leprosy were driven out of society because the disease was regarded as highly contagious. Leprosy was a disease with hideous results; the body of a leper was covered in sores and he even lost body parts like fingers and toes. These lepers had to live apart, outside the towns because everyone was afraid of them. Jesus, however, was not afraid of the lepers and did an unheard of thing. He touched a leper.

When the leper knelt before him and said, "Lord, if You are willing You can heal me," Jesus stretched out His hand and touched him. With this touch He demonstrated that He really cared for the leper. A miracle happened when Jesus touched the leper: the leprosy disappeared immediately and the man was healed.

While Jesus was on earth He reached out to all people. He helped them and healed them. Sometimes we avoid some people, but Jesus wants us to look at every other person with the same compassion with which He looked at the leper.

Your touch can mean so much for another person. Put your arm around the shoulders of somebody who suffers or give someone who is mourning a hug. By your touch you can show other people that you really care about them.

Lord Jesus, thank You that You really care about people. Give me that same caring love for others so that I can bring some sunshine into their darkness. Amen.

# Who do you say Jesus is?

When Jesus came to the region of Caesarea Philippi, he asked his disciples, " ... But what about you? ... Who do you say I am?"

MATTHEW 16:13, 15

When Jesus asked His disciples, "Who do the people say I am?" the answer immediately came, "Some say You are a prophet, some Elijah, Jeremiah or John the Baptist." It is always easy to report the words and opinions of other people.

Then Jesus came a little nearer to the disciples, "Who do you say I am?" He wanted to know.

The disciples had been following Jesus for a long time. They were in His proximity every day, they listened to the things He said every day, they were eye witnesses of the miracles that He did. In response to Jesus' question Peter gives a spontaneous and beautiful answer, "You are the Christ, the Son of the living God" (Mt. 16:16).

What would you answer if Jesus asked you this question today? Do you acknowledge Jesus as your Redeemer, your personal Savior? Do you love Him and do you live as He lived? Do you believe that He is truly the Son of God and that you, by believing in Him, will never be lost, but have eternal life?

If your answer is yes, you will have to be willing to live out your testimony.

Jesus is not on earth any more. The only way in which people can see Him now, is when they look at the behavior of His children.

Lord Jesus, I confess that You are the Christ, the Son of the living God. Help me to live so that other people can see You in me. Amen.

# Jesus must suffer and die

From that time on Jesus began to explain to his disciples that he must go to Jerusalem and suffer many things ... and that he must be killed and on the third day be raised to life.

MATTHEW 16:21

When Jesus explained to His disciples that the Way of the Cross was awaiting Him, Peter was presumptuous enough to take Him aside and rebuke Him, "Never, Lord! ... This shall never happen to You!" (Mt. 16:22).

It is nearly unthinkable that the same Peter who had just confessed that Jesus is the Christ is speaking here. However, Jesus came to earth to suffer and die so that we can live. He gave Peter a shattering answer, "Get behind me, Satan! You are a stumbling block to Me; you do not have in mind the things of God, but the things of men" (Mt. 16:23). In a matter of moments the rock on which the church would be built changed into the devil himself!

Like Peter, even people with the right beliefs and the best of intentions can sometimes be a stumbling block in the kingdom of God.

Jesus succinctly summarized the reason: we do not have the things of God in mind, but the things of men. You too must always test whether the things you want are in line with God's will. Beware that you – with your good intentions – do not sometimes stand in God's way.

*Lord Jesus, forgive me if on occasion I am a stumbling block to You. Help me first to test everything I want to do against Your will. Amen.*

# Jesus conquered death

"I am the resurrection and the life. He who believes in me will live, even though he dies; and whoever lives and believes in me will never die".

JOHN 11:25-26

When Jesus heard that His friend, Lazarus, was seriously ill, He did not go immediately to see him. When at last Jesus arrived in Bethany, Lazarus had already been dead for four days. Jesus' behavior must have been incomprehensible to Martha and Mary, Lazarus' sisters. They would definitely not have understood why Jesus allowed their brother to die, because they knew very well that He could have healed him if He had come in time.

However, Jesus had something better in mind for them. He comforted the two grieving sisters with the promise that He was the resurrection and the life, that whoever believed in Him would live, even if he died.

Jesus indeed raised Lazarus from the dead. When He Himself died on the cross and arose from the dead three days later, He conquered the power of death once and for all. Now death is no longer the end – for us who believe it has become only a transition to the true life.

Because we are mortal people, death awaits us all. Not one of us can avoid it. However, because Jesus has conquered death, He can take away our fear of death. You can peacefully await death now because you know that faith in Jesus ensures eternal life for you.

*Lord Jesus, thank You that You have removed the sting of death; that I no longer need to fear death, because one day I shall live with You for all eternity. Amen.*

# Jesus sends the Holy Spirit

"It is for your good that I am going away. Unless I go away, the Counselor will not come to you; but if I go, I will send him to you."

JOHN 16:7

In His human body Jesus could only be in one place at a time. However, with the coming of the Holy Spirit it became possible for Him to be with each one of His children forever and to be eternally present across the whole earth.

When Jesus' disciples were upset because He was going to leave them, He comforted them saying that it was for their own good that He was going away, because He would not let them stay behind alone. He would send the Holy Spirit to stay with them forever.

The Holy Spirit is living in every child of God. We now have Him with us forever. Because God is living within us, we need never be without God again.

Perhaps you have been wondering exactly what the Holy Spirit is doing in your life. He teaches you everything that Jesus did and said, He convicts you of sin, He also reminds you that Jesus is at the right hand of God and that His message is the truth.

However, there are certain responsibilities that you have concerning the Spirit. You have to listen to His words and obey His commands. Do not grieve the Spirit by ignoring Him. If you are willing to let Him, the Holy Spirit will lead, support and equip you every day.

Spirit of God, I praise You because You live in me and lead me, support me and equip me every day. Make me sensitive to sin and obedient to Your voice. Amen.

# Jesus intercedes for us

But because Jesus lives forever, he has a permanent priesthood. Therefore he is able to save completely those who come to God through him, because he always lives to intercede for them.

HEBREWS 7:24-25

In the Old Testament era the priests sacrificed a dove or a goat as reconciliation for the sins of the people. These sacrifices had to be repeated whenever the people sinned. There were a long line of priests as one succeeded the other

Jesus is the perfect high priest. He sacrificed Himself on the cross so that our sins could be forgiven once and for all. His sacrifice need never be repeated, unlike those in the Old Testament. Jesus is also the eternal priest. Because He exists forever, nobody need take over from Him. He saved us once and for all by His death on the cross.

Jesus is not only our high priest, but also our advocate with God. After His resurrection Jesus ascended to heaven and is now sitting at the right hand of God and pleads our case directly with God. Jesus prays for us. He remains the priest who intercedes with God for us.

The presence of Jesus in heaven is your guarantee that He is continually interceding for you, that your case is right with God because He has already paid for every one of your sins on the cross.

*Lord Jesus, thank You that You are interceding for me and that You have made it possible for me to be saved for eternity. Amen.*

# We must become like Jesus

And we, who with unveiled faces all reflect the Lord's glory, are being transformed into his likeness with ever-increasing glory, which comes from the Lord, who is the Spirit.

2 CORINTHIANS 3:18

If we live in obedience to Jesus it means that our lives will inevitably change; that we shall increasingly live and look like Him.

Children of Jesus should reflect His glory in their lives. How is this possible? By being like Jesus, acting like Him, speaking like Him and thinking like Him. To succeed in this, we have to make a careful study of His life here on earth.

If you have not yet done this and if your life does not yet reflect the glory of Jesus, you can start to read the four Gospels. Make detailed notes of the conduct of Jesus, of His relationship with His heavenly Father, of how He helped other people, how He never turned anybody away, how He was always willing to be the least and how He never looked down upon anybody. Then go and do as He did.

The life of Jesus on earth was a clear illustration of God's unconditional love for people. If you want to become like Jesus, you will have to follow in His footsteps. Just remember that you will never be able to do it by yourself, but the Holy Spirit will help you to do it.

You know that it is impossible for me to be like You in my own strength. Please help me to act like You and love others like You did. Amen.

# Jesus will return!

"Men of Galilee ... why do you stand here looking into the sky? This same Jesus, who has been taken from you into heaven, will come back in the same way you have seen him go into heaven."

ACTS 1:11

After Jesus' ascension the disciples stayed behind rather bewildered. They were lost without the inspiration and leadership of Jesus. However, two men dressed in white came to them with an encouraging message: Jesus will not be gone forever. He will come back!

I am sure most of us have wondered and speculated about the precise day and date of Jesus' Second Coming. However, there is only one fact of which we can be absolutely certain, and that is that nobody (not even Jesus Himself) knows when it will be. We do know that it will be unexpected and sudden.

The people of Jesus' time expected His Second Coming every day. However, when time passed and He did not come, they started to become impatient.

We have been waiting for over 2 000 years for Jesus to return. We must not become impatient or indifferent about it. We must keep expecting it every day, so that we shall be ready when it does happen.

Jesus' Second Coming is just as uncertain as the day of your death. It may be tomorrow, or next year. Live so that you will be ready. Stay wide awake and actively tell others about Jesus. Be His witness so that He will come soon!

Lord Jesus, thank You for the certainty in my heart that You will come again. Help me to be ready and active until the day of Your Second Coming. Amen.

# November

## Take off those masks!

The Dutch author, Marleen Ramaker, wrote a book on Romans 12 which she called *Leven zonder maskers*. Jesus often spoke about love during His time on earth. He spoke of true love, a love that makes it unnecessary to hide behind masks. This love makes it possible for us to be ourselves because it assures us that our lives are meaningful.

Romans 12 is the one Scripture passage that, more than any other, teaches us the method as well as nature of the Christian way of life. Self-sacrificing love is the essential quality that distinguishes a Christian from all other people.

Hopefully, by the end of this month you will have discovered how to live in love.

# Offer yourself to God

> Offer your bodies as living sacrifices, holy and pleasing to God – this is your spiritual act of worship.
>
> ROMANS 12:1

Being a Christian is not always easy. That's why all of us are tempted to do things that we know we shouldn't do. Today's verse challenges you to prove in all circumstances that you belong to God. Even if it requires sacrifices from you. But even more than that – you must also offer yourself as a sacrifice to God.

According to *The Message* you should give your whole life to Him, "Take your everyday, ordinary life – your sleeping, eating, going-to-work, and walking-around life – and place it before God as an offering" (p. 388).

Fortunately, God does not only give you this instruction, He also teaches you how to achieve it. Romans 12 provides a step-by-step explanation of the general principles that should characterize a Christian's life. Paul writes that we should prove to God with all of our lives how thankful we are for the salvation He gave us.

If you really begin to live like a Christian, you can expect resistance and persecution. In the Old Testament the sacrifice of an animal was the symbol of someone's surrender to God. If you are willing to offer yourself as a sacrifice to God, you will have to allow your entire life to be controlled by His Spirit.

Are you prepared to become such a living sacrifice?

*Lord Jesus, I want to give myself to You so that my entire life can be in Your service. Please make this possible for me. Amen.*

# Renew your mind

Be transformed by the renewing of your mind. Then you will be able to test and approve what God's will is – his good, pleasing and perfect will.

ROMANS 12:2

As God's children we must be different from the world. We must not only act and speak differently, but also think differently. We must allow God to change our thought processes and renew our minds so that we will know which things are in accordance with His will.

The renewal God wants to achieve in your life begins on the inside and eventually spreads to every part of your life. God will also teach you to distinguish between your own way and God's perfect will for your life; He will help you to surrender your will and to be obedient to Him.

When God renews your mind, you will discover that you will start thinking differently about many things. You will think differently about your religion, about your relationship with God and other people, about your calling in life. You will exchange your old, selfish way of life for a life in which other people are more important to you.

Slowly, in the cocoon of God's love, the caterpillar of selfishness changes into a butterfly gracefully displaying the glory of God's salvation in acts of sacrifice. Only then will you become the person God intended you to be.

*Heavenly Father, please teach me to think differently. Renew my mind and give me the wisdom to know and obey Your perfect will for my life. Amen.*

# Don't become arrogant

For by the grace given me I say to every one of you: Do not think of yourself more highly than you ought, but rather think of yourself with sober judgment.

ROMANS 12:3

Your church is where you practice self-sacrificing love and your attitude toward others should be right. Don't think more – or less – of yourself than you should. God gives gifts to each of us, and if you happen to have received more gifts than the rest of your friends, it is easy to forget that everything you have comes from God. It is even easier to become arrogant when people constantly praise and compliment you.

Christians should be humble and modest. After all, they are people who have discovered that their gifts and talents come from God, and should therefore use these gifts and talents in the church in His service and to His honor.

Consider your own position in your church. What are your gifts and how can they be used fruitfully in your church? Perhaps you are musical, then you can join the church choir; perhaps you have leadership qualities, and then you can offer to be chairperson of a committee.

Perhaps your gift is less evident, but you can still help by making yourself available to assist in the kitchen or to look after the children. Everyone has a gift. Find out what yours is and use it fully – without becoming arrogant in the process.

*Heavenly Father, thank You for the gifts and talents You entrusted to me. Help me to apply my particular gifts and talents to serve You and my church. Amen.*

# *Use your gifts*

We have different gifts, according to the grace given us. If a man's gift is prophesying, let him use it in proportion to his faith.

ROMANS 12:6

God gives a gift to each of us. You, too, have received a particular gift with which to honor Him. If you still don't know what your gift is, don't hesitate to ask a member of your family or your best friend what it is that you are really good at. Once you've done this, explore your gift and use it in your church.

Everyone's gifts are different and not everyone's gifts are equally evident. Some people's talents are much more spectacular than others. A big fuss is often made over such people. But everyone's particular gift is equally important in God's eyes.

The size or importance of your gift is not as important as what you do with it. Use your gift to the honor of God by using it in His kingdom in the best possible way and by serving other Christians with it.

Don't compare your gifts to those of others. People who compare themselves with others become bitter and dissatisfied because, in their own eyes, they always get the wrong end of the stick.

Rather realize that you received your particular gift from God and that it is not something you personally achieved. If you can achieve great things with your gift, you must realize that it has been given to you by God. Give Him the honor for it and serve Him with it.

*Heavenly Father, help me always to realize that my gifts come from You and that I have to serve You with them and give You the honor for them. Amen.*

# Love must be sincere

Love must be sincere.

ROMANS 12:9

Children of God are recognized by their love for God and for each other. Paul tells the Christians in Rome that their love must firstly be sincere. All of us are usually so busy with our own things that we have precious little time and attention left for other people. This is one of the reasons why our love is not always sincere. We pretend to be interested in other people's problems, while we actually only care about our own problems.

The original Greek text refers to an actor wearing a mask. Sincere love is therefore love without a mask. It is a love that is genuine and sincere, a love that puts others first, so that my own interests are less important.

In ourselves we are not capable of such a love, because it is the type of love with which God loves us. God is love, and only He can teach us to love like that; to see other people as He sees them; to look past the faults and shortcomings and love the people behind them.

Ask Him to give you this sincere love through His Holy Spirit who lives in you.

*Heavenly Father, I pray that You will make it possible for me through Your Holy Spirit to love other people sincerely, with the same love with which You love me. Amen.*

# Cling to what is good

Hate what is evil; cling to what is good.

ROMANS 12:9

The many instructions that Paul provides in Romans 12:9-16 help us to make visible the self-sacrificing love of Jesus through our actions in our lives and in our church. All these qualities were characteristic of Jesus' own life on earth. He always chose the best option.

If we see things through the eyes of Jesus, we will automatically hate what is wrong and cling to what is good. To hate what is evil means that you will choose to walk in the light of Jesus; that you will trust in Him and live every day in dependence on Him.

The prophet Micah wrote, "He has showed you, O man, what is good. And what does the Lord require of you? To act justly and to love mercy and to walk humbly with your God" (Mic. 6:8).

God requires you to fulfill your responsibility toward your brothers and sisters in Jesus; to look after them and to show them love and mercy. You must constantly test yourself to make sure that you are living according to God's will.

Religion is a way of life. If you are truly willing to hate what is evil and cling to what is good, your entire way of life will reflect your relationship with God.

Can this be said of you?

*Heavenly Father, I so much want to do what is good, but before I know it I have already done something wrong. Please forgive me and help me to live according to Your will. Amen.*

# Brotherly love and devotion

Be devoted to one another in brotherly love. Honor one another above yourselves.

ROMANS 12:10

Be good friends who love deeply; practice playing second fiddle" (*The Message*, p. 389-390). This is no easy task.

By nature we much rather tend to distrust each other, to be jealous of each other and to look after our own interests. This selfishness constantly impedes us when we want to obey the law of God.

After all, in His summary of the law Jesus says that we must love God above all things and our neighbor like ourselves. These two commandments are a summary of the entire law.

Only when your love for God is stronger than your love for yourself will you learn to be free to love and respect other people in the way God requires from you.

Only then can you (still with the help of God) love and respect other people unconditionally, even when they have fewer accomplishments and gifts than you do. Only then will the superior talents of your fellowman cease to be a threat to you – you will not begrudge them their talents and achievements.

After all, this is what Jesus did. Your attitude should be the same as that of Christ Jesus: Do nothing out of selfish ambition or vain conceit, but in humility consider others better than yourselves (Phil. 2:5, 3).

Are you up to this?

*Lord Jesus, I pray for the same spirit of humility and unselfish service that You had. Teach me to consider others better than myself. Amen.*

# *Never be lacking in zeal*

Never be lacking in zeal.

ROMANS 12:11

Christians often discover that the zeal and devotion they had when they started to serve the Lord gradually grows weaker until it dwindles away almost entirely.

"Yet I hold this against you: You have forsaken your first love Repent and do the things you did at first" (Rev. 2:4-5) is the message to the church in Ephesus.

This also applies to many marriages. When the honeymoon is over the spouses discover that they don't love each other as much as they initially thought. They are not prepared to work on their marriage, with the result that two out of three marriages end up in the divorce court.

How is your love for the Lord? Do you love Him as much now as you did when you were converted, or has your love for Him grown weaker with time? Do you find it a joy to talk to Him in prayer, to study your Bible and listen to His voice, or do you often fall asleep on your knees or constantly find excuses not to spend time in devotions?

This must never happen. If you have recently inadvertently started to stray from the Lord, make a U-turn and return to Him. Be prepared to work on your relationship with the Lord. He loves you and waits impatiently to be merciful to you.

---

*Heavenly Father, please forgive me for not serving and loving You with the same zeal as I did at first. I pray that You will return that enthusiastic first love to me. Amen.*

# Keep your spiritual fervor

Keep your spiritual fervor.

ROMANS 12:11

Never become lukewarm in your spiritual life. Rather, serve and love God fervently and eagerly. God will not tolerate lukewarm Christians. Because the church in Laodicea was spiritually lukewarm, they were unacceptable to Him.

"I know your deeds, that you are neither cold nor hot. I wish you were either one or the other! So, because you are lukewarm ... I am about to spit you out of My mouth," is how Revelation 3:15-16 puts it.

Fire played an important role in the spiritual sacraments of the Israelites. In the Old Testament sacrifices had to be burned with fire. God appeared to Moses in a burning bush and at night accompanied His people through the desert as a column of fire.

Fire therefore represented the holiness of God. Fire could purge and cleanse. The prophet Jeremiah writes that God's Word is like fire (Jer. 23:29). According to Marleen Ramaker, it is God's Spirit that wants to bring this word to life for us and that sees to it that this fire will touch and change us.

In order to remain fervent and enthusiastic about the things of the Lord, you will have to serve God with absolute devotion and read and obey His Word with the same devotion. You also need to make time for Him in your busy schedule. Only if you remain close to Jesus will He give you this fervent devotion to Him.

*Lord Jesus, I come to You to confess that I have become lukewarm in my relationship with You. Please forgive me and once again give me a fervent faith and devotion so that I will serve You with fervor. Amen.*

# Serve the Lord

Serve the Lord.

ROMANS 12:11

If we truly love God with devotion and fervor, it goes without saying that we will be willing to serve Him. Serving others was one of Jesus' most important qualities. "For even the Son of Man did not come to be served, but to serve, and to give His life as a ransom for many," Jesus tells His disciples in Mark 10:45.

Jesus' entire life was a life of service to others. His instruction that His children must be each other's servants still applies to all Christians today. And this willingness to serve should change the lives of His children irrevocably.

The example of Jesus should inspire you to be willing to serve others as He did. "Don't burn out; keep yourselves fueled and aflame," warns *The Message*. "Be alert servants of the Master, cheerfully expectant" (p. 390).

Service without love is impossible "Serve one another in love," Paul writes to the church in Galatia (Gal. 5:13). If you are willing to follow Jesus' example of service, not only serving God but also your neighbor, you must begin by truly loving your neighbor, in spite of the fact that they may differ from you and that they may harm you.

God will make it possible for you to do this if you make the decision to be willing to serve.

*Lord Jesus, I want to report for service. Make me willing to serve others as You did when You were on earth. Amen.*

# Be joyful in hope

Be joyful in hope.

ROMANS 12:12

Although Jesus experienced the uncertainty of the world, He never lost hope because He knew that His Father was in control. "In this world you will have trouble. But take heart! I have overcome the world," He tells His disciples (Jn. 16:33). In other words, Christians can succeed in living in hope in this world, even if things are not going well.

When Paul talks about hope here, he is referring to a fixed certainty that each Christian already has. This hope is not accompanied by a measure of uncertainty as we sometimes use it when we say "I hope my child will get a degree," or "I hope it will rain soon."

Christian hope is always entwined with God's promises, which He gives us in His Word. And we can trust in these promises because they are fixed and sure.

This is why God's children can be joyful in hope. They know that the things they hope for will come true.

"The Christian hopes with an eye on Jesus Christ and in the desire to live increasingly like Him. His hope is even more substantial: he hopes with his eyes on the clouds, the clouds of Jesus' Second Coming. The Christian is glad that his hope does not end in a grave but that it has the certainty of eternal life," writes Johan Smit.

Do you succeed in remaining joyful because of this hope that lives in your heart?

*Lord Jesus, thank You that I may live every day with hope in my heart because I know that You will keep every one of Your promises to me. Amen.*

# Be patient in affliction

Be patient in affliction.

ROMANS 12:12

In our own country we hardly know what the oppression the early Christians were subjected to must have been like. They were tortured and persecuted on account of their faith, and still they remained true to God. However, there are still many countries in which Christians suffer and are persecuted because they believe in Jesus. Paul tells these people to remain patient in affliction.

Although we are not physically oppressed, nobody can escape suffering. In everybody's life there are times when we fail to understand God; when, like Job, we want to know from Him why we have to be subjected to such suffering.

At times we also have to endure ridicule because we air our opinions on topics such as abortion, pornography and extra-marital sex – things that are accepted without question in our modern society. Remain steadfast in your convictions.

If you are currently experiencing such a moment of "oppression" because you professed your Christian faith; if people are avoiding you because you stood up for your faith, don't be disheartened. Try to wait patiently for God to deliver you. Paul's message also applies to you: you must remain patient. After all, you know that this oppression will only last a short time. God loves you and although He allows crises to arise in your life at times, He will provide deliverance in His good time and in His way.

*Lord Jesus, I am sorry for protesting when I sometimes have to sacrifice things for my faith. Help me to remain patient in affliction and to trust in You always. Amen.*

# Be faithful in prayer

Be faithful in prayer.

ROMANS 12:12

When we pray and don't receive any answer, we easily grow despondent and stop praying. But God wants us to continue praying, then more than ever. In His Sermon on the Mount Jesus says "Ask and it will be given to you; seek and you will find; knock and the door will be opened to you. For everyone who asks receives; he who seeks finds; and to him who knocks, the door will be opened," (Mt. 7:7-8). With these words Jesus tells us that we have to continue to seek God in prayer even when we don't immediately receive an answer to our prayers.

God is always there to listen to your prayers. But you must not lose hope and stop praying if He takes long to answer your prayers.

Abraham had to wait years for his heir, but he continued praying and believing even when it became physically impossible for him and his wife to have a child. Because Abraham persevered in faith and prayer, God gave him his promised heir.

God also wants to answer your requests, but only if you are willing to persevere in asking. He will answer your prayers when He deems fit. But remember: sometimes God's answer is different from the answer you would have liked. But even then you can know that God loves you so much that He wants to give you only what is best for you.

*Lord Jesus, please forgive me for growing despondent at times and for sometimes giving up when my prayers are not answered when I think they should be. Help me to persevere in prayer. Amen.*

# Share with those in need

Share with God's people who are in need.

ROMANS 12:13

When Jesus tells His followers to help each other, He means that we must help all people, starting with our fellow believers. Love for God cannot be separated from service to others. "Share with God's people who are in need," Paul asks. My husband likes saying that this text requires love with rolled-up sleeves. In Paul's time Christians often suffered and were dependent on fellow Christians for help.

This need Paul mentions is more than financial need. Need means that you are no longer in a position to handle your circumstances on your own. Fellow believers may live in a beautiful house with plenty to eat, but they may still have a need you can meet.

And precisely because we are so wrapped up in our own problems and crises, we are often oblivious to the needs of other Christians. Perhaps the time has come to tear your attention away from your own problems and focus on other people's needs. Get involved with other people. There are many people around you who need you. Support them, pray for them and encourage them.

Ask the Lord to open your eyes and ears to their need; to enable you to be at the disposal of people in need and to play an active part in helping them.

*Heavenly Father, I come to You to confess that I am so busy with my own things that I am often oblivious to the needs of others. Please forgive me and help me to see their need in future and to do something to help them. Amen.*

# Practice hospitality

Practice hospitality.

ROMANS 12:13

While I was studying this Scripture passage, it struck me how often our own activities prevent us from treating others as God wants us to. Hospitality is an instruction from God. "Offer hospitality to one another without grumbling," Peter writes in 1 Peter 4:9.

The Jews were very proud of their tradition of hospitality and this custom was built into several of their laws. Read with what hospitable abandon Abraham received the three foreign visitors in Genesis 18. This custom is sadly disappearing from our Western civilization. When we hear that somebody wants to visit us, we often think first about the time, effort and expense it will require from us. Some of us would much rather give money than open our homes to others.

True hospitality involves much more than this. It means that you will also be prepared to open your heart to visitors to make them feel truly welcome.

Unfortunately the type of society in which we live today makes it almost impossible to open our doors to strangers as people could do in the past. But this does not mean that we cannot at least try to be more hospitable to our acquaintances; to care more for each other. We need to be more genuinely compassionate toward each other; to receive our friends and acquaintances in our homes with more hospitality.

Are you willing to try?

*Lord, I am sorry for often being so inhospitable toward others. Make me willing to open my heart and my home to others. Amen.*

# Bless your persecutors

Bless those who persecute you; bless and do not curse.

ROMANS 12:14

We so easily fail when it comes to Jesus' most important instruction to love our neighbor. Loving the people who love you isn't always all that easy, but to love those people whom you hate, just seems like too much to ask. No one likes to come off second best, and usually we are quite indignant when we do. Because we are only human, we find it virtually impossible to bless those who have persecuted us.

And yet the Lord asks it of us. Jesus was willing to pray for and bless the people who persecuted Him time and again. Even on the cross He prayed to God to forgive His persecutors because they did not know what they were doing.

In His Sermon on the Mount He similarly states that His children should love their enemies, "But I tell you: Love your enemies and pray for those who persecute you" (Mt. 5:44).

To obey this command is impossible if you are not yet a child of God. It is only He who can enable you to conquer your innate selfish nature and to love and bless those people for whom you feel no love. Are you able to wish your persecutors well yet? If not, God would like to make it possible for you to do so.

*Heavenly Father, You know that I cannot bless those people who persecute me. Please enable me to love them because You loved me first. Amen.*

# Rejoice with those who rejoice

Rejoice with those who rejoice.

ROMANS 12:15

It is easy to be happy when joyful events take place in our lives. We celebrate the marriages of our children with great gladness and we radiate joy when our grandchildren are born. We love hearing that our husbands got a promotion at work; that our children passed their exams with flying colors.

But it is rather more difficult to be joyful for other people and to congratulate them from the heart when one of your colleagues received the promotion that you expected to get, or when one of your friends' children gets much better results at school than your child.

Paul's instruction to rejoice with those who rejoice goes against the grain of our innate selfish nature, just as all the other instructions in Romans 12.

The only way in which we will really be willing to share spontaneously in other people's joy is when we become truly emotionally involved with these people; when we start caring for them from the heart and start loving them with the same unselfish love that Jesus shows toward us.

And this, unfortunately, is impossible. But by this time you should know the solution to the problem. The Holy Spirit who lives within you can help you to accomplish this goal. Ask Him right now to do this and immediately start to assure other people that you rejoice with them when something exciting happens in their lives.

*Lord, make it possible for me to love other people so much that I will truly rejoice with those who rejoice. Amen.*

# Mourn with those who mourn

Mourn with those who mourn.

ROMANS 12:15

Selfish people find it much easier to mourn with others than to rejoice with others. And yet it requires sincere compassion to really cry with someone who is sorrowful because this sympathy should go much deeper than a little card or a few words of condolence.

What do you do when someone close to you loses a loved one? When your neighbor's wife succumbs to a serious illness, or when an acquaintance's new grandchild turns out to be disabled? It is all too easy just to mumble a quick "I'm sorry" in passing, rather than to become truly involved or sincerely mourn with people who are sad.

Jesus truly cared for the people around Him. It did not matter to Him whether they were cast out by society. He loved everyone unconditionally. He always helped people, healed the sick, reached out to people who were sorrowful.

And you ought to do the same. If you have suffered in your own life, you are even better equipped to mourn with those who mourn, because then you are able to console them from your experience.

Ask the Holy Spirit to teach you and lead you to reach out to those people who need your compassion most. Show a sincere interest in the people around you. Make yourself available to them. Know when things are not going well for them and offer your sympathy and help.

*Lord Jesus, make it possible for me truly to have sympathy with people who are sorrowful and make me willing to help them in a practical way. Amen.*

# Live in harmony

Live in harmony with one another.

Romans 12:16

When Paul writes that Christians should live in harmony with one another, he doesn't mean that we should all be the same; that we should all think alike and surrender our own identities to become replicas of each other. Rather, he means that we should think and act from our mutual love for God, the glory of our King and our aspiration for His kingdom here on earth to grow.

In Philippians 2:2-4 this spiritual harmony is explained beautifully, "Make my joy complete by being like-minded, having the same love, being one in spirit and purpose. Do nothing out of selfish ambition or vain conceit, but in humility consider others better than yourselves. Each of you should look not only to your own interests, but also to the interests of others."

Unfortunately we hear much more about division among Christians than about harmony. In just about every church disputes among God's children regularly occur. And the reason for these disputes are, once again, selfishness and self-interest. When you are so involved in your own life and interests that there is no room for other believers in your life, you are disobedient to God's command.

The same is true when you are unable to live in peace with other Christians. But if you are willing to live in harmony with your fellow Christians, as God commands you, you will gladden God's heart because you will be glorifying His Name.

*Heavenly Father, forgive me for not living in harmony with my fellow believers. Help me to be one in spirit and purpose with other Christians. Amen.*

# Do not be proud

Do not be proud.

ROMANS 12:16

"Get along with each other; don't be stuck up," is how *The Message* (p. 390) interprets this command. People who are proud believe that they are just that little bit better than everyone else. They believe that they are always right and they tend to look down on other people. We all know Christians who fit this bill.

They are usually those people have been extremely successful in their career, people others look up to, people who have achieved much – at least in worldly terms. But God does not tolerate pride in His children. At the beginning of Romans 12 Paul writes without mincing words, "Do not think of yourself more highly than you ought, but rather think of yourself with sober judgment, in accordance with the measure of faith God has given you" (Rom. 12:3).

What is your position? Are you successful and popular? Do other people make a fuss of you? If you have accomplished much in life; if the things that you have achieved tend to make you conceited, just remember that you have nothing that you didn't receive from God. All your abilities and talents come from Him; your success and achievements are all His work. It is He who helped you to become what you are today. And for this reason you have no right to think too much of yourself. Rather, you should always give the honor for the things that you have accomplished to God.

Do you?

*Heavenly Father, forgive me for occasionally being conceited about my successes and achievements. Teach me that all these things are undeserved grace from Your hand. Amen.*

# Associate with the humble

Be willing to associate with people of low position.

ROMANS 12:16

One of Jesus' most outstanding characteristics was His absolute humility. "Christ Jesus ... being in very nature God ... made Himself nothing, taking the very nature of a servant, being made in human likeness," as Paul writes (Phil. 2:5-7). Despite the fact that He was God Himself, He was willing to come to the world as an ordinary human being. He was prepared to be born here in a dirty stable, to wash His disciples' feet and to die the cruelest death conceivable, so that sinful human children could return to a holy God.

And this attitude of Jesus, Paul writes, should also be in every one of His children. We sometimes think that humble people are rather cowardly, that they are people who are too afraid to assert themselves. But this is far from the truth. People who are truly humble are willing to put other people's interests before their own, and this takes a tremendous amount of courage.

God wants you to be willing to be associated with humble people. "All of you, clothe yourselves with humility toward one another, because, 'God opposes the proud but gives grace to the humble,'" as Peter writes (1 Pet. 5:5).

It is not that difficult to be humble if you see yourself as God sees you. Each one of us is born in sin. In your own strength you can accomplish nothing that is good and right. You have nothing that you haven't received from God. Ask Him to help you to live humbly from now on.

*Heavenly Father, forgive me for struggling so much to be truly humble and to hold others in higher regard than I do myself. Please make it possible for me to accomplish these goals. Amen.*

# *Do not be conceited*

Do not be conceited.

ROMANS 12:16

**W**hat exactly does it mean to be conceited? Marleen Ramaker summarizes it succinctly. To be conceited is to:

☀ always know better than anyone else.
🧠 be convinced that you are always right.
🖐 have a tendency to always correct others.

People who are conceited find it very hard to put themselves in other people's shoes because in their own reckoning they always know best about everything.

The wisdom of which the Bible speaks stands in direct opposition to conceit. This wisdom means to rely on God to help you distinguish between right and wrong. James asks, "Who is wise and understanding among you? Let him show it by his good life, by deeds done in the humility that comes from wisdom" (Jas. 3:13). He continues to explain exactly what this wisdom involves, "But the wisdom that comes from heaven is first of all pure; then peace-loving, considerate, submissive, full of mercy and good fruit, impartial and sincere" (Jas. 3:17).

Do you perhaps think that you always know best; that you possess all the wisdom in the world? Always remember that all people are fallible and make mistakes. That includes you! In future, be prepared to listen to others and to admit that you might be wrong. Acknowledge and pray for God's wisdom in your life. Contemplate the Scripture verses quoted above and ask God to exchange your conceit for His wisdom.

*Lord Jesus, forgive me for sometimes thinking that I am always right. Grant me the wisdom that comes from You and help me to give others a chance. Amen.*

# Do not repay evil with evil

Do not repay anyone evil for evil.

ROMANS 12:17

If someone has wronged you or someone close to you, you naturally want to take revenge on that person. But Paul insists that Christians should not repay evil with evil.

To be able to forgive and not harbor bitterness you will have to start with your thoughts, because if you harbor vengeful thoughts toward someone, you find that before long those thoughts are transformed into deeds.

Do you remember that earlier this month you undertook to dedicate yourself completely as a sacrifice to God? To love other people just as much as Jesus loves you?

If so, you should also be willing to wholeheartedly forgive people who have wronged you. People who cannot forgive and forget the wrongs that others have done to them cannot truly love other people.

It is natural to wish suffering on people who have treated you unjustly. It is also natural to want to have a hand in their suffering; to get back at them. But if you are sincere in your commitment to God, you will undertake not to repay evil with evil.

Are you prepared to offer your love and forgiveness to people who have wronged you? You will never be able to do it in your own strength, but God will enable you to do it.

*Heavenly Father, You know that it sounds very unfair to me that those who have wronged me will come off scot-free. Please help me to relinquish all my vengeful thoughts and to forgive them. Amen.*

# Do what is right

Be careful to do what is right in the eyes of everybody.

ROMANS 12:17

This instruction would have been much easier if only Paul had left out the word "everybody." To do right to people who do right to you is not that difficult, but to do right to everyone complicates matters somewhat!

In this context, to do what is right means to have a benevolent attitude and demeanor toward all people, to wish only the best for other people and to do everything in your power to give it to them, as Johan Smit writes.

In God's eyes a benevolent attitude should always be accompanied by good deeds. It serves no purpose to have a friendly word for everyone, but no good deeds to confirm the authenticity of your words.

As far as this instruction is concerned you can once again turn to Jesus' example. He did right to all people, including His persecutors, the people who betrayed and killed Him, and His disciples who betrayed and deserted Him.

With what attitude do you view other people? Do you distrust everyone without exception, or do you trust people? Do you live a selfish life that is focused only on your personal gain, or do you have a benevolent attitude towards other people? Can you honestly say that you do right to those people who steal your little spot in the sunlight?

Make benevolence toward all people a part of your life. See the good in others and develop it. Give other people a fair chance – just as God is willing to do for you every day.

*Heavenly Father, thank You for always seeing the good in me and for forgiving my sins time and time again. Help me to be prepared to do the same for others. Amen.*

# Live at peace with everyone

If it is possible, as far as it depends on you, live at peace with every-one.

ROMANS 12:18

To live at peace with other people implies that you should do your best, in so far as it is possible from your side, to maintain good relationships with other people. And yet again Paul includes that pesky little word "everyone"! You will therefore have to do your best to live in harmony with all other people and undertake to act as peacemaker in the lives of others.

In His Sermon in the Mount Jesus says, "Blessed are the peacemakers, for they will be called sons of God" (Mt. 5:9). It is therefore not enough merely to live at peace with others. You should also be willing to be a peacemaker, to resolve and put to rest the disputes among other people.

The peace of which the Bible speaks refers to something that transcends worldly peace, which actually requires nothing more than a truce. The peace of the world means simply concluding an agreement with someone, but biblical peace means reconciliation, reaching out to one another in love, putting an end to conflict, being prepared to forgive the other person wholeheartedly.

However, making peace does not mean that you should be willing to relinquish your Christian principles. Live in peace as far as it depends on you, Paul writes. Sometimes the other party will refuse to take the hand of goodwill that you extend to him, precisely because your viewpoints differ so radically.

*Lord Jesus, I pray that You will grant me Your peace in my life and that I will be willing to pass this peace on to other people, so that I may be a peacemaker for You in this world. Amen.*

# Do not take revenge

Do not take revenge, my friends, but leave room for God's wrath, for it is written: "It is mine to avenge; I will repay," says the Lord.

ROMANS 12:19

Paul filled Romans 12 with extremely difficult instructions! None of us wants to wait until the Lord one day sets things right for us. We want to do it right now. But God asks His children to leave all reprisal to Him.

In all of our lives there is at least one thing that we struggle to deal with and to forgive. In my own life it was something that someone did to my husband years ago. I simply couldn't manage to forgive that person. And what's more, I kept thinking that the Lord would ultimately see to it that that person would get what he deserved.

It took long years for me to realize that this is not at all what Paul means in this passage. You should not dredge up the pain from the past time and again, and make elaborate plans to get back at the person who wronged you. You should also not delight in the thought that God will take revenge for you. If you are obedient to God's commands, you will be willing to surrender this thing that torments you completely to God. He will deal with the matter in His own way and in His own time.

Make a conscious decision to forgive the person. God will enable you not only to forgive the injustice, but also to forget it.

*Lord, You know that there are things in my past that still hurt me. Grant me the mercy to forgive the people responsible for my pain, and to forget it altogether. Amen.*

# Feed your enemy

"If your enemy is hungry, feed him; if he is thirsty, give him something to drink. In doing this, you will heap burning coals on his head."

ROMANS 12:20

When you have an enemy, that person actively campaigns for your destruction; he will do everything in his power to harm you. And the Bible expects you to do good to your enemy in return!

This verse compares the effect of doing good to your enemy to heaping burning coals on his head. In Paul's time people used little stoves that generated heat from hot coals to cook their food. When someone ran out of coals, he had to go out and find more coals.

These burning coals were carried in a container on the head, and generous people who had enough coals for their own use often supplemented such a person's supply of coals by placing hot coals in this container.

It was this same benevolence toward his enemies that Jesus manifested when He healed Malchus's ear that had been severed by Peter's sword. If the love that lived in Jesus is also present in your own heart, you will be willing to do good to those people who are actually your enemies.

Are you doing this yet?

*Lord Jesus, I don't always like helping those who are my enemies. Please enable me not only to help them, but also to love them. Amen.*

# Do not be overcome by evil

Do not be overcome by evil.

Romans 12:21

We have already seen that that the concepts of "evil" and "good" actually refer to the attitude of your heart.

This is the place where the good and the evil things in your life reside. In itself your heart is filled with darkness. Paul writes in Romans 3:12 that "there is no one who does good, not even one." And yet God makes our hearts new, and His love enables His children to pass this love on to others, to live lives filled with goodness.

When we look at the world around us, it is all too obvious that evil reigns supreme in contemporary society. When we open the newspaper, we read of people being murdered and assaulted, of thefts and break-ins, of white-collar crime and fraud. It would appear as if evil has already claimed the victory.

Fortunately this is not the case. But there is good as well as bad news. Even if you think that your life isn't going altogether badly, you can never pass the test in God's eyes. All people are sinners, and because God hates sin, he punishes it with death. Fortunately for you Jesus has already taken your punishment on Him through His crucifixion.

Because He died for you, God is willing to forgive your sin. Do you think you will be able to deal evil a death-blow by living a life dedicated to God from now on?

*Lord Jesus, thank You for enabling me to get the upper hand over the evil in my life through Your crucifixion. Help me to live only for You every day. Amen.*

# Overcome evil with good

But overcome evil with good.

ROMANS 12:21

Y ou have already discovered that you can conquer evil because Jesus has enabled you to do so through His death on the cross.

But in this verse Paul provides you with another weapon that you can use with good effect against evil: overcome evil by doing good; by fighting the evil nature that is still a part of you; by saying no every time you are tempted to commit a sin.

You can fight the evil in you and around you with the love that God Himself has put in your heart. You can take a stand against things which you know run counter to biblical standards. You can obey God's law. You can choose your friends, your television programmes and your reading material carefully. You can tell people that you do not agree with things like abortion, pornography and fraud.

You can also do what is good by filling your life with positive things, by blocking all negative things from your thoughts. You can live as a child of God by helping and supporting others; by making a positive contribution to society.

If you succeed in doing this – with God's help and in His strength – then you have already managed to overcome evil with good. And then you have fulfilled Peter's instruction: "He must turn from evil and do good; he must seek peace and pursue it" (1 Pet. 3:11).

*Lord Jesus, I pray that You will enable me to conquer the evil in my own life as well as the evil that reigns supreme in the world through Your strength. Amen.*

# People owe one another love

Let no debt remain outstanding, except the continuing debt to love one another, for he who loves his fellowman has fulfilled the law.

ROMANS 13:8

*The Message* paraphrases this verse as follows: "Don't run up debts, except for the huge debt of love you owe each other. When you love others, you complete what the law has been after all along" (p. 391). If you love other people, you have fulfilled the entire law of God. This debt of love is a debt that you will be paying off for the rest of your life! If you are a child of God, you will never be able to settle this debt completely. It has to be paid off day by day and moment by moment.

And this is a formidable debt. You know exactly what your love for other people should be like. This love must be sincere, it must not be put-on, or the kind of love that wears masks. You cannot simply pretend that you care for other people. You should love them unconditionally, even those who anger you or wrong you.

Furthermore, you should also be willing to transform your love into deeds, to roll up your sleeves and to help people in distress, "Let us not love with words or tongue but with actions and in truth" (1 Jn. 3:18).

Sincere love can never remain a mere theory; it must always be transformed into deeds. It is precisely in this active kind of love that people will be able to see that you belong to Jesus. Love is the hallmark of the Christian.

How much of your debt of love have you paid off already?

*Lord Jesus, thank You for loving me unconditionally. Grant me more and more of Your love so that it will run over to others, thus enabling me to start paying off my debt of love. Amen.*

# *T*ime for love

Christmas is the one time of the year that all of us look forward to. Not only is it the holiday season and we usually have all our loved ones with us, but each Christmas we are also reminded of the coming of Jesus to the world and of what this fact means for us personally.

Joan Anglund wrote a little poem about Christmas that captures its enchantment very well:

> *C*HRISTMAS IS ...
> But for everyone.
> Christmas is a time of magic
> when troubles melt and once again the world is young.
> It is the time above all other
> when peace may visit earth
> and find a dwelling place in every heart.
> Christmas is a time of giving ...
> A time of hope,
> A time of joy.
> Christmas is a blessed time of love.

Wouldn't you like to make the hope, joy and love of Christmas an inextricable part of your life and pass it on to everybody who is going to celebrate Christmas with you this year?

# The Word becomes flesh

All Scripture is God-breathed and is useful for teaching, rebuking, correcting and training in righteousness.

2 TIMOTHY 3:16

"The Word became flesh and made His dwelling among us" John says about the birth of Jesus (Jn. 1:14). In December we celebrate the birth of Jesus, the Word that became flesh and made His dwelling among us.

When Jesus was born, God's Word, God's sermon for humanity, took a human shape. Jesus is God's love for humanity personified. The coming of Jesus made an immense difference in the world. Now sinners can become children of a holy God because He paid their debt of sin on the cross. After His ascension Jesus, the man, is no longer with us, but we do have His Word through which He speaks to us every day.

Paul writes to Timothy that the Word teaches us to live the way God wants us to. In this way we can know what God expects from us and how we can help to expand His kingdom here on earth.

What are you doing with the Word that became flesh? Do you believe in Him and do you love Him? What are you doing with His Word, in which He teaches you how you should live? Do you make enough time to study that Word and do you obey what Jesus commands in that Word?

If you cannot yet answer positively to these questions, don't you want to make a change for the better this Christmas season?

*Lord Jesus, I praise You for being the Word of God who became flesh, so that I may come to God. Please speak to me through Your Word. Amen.*

# Remain in Jesus

If you remain in me and my words remain in you, ask whatever you wish, and it will be given you. This is to my Father's glory, that you bear much fruit, showing yourselves to be my disciples.

JOHN 15:7-8

Every child of Jesus remains in Him, and Jesus remains in them. Both are in an intimate relationship with each other. Only in this relationship – as close as the branch to the vine – can people ask things of Him and He will give these things to them; only in this relationship will His children really be able to bear fruit for Him.

To be in Jesus and have His words in you means to be saturated with His will. His will becomes your will. If therefore you ask something from Him, it is really His will that you are speaking in the words of your prayer.

Your prayers are heard because they form part of God's will. If you then bear fruit for God, it only means that you are obeying the divine command. The purpose of this fruit is always to glorify God.

If the child of Bethlehem is really the King of your life, if you remain in Him and His words remain in you, it will change your way of life. If that happens, God's dream for you can become true; then the Father can be glorified in your life because your prayers will be heard, you will bear much fruit and will be His disciple.

Lord Jesus, I dearly want to remain in You as the branch in the vine. Allow Your words to remain in me so that my prayers can be heard and I can bear much fruit for You. Amen.

# Thus you must live

But the fruit of the Spirit is love, joy, peace, patience, kindness, goodness, faithfulness, gentleness and self-control.

GALATIANS 5:22-23

The branch that remains in the vine is the branch that bears fruit. If you remain in Jesus and His words in you, if you live in an intimate relationship with Him, His fruit should be seen in your life. In Galatians 5:22 Paul describes this fruit: it consists of love, joy, peace, patience, goodness, faithfulness, gentleness and self-control.

If you are willing to bear fruit for God the list of characteristics mentioned here will be evident in your behavior. People will see God's love in your deeds and relationships. They will see that you radiate His joy, that His peace is living in you, that you are patient, friendly, kind, and faithful to other people, that you are gentle and can control yourself.

All these characteristics are brought into your life by the Holy Spirit. You cannot earn them yourself, but they become part of you if you become one with Christ and follow His example every day.

Mark each of the characteristics that are already present in your life. When you have done this, tackle those characteristics that you still lack.

If you are willing to live out God's Word and bear fruit for Him, your life will make a positive difference to the world around you. See to it that it becomes true of you during this Christmas season.

*Lord Jesus, I dearly want to bear fruit for You. Make me loving, joyful, peaceful, patient, friendly, kind, faithful, gentle and self-controlled, so that other people can see You in me. Amen.*

# *Keep in step with the Spirit*

Since we live by the Spirit, let us keep in step with the Spirit.

GALATIANS 5:25

If you are a child of God you already have the Holy Spirit in your life, and He wants to have a say in the way you live. He wants to see to it that all nine parts of the fruit of the Spirit are present in your life. Unfortunately not every child of God allows the Holy Spirit to take control of his life.

When you drive a motorcar you can do it in three ways: You can get into your car and drive to the place where you want to go; you can pick up somebody else and drive to the destination indicated by the passenger; or you can allow your passenger to drive your car and go where he or she wants to.

The last possibility is a picture of the Holy Spirit in our lives. He does not want you to do just as you like. He also does not want to be only a passenger in your car. He wants to take control of your car and point out God's road for you.

He is the only Person who can show you God's will for your life. Are you willing to leave the driving completely in His hands? Then He will lead you day by day to live according to God's will.

*Holy Spirit, I pray that You will make me willing to allow You to determine my behavior and to control my whole life so that I can do God's will every day. Amen.*

# Live according to the will of God

Whether you turn to the right or to the left, your ears will hear a voice behind you, saying, "This is the way; walk in it".

ISAIAH 30:21

When your life is controlled by the Holy Spirit, you will know and obey God's will. By revealing the truths of the Scripture to you, the Holy Spirit helps you to know God's will. When you pray and ask God's will about a certain matter, He will reveal it to you. When you are still unsure, it always helps to discuss it with other Christians.

When at times you deviate from the right course and wander away from God, you will certainly hear the voice of the Holy Spirit saying to you, "Now you are on the wrong road, it is time to turn around!" The guidance of the Holy Spirit will direct you to the right way every time.

Be careful not to ignore the voice warning you about your wrong ways. The Holy Spirit is not going to force Himself on you. The more you ignore His voice, the less you will hear Him speaking to you.

In this time of celebration there are many more occasions to ignore God's will for your life and to do your own will. Be especially sensitive to the voice of the Holy Spirit in your life at this time, so that you may know for certain what God's perfect will for you is.

*Holy Spirit, I pray that I might know God's will for my life; that You will warn me if I embark on a wrong road and make me willing to obey Your voice. Amen.*

# Reason for joy

"As soon as the sound of your greeting reached my ears, the baby in my womb leaped for joy. Blessed is she who has believed that what the Lord has said to her will be accomplished."

LUKE 1:44-45

When the angel told the young Mary that she was going to have a baby, and that this baby would come from the Holy Spirit and be the Son of God, she immediately declared herself available to God. However, she must have realized that this willingness would cost her dearly in the future.

When the promised child became a reality and Joseph wanted to leave her, when the people of Nazareth didn't believe her story, Mary must have wondered whether she hadn't perhaps misunderstand the message of the angel.

What great joy Elizabeth's joyful greeting must have brought her! Here at last she had the affirmation that the message of the angel was really a message of joy; that the one who believed that the promise would be fulfilled was blessed.

Mary's faith shone forth from the time of the annunciation up to the birth of Jesus. She was willing to sacrifice, to lay her reputation on the altar for her faith. And it was a joy for her all the way. In her song of praise she says, "From now on all generations will call me blessed, for the Mighty One has done great things for me" (Lk. 1:48-49).

If you, like Mary, are willing to obey God's will, you will have reason for joy this Christmas season.

*Heavenly Father, make me willing to say yes to Your plan for my life without thinking about what I can benefit from it. Make me available as Mary made herself available. Amen.*

# Jesus makes you a person of joy

And Mary said: "My soul glorifies the Lord and my spirit rejoices in God my Savior, for he has been mindful of the humble state of his servant."

LUKE 1: 46-48

When the two expecting mothers saw each other, they shared in each other's joy for the children God had promised them. The Holy Spirit made it clear to Elizabeth that the child Mary expected was the long expected Messiah. Even the unborn baby in Elizabeth's womb was excited about the coming of the Savior. Elizabeth told Mary that the child in her womb leaped for joy.

Although both Elizabeth and Mary lived in a dark time in the history of Israel, they knew that the two boys promised to them were going to make a big difference in the world. For this reason both of them were filled with joy.

When Elizabeth's husband, Zechariah, sang about the Messiah who was going to be born, he said that through this Child "the rising sun will come to us from heaven to shine on those living in darkness and in the shadow of death" (Lk. 1:78-79). Mary too sang a song of joy because of God's mercy in her life.

At present we are again living in dark times. However, Jesus is still the light of the world. Our obedience to Him always brings joy into our lives. This Christmas Jesus wants to offer His joy to you and once again bring light into your darkness.

Are you going to allow Him to do this for you?

*Lord Jesus, thank You very much that You are the light of the world, and that I can live joyfully each day because You are the light in my darkness. Amen.*

# The Child is born!

---

For to us a child is born, to us a son is given, and the government will be on his shoulders ... Of the increase of his government and peace there will be no end.

ISAIAH 9:6-7

---

In Jesus' time life was dismal. Israel suffered under Roman domination, superficial religion and poverty were rampant and still the promised Messiah did not come. But Isaiah had prophesied the birth of a special Child, a Child who would rule and whose presence would ensure eternal peace and prosperity for God's people.

In Isaiah 8 and 9 Israel is invited to look beyond the present darkness and to marvel at God's wonderful future. Israel did indeed live in darkness, but God saw a different picture from what they did. In truth, His restoration programme had already started in Paradise when He promised Adam and Eve that one day Somebody would come who would crush the snake's head. The prophet Isaiah prophesied that this Child would soon be born.

The birth of Jesus was a miracle that would change world history. While Adam and Eve were departing through the gates of Paradise, God was already planning the birth of our Savior.

Christmas reminds you that Jesus was born, but also that He will someday come again. Your life today is in reality only a waiting period before the Second Coming of Jesus. You can celebrate Christmas because you have an eternal future; because you are going to dine at the wedding feast of the Lamb one day.

*Lord Jesus, how wonderful that Christmas not only points to Your birth, but also to Your Second Coming. Thank You that I can now already look forward to the marriage of the Lamb. Amen.*

# Who is Jesus for you?

After Jesus was born ... Magi from the east came to Jerusalem and asked, "Where is the one who has been born king of the Jews? We saw his star in the east and have come to worship him."

MATTHEW 2:1-2

Even before the people of Israel knew who Jesus was, the Magi from the east knew that the Child who was born in Bethlehem was the King of the Jews. They made a long journey to come and worship Him.

Who is Jesus for you when you celebrate Christmas: a Child, or the King of your life? For many people Jesus is still the Child lying in the manger portrayed in many nativity plays.

However, you must always realize that this Child in the manger is also the King of the world. He is not small and defenseless, but great and powerful. He is the Son of God who died on the cross and was resurrected from the dead, the Son of God who will one day come again as King.

Annelise Wiid sings a beautiful song about this: "Today at Golgotha a Son was given us. Immanuel, wrapped in linen cloth lies in a foreign grave."

It's fine to be sentimental about Christmas and the coming of the Child, but don't stay focused on the manger and the cloths in which Jesus was wrapped. Remember the victory of the strips of linen lying in Jesus' grave. Jesus conquered death for you.

*Lord Jesus, forgive me that every Christmas I see You as a small baby lying in a manger and forget that You are the King who has conquered death and will one day come again. Amen.*

# The Child is a King

> The government will be on his shoulders ... Of the increase of his government and peace there will be no end. He will reign on David's throne and over his kingdom, establishing and upholding it with justice and righteousness from that time on and forever.
>
> ISAIAH 9:6-7

When Isaiah prophesied that a child would be born, he did not doubt for a moment that this child would be a king. This child would rule as king, sitting on the throne of David and upholding his kingdom forever.

Isaiah's prophecy was probably directed at a historical king who would be born in his time and who would again bring peace and prosperity for the exiled people.

However, the prophecy is also about Jesus. When we carefully read the description of the child, the Child of Bethlehem can be clearly recognized in it. "Of the increase of His government and peace there will be no end," Isaiah prophesied.

The Israelites accorded great significance to names. The character of this king who would be born was thus described in His names: Wonderful Counselor, Mighty God, Everlasting Father, Prince of Peace (Is. 9:6).

When you want to celebrate the King who was born, you should understand that this King wants to rule your life every day. You will have to recognize Him as King, submit yourself to His Word, and live according to His will. Are you ready for it?

*Lord Jesus, I worship You as the Child who was born, but also as the King of my life. Help me to obey Your Word and to live according to Your will. Amen.*

# God of miracles

For to us a child is born, to us a son is given, and the government will be on his shoulders. And he will be called Wonderful Counselor.

ISAIAH 9:6

Jesus was to be called Wonderful Counselor. The word used here for wonderful is the same as the word that was often used in the Psalms for miracle. When the psalmists called upon the people to think of the great deeds of God in the past, they described these deeds as miracles. For them the greatest miracle of all was being set free from bondage in Egypt.

A miracle is something that cannot be conceived by human understanding and cannot be done by human hands. Only God can perform miracles because He is a wonderful God. Jesus' life on earth was a miracle, from His virgin birth to the miracles He did on earth. He healed the sick, made the blind see, woke the dead and controlled nature by calming the waves and the wind.

For us the greatest miracle happened on Golgotha when God's Son redeemed us from the power of sin because His blood flowed for us on the cross. Jesus is still the same God of miracles. He can still do the same things as those He did when He was on earth, if your faith in Him is strong enough.

Every year at Christmas we worship the Wonderful Counselor, Jesus who came to make the miracle of God's love for sinners true – God becoming man and coming to live among us. Is it still a miracle for you?

*Lord Jesus, I worship You as the Wonderful Counselor who came to make the miracle of God's love true for me. Please let Your birth remain a miracle for me. Amen.*

# The God who counsels

For to us a child is born, to us a son is given, and the government will be on his shoulders. And he will be called Wonderful Counselor.

ISAIAH 9:6

Jesus is our Counselor. He does not need counsel from other people, because God is His Counselor. He will always have advice for all of our problems.

The most important characteristic that an Old Testament king could have was wisdom so that he could rule his subjects justly. Solomon was an exceptional king. When he could choose from different gifts, he chose wisdom. All the kings had counselors, wise men who could give advice when problems arose. However, our King does not need them. He is a Counselor Himself.

Jesus was born into a confused world where God's people were seeking solutions to their many problems. We, too, often need advice in the world in which we live. There are so many questions that we cannot answer, and therefore we need a Counselor, somebody who can solve our problems with His wisdom and insight.

The King you worship has all the knowledge, wisdom and insight in the world and He wants to make it all available to you. He gives you His Word to show you how to live and what His will is. If you know and love Him, you need never be bewildered again – He is willing to advise you every day.

Is Jesus your Counselor?

*Lord Jesus, I praise You that You have answers to all my problems; that You are always there for me when I need advice, wisdom and insight. Amen.*

# The God who can do everything

For to us a child is born, to us a son is given, and the government will be on his shoulders. And he will be called ... Mighty God ...

ISAIAH 9:6

Isaiah says that Jesus will be called Mighty God. He is God's representative on earth. Whoever sees Him, virtually sees God Himself.

The Jews had a big problem with this specific name that Isaiah gave to a baby who was still to be born. No earthly king would dare to have called himself God. In their eyes it was a violation of the first two commandments. One of the reasons why they had Jesus crucified was because He called Himself the Son of God. Fortunately this name poses no difficulty for us. Jesus *is* the Mighty God.

The word translated here as "mighty" literally means "hero." Heroes, those people who periodically came to the fore in Israel to save the people out of their predicaments, held a very important place in history.

Jesus is omnipotent, He can do everything. He is the Hero-God, bringing redemption for us. He proved His heroic courage on the cross when He died so that we can live. He also rose from the grave and ascended to heaven. Now He is ruling in heaven where He is sitting at the right hand of God.

Jesus dearly wants to save you from the power of sin that keeps you in bondage. He is the Hero who came to earth to liberate you forever. Through Him you have the power of God available to you. Is Jesus your Hero?

*Lord Jesus, I worship You as the Hero-God who made redemption possible for me and who makes Your great power available to me every day. Amen.*

# *Father for ever*

> For to us a child is born, to us a son is given, and the government will be on his shoulders. And he will be called ... Everlasting Father.
>
> Isaiah 9:6

The Child who was to be born would be a father to His people and would provide for their needs and look after them every day. According to commentators "Everlasting Father" can have two meanings. It can mean that Jesus is the eternal Creator, the One from whom everything originated, or it can mean that God has become our Father through Jesus.

Although every one of us has a different father-image, the most prevalent concept is that of love, provision and protection. We have God as our Father, the God who provides for us and protects us, who showers His children with His love and goodness every day.

The security of this Father is absolute. He can never go bankrupt or disappoint us like our earthly fathers sometimes do. We have His promise in His Word that He will always protect His children and keep His arms around us.

In the Lord's Prayer Jesus teaches us to address God as Father. This word for father we can also be translated as daddy. God is the Dad who will provide our daily bread, the Forgiver of our sins, the Protector against the evil one.

God still wants to do this for you. He wants to be your Dad forever. You can go to Him with each of your needs. He is there for you always. Have you accepted Him as your Father?

*Heavenly Father, it remains a miracle that I can have You, who are so great and almighty, as my eternal Father. Thank You for loving me and providing for me every day. Amen.*

# *Jesus brings peace*

For to us a child is born, to us a son is given, and the government will be on his shoulders. And he will be called ... Prince of Peace.

ISAIAH 9:6

The last name Isaiah gives to the Child, is Prince of Peace. This child would break down the enmity between God and man, between man and man, and between man and nature. Under His rule there would be complete harmony in creation, so that every person would be able to serve God without hindrance.

The Old Testament word for peace means to be whole, to be a fulfilled person. Indeed, the coming of Jesus made us fulfilled people.

In verse 7 Isaiah gives a brief CV of this Prince of Peace: His government will increase, He will bring peace and prosperity for ever, He will eternally reign over His kingdom on David's throne, establishing and upholding it with justice and righteousness.

In today's world we no longer know true peace. We have never experienced it. After the creation there was complete harmony, but the harmony was disturbed when sin drove away peace. Sin breaks the relationship between God and man and between man and man. Jesus came to restore that relationship.

In this disordered world in which we live we have an urgent need for peace. We don't have peace with God, man or nature any longer. You, too, urgently need peace in your life, and you can obtain it if Jesus, the Prince of Peace, becomes the King of your life.

*Lord Jesus, I worship You as the Prince of Peace. Thank You for restoring the relationship between God and me and between other people and me. Amen.*

# Reconciliation

---

"And I will put enmity between you and the woman, and between your offspring and hers."

GENESIS 3:15

---

There is a lot of talk about reconciliation these days, but we see few results. Since the Fall there have been broken relationships, enmity between man and nature, between man and man and between man and God. In many countries around the world there are broken relationships between people and between groups.

For most people reconciliation means an essential process of healing between different political, religious or racial groups. However, for Christians reconciliation means something totally different: true reconciliation is only possible through Jesus. Only once we believe in Him, will He make reconciliation possible in our hearts and lives.

Jesus wants you to be a leader in reconciliation this Christmas. Broken relationships are never healed by writing about them or arguing about them, but only by bringing people together again. For true reconciliation it is necessary that we forgive other people for their past mistakes, that we turn to each other and reach out to each other.

Reconciliation is always the gateway to peace; the peace that is needed so urgently in many countries. Are you willing to do what you can to promote reconciliation?

*Lord Jesus, I pray that You will make me willing to turn to other people and reach out to them in love, so that I can promote reconciliation between people. Amen.*

# Jesus brings reconciliation

He is the atoning sacrifice for our sins, and not only for ours, but also for the sins of the whole world.

1 JOHN 2:2

To make true reconciliation a reality, we should firstly realize that Jesus not only made reconciliation with God and other people possible by His death on the cross, but that He Himself was the atoning sacrifice for our sins. To experience true reconciliation we must know Him and obey His Word.

In the Old Testament the priests sacrificed a lamb as atonement for the sins of the people. Jesus is God's sacrificial Lamb, making possible the atonement for our sins by His death on the cross. His sacrifice never had to be repeated, "All this is from God, who reconciled us to Himself through Christ and gave us the ministry of reconciliation" (2 Cor. 5:18).

In 1 John 2:6 we receive a rather difficult command: true reconciliation with God and man is possible only when we are willing to live like Christ every day.

This is precisely God's dream for you this Christmas: that you will be reconciled with Him and the people around you by being obedient to His commandments and becoming more and more like Jesus every day. Don't you want to succeed in this with the assistance of the Holy Spirit this Christmas?

*Heavenly Father, will You please make it possible for me to be a bearer of Your reconciliation this Christmas, so that I can become more and more like Jesus every day. Amen.*

# The price of peace

---

Suddenly a great company of the heavenly host appeared with the angel, praising God and saying, "Glory to God in the highest, and on earth peace to men on whom his favor rests."

LUKE 2:13-14

---

In the Old Testament we find the expectation that the Messiah to come would bring world-wide peace. But the birth of Jesus did not bring the hoped-for peace. The prevailing hatred between Jews and Romans endured. Shortly after the birth of Jesus thousands of Hebrew baby boys were cruelly murdered by Herod. To us it seems as if the angels' promise of peace was not fulfilled. Peace does not simply come into this world with the song of the angels every Christmas.

The truth is that peace is terribly expensive – it always demands a high price. The Prince of Peace first had to die on a cross before peace on earth could become a reality. Jesus brought peace by breaking down the wall between God and you.

Biblical peace always results in reconciliation. It demands something from you, because it means that you will have to be willing to give up your own demands in favor of those of others.

Bethlehem and Golgotha meet in the Sermon on the Mount where Jesus spells out the price of peace for His children. We must be willing to turn the other cheek, to love our enemies.

Followers of the Prince of Peace are always cross bearers. The only way to reconciliation is the way of self-sacrifice.

Are you willing to do it?

*Lord Jesus, make me willing to pay the price for peace by putting other people first and by loving my enemies. Amen.*

# *Jesus, King of righteousness*

"The days are coming," declares the LORD, "when I will raise up to David a righteous Branch, a King who will reign wisely and do what is just and right in the land."

JEREMIAH 23:5

The spiritual and political leaders of Jeremiah's time all forsook their duty, and there was no one to see that justice was done in the land. Jeremiah announced God's judgment on these bad leaders – they had caused the people of Israel to be killed and scattered.

However, God promised His people that He would bring them back to their country and that one day He would send them a just king, "In His days Judah will be saved and Israel will live in safety. This is the name by which He will be called: the Lord Our Righteousness," writes Jeremiah (Jer. 23:6).

After the exile Israel was resettled in their country, but the birth of the promised king was totally different from their expectation. Only when Jesus was born did God's promise for His people become true.

He is the King who brings us into the right relationship with God and therefore He can claim the name the Lord Our Righteousness. God made a new beginning by bringing righteousness to us through Christ. Therefore Christ's birth and death became the pivotal point in history.

By the birth of His Son God wants to bring about a revolution in your life. He wants to renew your life by bringing righteousness into your life through Jesus.

*Lord Jesus, thank You that You are God's righteousness. Thank You that I, by believing in You, can live in the right relationship with God. Amen.*

# The source of our hope

---

May the God of hope fill you with all joy and peace as you trust in him, so that you may overflow with hope by the power of the Holy Spirit.

ROMANS 15:13

---

Hope played a very important part in the ministry of Paul. The reason why hope was so important to him was because he was living in a time of religious and political persecution. Conditions were dismal for the Christians and they were persecuted and oppressed. When conditions are bad, it is easy to lose heart and the early Christians were on the point of completely losing trust in God and their neighbor.

The political and economic conditions of the times in which we are living also cause us to become despondent. God's children can become joyless and disheartened as well when they look at the negative conditions around them. Fortunately, God remains our source of hope. When we cling fast to Him and trust Him completely He will save us.

The future should always be an adventure for the Christian because he is living with hope in his heart. "Hope works," Piet Naude writes, "not because it is cheap escapism in religion. It looks at reality in the light of Reality. It does not depend on my predisposition or my opportunity. It depends on God."

Although there may still be many unknown tomorrows before you, it is a well-known God who will be accompanying you. Therefore, you need not fear.

*Lord Jesus, thank You for the assurance that I need not fear the future or disasters that may hit me because I can always hope in You despite what happens around me. Amen.*

# A spirit of unity

May the God who gives endurance and encouragement give you a spirit of unity among yourselves as you follow Christ Jesus.

ROMANS 15:5

Jesus is our source of hope, and through His life God's promises have been realized. Even more, He lives in us, He is our hope for the glory that God promised to His children (see Col. 1:27). Paul told the Christians of his time that a spirit of unity was required if they wanted to share in this hope. He spoke about those things that could cause us to lose sight of God and at the same time he called the congregation to mutual tolerance and unity.

In Paul's time there were great differences between the Jewish and Roman Christians. The Jewish Christians adhered strictly to the laws of Moses and looked down on other Christians, whereas the Roman Christians did not pay attention to inherited traditions.

The Christians of today are still divided and often the differences are small. It is however necessary that we should have a spirit of unity in our faith, that we, as Paul asks in Philippians 2:2, be "like-minded, having the same love, being one in spirit and purpose."

What place does Jesus occupy in your life? This Christmas, try to look at Christians across church boundaries. Have a spirit of unity in Jesus, take each other's hands and reach out to each other because you all love the same Lord.

*Lord Jesus, thank You that You are my hope for glory. Help me to reach out to other Christians across church boundaries. Give us a spirit of unity because You love us. Amen.*

# Hope in Jesus

Now faith is being sure of what we hope for and certain of what we do not see.

HEBREWS 11:1

Jesus is our hope of glory. We celebrate Christmas every year because of this hope. That is how hope works: we cannot see the things we hope for, but are sure that they will become true for us in the future. Hope is always a matter of faith. We can always keep on hoping even if matters seem rather hopeless at the moment.

When you think of God's promises, your faith works like a title-deed for a property: it gives you the guarantee that you are the owner of God's promises already, although at the moment they may still be invisible to you. You indeed have the title-deed, your faith, which is your proof that all God's promises for you will be realized in the future. To that you may fasten your hope.

The heroes of faith of whom this chapter speaks, succeeded in this, "Against all hope, Abraham in hope believed and so became the father of many nations" (Rom. 4:18).

Renew your hope this Christmas and believe that all God's promises for you will be fulfilled.

*Lord Jesus, thank You that You made it possible for me to keep on hoping in You even though my circumstances may sometimes be hopeless. Thank You for the promise that my hope in You will never be disappointed. Amen.*

# A messenger of mercy

"And he [John the Baptist] will go on before the Lord ... to turn the hearts of the fathers to their children and the disobedient to the wisdom of the righteous – to make ready a people prepared for the Lord."

Luke 1:17

When the angel told Zechariah that he would have a son he said that this son would be a guidepost. He would bring the disobedient people back to the right road again. In Zechariah's song of praise he proclaimed that this child would go on before the Lord to prepare the way for Him.

John's name means "The Lord is merciful" and he spread this message among the people. Christmas is about God's mercy toward people. Ask God to help you proclaim His message of mercy this Christmas time.

Christmas has become largely a commercial festival where the emphasis is placed on big and expensive gifts. We are tempted by advertisements to spend more money than we can afford. As Christians, we should not be sidetracked by worldliness but always make Christmas a Christ-feast.

What difference does the fact that you are a Christian make to the way you celebrate Christmas? Are you changing the world around you because you believe in Jesus? You can always be a guidepost pointing the way to Jesus, especially at Christmas. Make people happy this Christmas because you proclaim the joyful message of Jesus.

*Lord Jesus, make me a messenger of Your mercy and let people come to know You through me. Amen.*

# God is coming!

Be patient, then, brothers, until the Lord's coming ... You too, be patient and stand firm, because the Lord's coming is near.

JAMES 5:7-8

We are living between the first and the second coming of Jesus. It is rather difficult for God's children to wait patiently until He comes again. The world around us is so unbelieving. It does not believe that God can really make a difference to the lives of people.

Furthermore, we are living in unsure, difficult circumstances. Sometimes it seems as if God has forgotten about us, or that He has turned His back on us and does not see our hardship. Then again it seems to us as if life is much more prosperous for unbelievers than for people who love God and obey His commandments.

James warned the Christians of his time to wait patiently for the Second Coming of the Lord, as a faithful grain farmer waits for rain. This time of waiting is not an idle time, but a time of hard work.

Tomorrow we celebrate the Lord's coming over 2000 years ago. The fact that you can celebrate Christmas is proof that God really cares about the world. In this Christmas season, focus on God and the Second Coming of Jesus.

Do not be disheartened when the waiting period is longer than you initially expected – for you the coming of Jesus might be nearer than you expect. Make sure that you expect Him every day.

*Heavenly Father, I praise You that You sent Jesus to the world so that I may believe in You. Make me willing to wait patiently for His coming. Amen.*

# God with us

"The virgin will be with child and will give birth to a son, and they will call him Immanuel" – which means, "God with us."

MATTHEW 1:23

Matthew had two messages that he wanted to bring clearly to his readers: the Baby to be born in Bethlehem would be truly human and truly God. The angel told Joseph that the name of the Child was to be Immanuel, God with us. Therefore, Jesus is completely God and completely human, as the Heidelberg Catechism puts it.

By the birth of His Son God came to live among people. The people of Matthew's time really needed this message. They lived in difficult conditions, just as we do today. Matthew wanted to tell these people, "God is with you in your hardship."

In the last chapter of his Gospel he underlines this fact again. When Jesus sent His disciples to make people His disciples, He promised them that He would be with them to the end of the world. Through His Holy Spirit He is still living in each of His children.

"God gives us the light during Christmas – it is faith; the warmth of Christmas – it is love; the faith in Christmas – it is truth; the sum total of Christmas – it is Christ," Wilda English writes. This Christmas you may know for certain, the Jesus who was born 2000 years ago in a stable is truly God and truly human. He will be with you for the rest of your life.

*Lord Jesus, how wonderful that You will be with me every day for the rest of my life to teach and help me. Thank You that I can celebrate it this Christmas. Amen.*

# God gives you a sign

> "'If you do not stand firm in your faith, you will not stand at all.'
> Therefore the Lord himself will give you a sign: The virgin will be
> with child and will give birth to a son, and will call him Immanuel."
>
> ISAIAH 7:9, 14

King Ahaz and the people of Israel were terrified of the two gentile kings Resa and Peka who threatened to invade their country.

However, God came to reassure them through the prophet Isaiah that the invasion would not take place. He gave them a sign to underline His promise: someday Immanuel would be born, and He would make all fear unnecessary because He would be the Savior of His people. Through Him they would have God Himself with them every day.

The promise of verse 4 is true even today for God's children "'Be careful, keep calm and don't be afraid.'" As it was unnecessary for Israel to be upset about the "two smoldering stubs of firewood" as Isaiah called the two gentile kings, it is also not necessary for us to fear anything. We know for certain that we have God on our side.

Close to the beginning of another new year your courage sometimes diminishes. However, Jesus has already been born. He is God with you. In contrast to Ahaz, you and I are living on the other side of the cross. We know Jesus and so fear is unnecessary because heaven is waiting for everybody who believes in Him.

*Lord Jesus, thank You that You have come to take away all my fears. Make it possible for me to be calm in the certain knowledge that You will look after me. Amen.*

# The way of sanctification

For this reason, since the day we heard about you, we have not stopped praying for you.

COLOSSIANS 1:9

The great success that Paul had in his ministry could possibly be ascribed to the fact that he prayed faithfully and regularly for the congregations in which he worked. There are eight things for which Paul prayed for the church at Colosse. He prayed that they would:

❊ have the wisdom and understanding of the Holy Spirit in their lives.
❀ gain knowledge of God's will.
❀ live to the honor of God by doing only His will.
❀ bear fruit for God.
❀ grow in the knowledge of God.
❀ be strengthened to endure patiently.
❀ always joyfully give thanks to God.
❀ have hope for the future to share in the inheritance of the saints prepared by God.

If you want to make progress in sanctification you should make these eight points a reality in your life. Read them again carefully and make a mark next to those on which you must still work. Then ask the Lord to help you to make Paul's prayer a reality in your own life every day.

Lord Jesus, I pray that You will help me to have these eight qualities in my life. Thank You for sanctifying me. Amen.

# In good and bad times

When times are good, be happy; but when times are bad, consider:
God has made the one as well as the other.

ECCLESIASTES 7:14

It is a human trait to believe that prosperity and success are rightfully ours, but as soon as misfortune comes knocking at our door, we immediately want to blame somebody else.

Job is a very good example of how we should act in crisis situations. When he lost all his possessions and his children, he still succeeded in professing, "The LORD gave and the LORD has taken away; may the name of the LORD be praised" (Job 1:21). By this Job proves that one can love the Lord for what He is and not for what He gives.

All of us experience prosperity as well as misfortune. Not one of us knows what is waiting for us in the future. We do know, however, who has the future in His hands. When you give control of your life to God, you need not fear misfortune. God is with you also in the midst of the crisis. His hand supports you.

God sometimes uses crises in your life to bring you closer to Him. For this reason hardship is profitable because it teaches you to get to know God better and to trust Him more.

You may trust God every day in the new year that is soon to begin. He has prosperity and misfortune in His hand and in the end He will work out everything for your good.

*Lord Jesus, I am extremely thankful that I need not fear the new year lying before me but that I may trust You unconditionally in prosperity and misfortune because You will provide for me. Amen.*

# Be calm

Calmness can lay great errors to rest.

ECCLESIASTES 10:4

All of us occasionally become upset or angry and then say things which we regret bitterly afterwards. Our family still laugh over a favorite comic strip in which Helga shouts at Hägar. "Don't step on my shadow!" Times of irritation make us say strange things.

Calmness can lay great errors to rest, writes the wise Teacher of Ecclesiastes. There is a reason that patience is one of the components of the fruit of the Holy Spirit. If you can succeed in staying calm in all circumstances, you will be able to avoid many difficult situations.

The Greek word for patience really means to give somebody else another chance. Ask the Lord to give you His peace in your life, to make you calm, so that you will succeed in defusing problems with your calm conduct.

Scientists maintain that if you have done something more than forty times, it forms a "path" in your brain, so that in future you do it automatically. If you have trouble staying calm in a crisis, train yourself to count slowly up to ten before you explode. Before you know it, you will be able to make a difference in the world around you with your peacefulness and calmness.

Heavenly Father, You know that my impatience has caused me to make great errors already. I pray for Your peace and calm in my life, so that with Your wisdom, I will be able to act calmly in problem situations. Amen.

# Let go of the worries

"What I feared has come upon me; what I dreaded has happened to me. I have no peace, no quietness; I have no rest, but only turmoil."

JOB 3:25-26

When you look back on the past year, there are two things that will probably strike you. Many of the things you feared did not happen to you. At the same time, those times when you were negative and despondent, things definitely got worse than when you were positive and full of hope.

When you are waiting for a disaster to happen to you, it often does. Disasters and afflictions very soon cause you to lose your composure and calmness. Read verse 26 again: it may just as well be a classic description of the stress and depression of which so many modern people suffer. It also does not bode well for your medical health, because scientists have recently discovered that 90% of all diseases are stress-related.

Nevertheless, you can rectify this cycle of depression in the coming year by following Peter's advice, "Cast all your anxiety on Him because He cares for you" (1 Pet. 5:7).

If you can succeed in taking all the things you fear, all the things you worry about to Jesus and leaving them with Him, He undertakes to care for you. Then you will also discover that your stress and depression will be replaced by the calmness and peace of Jesus.

Don't delay in asking Him to help you.

*Lord Jesus, You know about all the things that make me despondent and depressed. I want to bring every one of them to You now and allow You to care for me in the year ahead. Amen.*

# God is on your side

With God we will gain the victory, and he will trample down our enemies.

PSALM 108:13

In Psalm 108 the psalmist is praising the Lord because He saved him, because He gave him and His people victory every time, because He was on their side.

Today is the last day of the year. You have most probably had your shares of successes and failures in the past year. Have you given God the honor for the successes, or do you think that your achievements were your own doing? Always remember what is written in 1 Corinthians 4:7 "What do you have that you did not receive?" Everything you have achieved in this year you were able to do because God gave you the talents and the strength to do it.

Concerning the failures: Not one of us escapes them. Don't allow your failures of the past year ever to defeat you. A failure is only a failure if we cannot learn something from it, somebody said. Thus, learn from yours.

As a Christian, you have most probably experienced that God has been with you every day of the past year and that He carried you, helped you and encircled you with His love. With Him on your side you discovered time and again that indeed you are more than a conqueror.

In the coming year you can cling to the same promise. In the new year you will be victorious if you have God on your side. Don't enter the new year without Him.

Heavenly Father, thank You for the assurance that You are on my side and that for this reason I will be more than a conqueror in the year ahead. Amen.